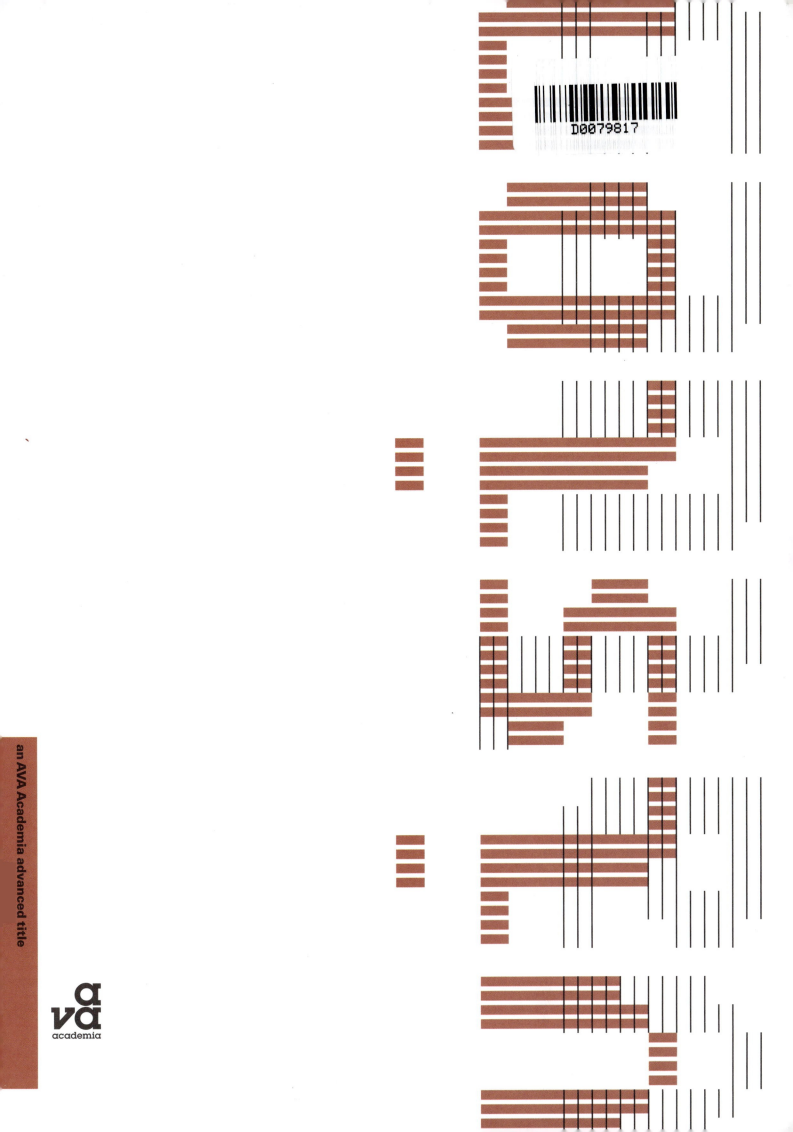

an AVA Academia advanced title

ava
academia

An AVA Book
Published by AVA Publishing SA
Rue des Fontenailles 16
Case Postale
1000 Lausanne 6
Switzerland
T +41 786 005 109
E enquiries@avabooks.ch

Distribution (ex-North America)
Thames & Hudson
181a High Holborn
London WC1V 7QX
United Kingdom
T +44 20 7845 5000
F +44 20 7845 5055
E sales@thameshudson.co.uk
www.thamesandhudson.com

Distribution (USA and Canada)
Ingram Publisher Services Inc.
1 Ingram Blvd.
La Vergne, TN 37086
USA
T +1 866 400 5351
F +1 800 838 1149
E customer.service@
   ingrampublisherservices.com

English Language Support Office
AVA Publishing (UK) Ltd.
T +44 1903 204 455
E enquiries@avabooks.ch

Design
Rupert Bassett

Index
Compiled by Indexing Specialists (UK) Ltd.

Production
AVA Book Production Pte. Ltd.
Singapore
T +65 6334 8173
F +65 6259 9830
E production@avabooks.com.sg

Copyright

ISBN
978-2-940373-79-6

10 9 8 7 6 5 4 3 2 1

Vision and Values in
Design Management

David Hands

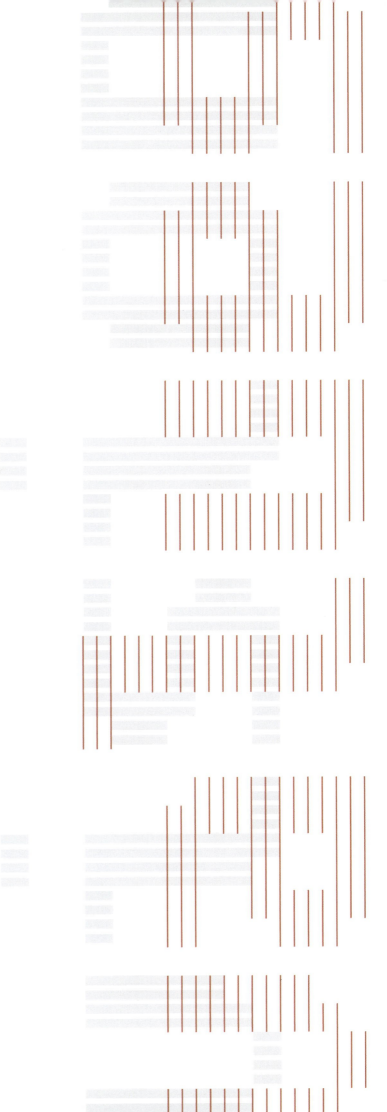

an AVA Academia advanced title

academia

**Vision and Values in
Design Management**

Design
directions

Design
transformations

Design
advocacy

Design
alliances

Table of contents

Chapter one   12
Design directions

Chapter two   50
Design transformations

Introduction   6

The value of design   14

Connecting different meanings   52

How to get the most out of this book   8

Interview   22
Richelle Harun

Case study   56
**Transforming perception
through design**

Foreword   10
Professor Rachel Cooper

Quantifying the benefits   24

Applying a holistic approach   64

Interview   34
Dr Alison Prendiville

Interview   68
Andy Cripps

Communicating the vision   36

National design policies   70

Case study   42
**Transcending organisational
boundaries**

Interview   74
Gavin Cawood

Chapter summary   48

International design
collaboration   76

Case study   84
**Coordinating growth
through design**

Chapter summary   92

Chapter three   94
Design advocacy

Chapter four   144
Design alliances

Design leadership   96

Emergent issues in design   146

Conclusion   182

Interview   102
Alan Wall

Interview   152
**Dr Caroline Davey and
Andrew Wootton**

Contacts   184

Driving innovation through design   104

CSR and design   154

Picture credits   185

Case study   112
**Product success through
design leadership**

Case study   158
**Design thinking:
designing against crime**

Glossary   186

Design strategy   120

Innovation in services   166

Index   188

Case study   126
**Innovation through
collaboration**

Interview   172
Dr Cristiaan de Groot

Quotation sources   191

Design collaboration   134

Where next?   174

Acknowledgements   192

Interview   140
Peter Quinlan

Interview   178
Professor James Woudhuysen

Chapter summary   142

Chapter summary   180

**Vision and Values in
Design Management**

Design
directions

Design
transformations

Design
advocacy

Design
alliances

Introduction

The business imperative for design is compelling, suggesting that its sophisticated and thoughtful utilisation can offer long-term benefits for an organisation. The benefits can be both tangible and intangible, adding value to both products and services and indeed, to the organisation itself. However, in order to achieve this understanding and application of design, the organisation needs to plan and implement a framework for the way design is going to be successfully harnessed. Using design effectively in this way will enable the company to increase the perceived value of its product offerings and maintain long-term competitive advantage.

Section one
Design directions

Design directions introduces the ongoing debate of valuing the true worth of design and how it can be applied throughout a variety of contextual environments. Design has progressed considerably since the days when it was used to modify existing products and was considered worthwhile and important mostly at project level. Two contributors discuss how they perceive the value of design in business, arguing passionately that it can make a significant and meaningful contribution to organisational performance. This section concludes with a case study that illustrates the importance of design and how it was used to full effect in the development of a value-added and highly innovative shower range by Trevi Showers.

It is widely accepted that the successful organisation will no longer focus on lowest cost, but will strive to provide value-rich products and services that are distinctive and appealing. Customers are now far more demanding due to increased spending power and the proliferation of choice – therefore the company needs to anticipate, respond to and, more importantly, exceed the customer's expectations.

Trends indicate that design expertise may be especially critical for competitive and growth purposes within global markets. Designers may conceive, shape and communicate new innovative products and visualise brands, but design often needs to be coordinated and carefully aligned with the firm's strategy and core competencies.

Careful attention to design and its effective management can lead to the development of new and innovative products and services; stronger company image by the enhancement of brand values and corporate identity; and the ability to design and manufacture products utilising new technologies and innovative production techniques. However, design has equally stronger 'softer' benefits that are harder to measure and quantify, but when viewed and understood within a wider organisational context, its value and ability to transform is considerable.

This book is divided into four sections, with each section focusing on a particular aspect of design and design management, offering a rich overview of the complexities and nuances of design in everyday practice and strategic utilisation.

When viewed in entirety, it is hoped that the reader gains a 360° contextual understanding of strategic design management and the many benefits it has to offer.

This book does not aim to offer firm conclusions on what constitutes design management, but to raise its value by discussing its worth and position within the organisation. It is hoped that the reader can explore the many issues and viewpoints offered and form their own interpretation and understanding of design management, taking this into their own professional practice. Through critical debate and analysis, it is hoped that a common consensus can be both established and agreed, whereby design management can take its next evolutionary step towards maturity and relevance in today's ever-changing world.

Section two
Design transformations

Design transformations illustrates how design and design management has many different interpretations and methods of strategic application. Used in a visionary manner, it has the power to transform the way an organisation views itself, leading to endless possibilities of change and corporate success. Two international perspectives of design management are offered; one from Mexico and the other from China. Each viewpoint articulates how design management is aligned to its specific contextual need, adapting to suit industry activity and business operation. To complement international comparisons, case studies are drawn upon to provide a unique insight into how design enhancement radically transformed two leading organisations throughout every aspect of business practice.

Section three
Design advocacy

Design advocacy raises the issue of how design champions are key drivers of change within the organisation. What are design champions and how do they contribute to strategic change and business growth? Leadership by design can drive innovation not only within the organisation but by reaching out to partners within the extended supply chain. With the ability to foster a climate of creativity and innovative activity, new and sustainable strategic futures are created, enabling endless possibilities for the organisation. The recent emergence of design leadership as an evolutionary advancement of design management raises many questions. Is it design management with new clothes or a logical developmental step in its ongoing maturity? Moving on to innovation and, in particular, the role of design and how it can draw upon expertise and knowledge within the supply chain, provides further weight to the argument that design is a strategic resource and should be represented at boardroom level in the planning process.

Section four
Design alliances

Design alliances concludes by focusing forward into the future, asking where next for design? Assaulted by continual change and complex socio-technical forces, organisations are having to adapt and adopt new ideas and experimental methodologies to compete and flourish on a global playing field. One sizable driver for change is the constantly shifting political landscape with new economies arising and others being dramatically reconfigured. One only has to look towards south-east Asia and the Indian sub-continent where a significant proportion of the world's manufacturing takes place, along with the outsourcing of technology-orientated workplace activities. With new market opportunities opening up on a daily basis, demographers and marketers are continually compartmentalising and slicing markets into ever smaller sizes based on individual lifestyles and personal aspirations, thus in turn forcing the designer to understand and produce designed solutions that excite customers and end-users throughout a variety of different points of engagement.

**Vision and Values in
Design Management**

Design
directions

Design
transformations

Design
advocacy

Design
alliances

How to get the most out of this book

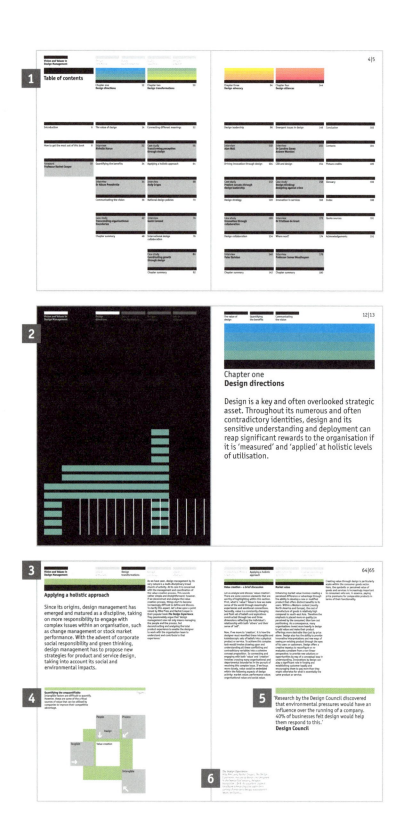

1 Structure
The table of contents reveals the overall structure of the book, consisting of four main chapters, with key elements colour-coded to aid navigation.

2 Chapters
Each chapter introduces a different aspect of design management, broken down into sections and accompanied by relevant photographs, diagrams and quotations.

3 Headings
The highlighted headings running across the top of each spread provide a continuous aid to navigation.

4 Diagrams
Some of the more complex concepts of design management described in the book are explained using simple diagrams.

5 Quotations
Highlighted quotations provide additional insight into the issues being discussed.

6 Glossary
In addition to the glossary at the end of the book, key names and terms are defined on the page where they appear.

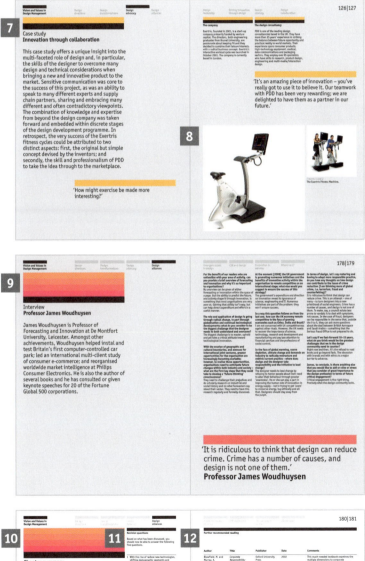

7 Case studies
The six chosen case studies illustrate the application of design management in different contexts.

8 Photographs
Many of the subjects described in the book are illustrated by photographs supplied by leading practitioners.

9 Interviews
Within each chapter there are interviews with leading design management academics and practitioners.

10 Summaries
The main points of each chapter and case study are captured in a concise summary paragraph.

11 Questions
Each chapter and case study has an accompanying set of revision questions.

12 Reading list
Each chapter and case study has a recommended reading list to help you explore further the issues covered in the chapter.

**Vision and Values in
Design Management**

Design
directions

Design
transformations

Design
advocacy

Design
alliances

Foreword
Professor Rachel Cooper

'Design faces many new challenges and opportunities in today's turbulent and globalised marketplace.'

Design management is a discipline in continual motion, changing, responding and adapting to the ever-increasing dynamics of social and business transformation. Its value as a force for change and thinking is growing in prominence, reaching far beyond the realm of industry and commerce, forging a strong presence within public sector institutions and not-for-profit organisations.

The value of understanding and being sensitive to design is now far better appreciated than when the first faltering steps were taken in the late 1970s. The manufacturing sector embraced design management as a key strategic tool in a quest for long-term survival within the midst of economic decline and increased overseas competition. Through the recessionary 1980s to the new millennium, its advancement was considerable, leading to the development of MBA modules and new educational courses, preparing students for design leadership roles in industry and commerce. Slowly, the influence of design began to permeate throughout every area of organisational activity, taking on and overcoming complex business challenges. The UK Design Council launched a host of initiatives aiming to bridge the divide between design and business; knowledge providers such as higher education institutions and the commercial sector placed design at the centre of the corporate agenda. Alongside these collaborative partnerships, national policies on harnessing the latent potential of design were being endorsed and supported by No.10 Downing Street, in a bid to foster a climate of creative engagement with emergent organisational and international developments.

Design champions were gaining prominence both within and beyond the organisation, strongly advocating the many benefits that design has to offer throughout a diverse range of applications. Its movement from design enhancement in a quest to continually differentiate products through to the creation of branded environmental 'experiences' has been both swift and timely. However, design faces many new challenges and opportunities in today's turbulent and globalised marketplace. The combined transformative forces of both technological and demographic change are demanding a reorientation of design within everyday practice, requiring new vocabularies that transcend geographic and cultural boundaries. Technological convergence is forcing a radical reappraisal of how we consume and interact with common everyday products and services. For example, the mobile phone handset is markedly different to the original handsets that we used in the 1980s, with miniaturisation and increased processing technologies altering our connection with the product experience and the services that we can now access and enjoy.

The rise of service innovation repositions our existing and long-held relationship with organisations, creating new modes and forms of engagement, supporting our ever-increasingly individualised lifestyles and personal tastes. Design not only supports innovation within the service sector but also within the extended supply chain, driving innovative activity through the transference of knowledge and technologies from one sector to another. This is particularly more acute and pertinent with the advent of new ICT technologies and distributed design teams, learning and sharing knowledge beyond geographic and cultural boundaries. Through this accelerated rate of development, visionary leadership of design is becoming a prerequisite for business success.

Design leadership is not only the sole preserve of business practice, but is also being recognised as an increasingly valuable contribution to the public sector, none more so than in the healthcare system. This is mostly achieved through better designed healthcare environments, more user-friendly medical products and enhanced communication material that increases efficiencies in the delivery of a more personalised service to the end-user. Taking this further, design is playing an increasing role in the fight to combat crime and anti-social behaviour, offering unique perspectives within the problem-solving process. Design can provide a holistic insight into the wider context of how a product or service is used and potential failing points, removing opportunities for subsequent criminal activity. With the rise of corporate social responsibility and the demonstration of commitment by organisations to their wider audiences and society as a whole, a broader, more understanding mindset is required. Rather than viewing corporate social responsibility as an unnecessary burden or limitation, the role of design is being used to meaningfully contribute to this critically important debate.

This book offers a unique set of perspectives by the author and leading contributors, exploring all these emergent issues from a variety of perspectives. Design management is in a constant state of flux, responding to the dynamics of change and social transformation, with its value and worth requiring constant reappraisal. I hope that you, the reader, can immerse yourself within these issues and rise to the challenge of championing design throughout everyday practice in your career.

Professor Rachel Cooper
Co-director
Imagination@Lancaster University

Professor Rachel Cooper
Rachel Cooper is a professor of design management and author of six books and over 200 research papers. Her research interests cover design management; design policy; new product development; design against crime and CSR.

**Vision and Values in
Design Management**

Design
directions

Design
transformations

Design
advocacy

Design
alliances

The value of
design

Quantifying
the benefits

Communicating
the vision

12|13

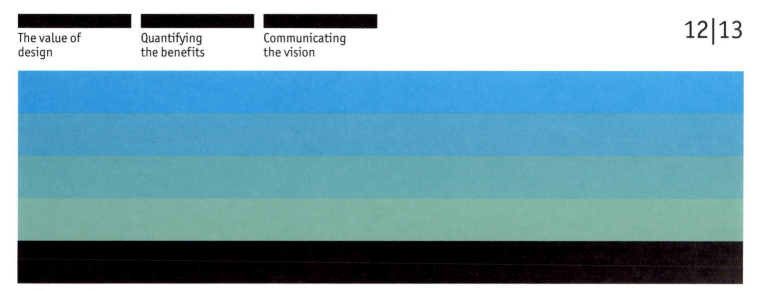

Chapter one
Design directions

Design is a key and often overlooked strategic asset. Throughout its numerous and often contradictory identities, design and its sensitive understanding and deployment can reap significant rewards to the organisation if it is 'measured' and 'applied' at holistic levels of utilisation.

The value of design

Communicating the benefits of design has been a slow and arduous task. However, organisations that fully recognise the benefits that design can offer tend to prosper and succeed in marketplaces that are often difficult. This section describes the 'softer' and arguably more 'potent' benefits of design within the organisation.

Despite a plethora of indigenous design talent, the UK has been slow to realise the full potential benefits that design can provide in the quest for successful new product introductions and commercial competitiveness. Other countries, in particular Germany, Japan and the USA have progressed by integrating design at a strategic level, rather than employing it solely as a tool to enhance the aesthetic appearance of existing products or surface decoration. In an increasingly competitive marketplace, organisations are continually required to develop and create the 'competitive edge'.

Percentage of firms saying design, innovation and creativity has contributed to these areas during the last three years.
Percentage of firms where design made a contribution. More than one answer possible, so percentages may add up to more than 100%.

Table 1

	%
Increased turnover	51
Improved image of organisation	50
Increased profits	48
Increased employment	46
Improved communication with customers	45
Improved quality of services/products	44
Increased market share	40
Development of new products	40
Improved internal communication	28
Reduced costs	25

Source: Design Council research by PACEC, 2001

Main sources for ideas to improve or change business

Table 2

	%
Customers	63
Internal discussions with staff/management	31
Suppliers	23
Publications/journals	11
Competitors' actions/plans	8
Other	8
Internal research and development	5
External consultancy	2

Source: Design Council research by PACEC, 2001

The value of
design

Quantifying the
benefits

Communicating
the vision

14|15

The company that does not plan for the future, operating solely on a day-to-day basis, will never unlock its true potential for sustainable growth and commercial success. Design and the many benefits it has to offer are often misunderstood by many organisations. Design can significantly contribute by:
— reducing production and manufacturing costs, minimising the use of expensive materials
— increasing customer loyalty, often by designing-in features that offer real tangible benefits to customers
— developing new and innovative products and services that could increase market-share in highly competitive markets
— reducing customer complaints by better design of information
— changing the perception of the organisation by utilising the way the customer experiences business in line with the **brand**.

The benefits

Research undertaken for the Design Council (2001) by **PACEC** highlights the many benefits that design can actively contribute to the organisation (see Table 1). This research provides strong evidence to date that good design can boost a company's operating performance and commercial growth. As a consequence of the recession in the early 1990s, companies were forced to develop new, often radical ways of competing in difficult and often tumultuous marketplaces. The vicissitudes of global forces and unrestricted movement of international capital present unforeseen problems for an organisation. Many organisations responded to the effects of 'change' and positively flourished, but for others, 'change' caused adverse effects on the company's ability to compete, survive and prosper. The benefits of design investment at a strategic level to greatly assist innovation are well publicised (Cooper & Press, 1995; Oakley, 1990; Walsh et al, 1992; Bruce & Bessant, 2002) illustrating how design can significantly add value to the organisation's product/service offerings.

Again, research by PACEC for the Design Council (2001) has quantified the benefits of innovative behaviour and product introductions to organisations, identifying the key drivers that force innovation (see Table 2).

Organisations utilise design in a variety of ways, providing many benefits in the way they behave and communicate to their customers. Design can be a powerful tool for managing and coordinating how the business looks and communicates to its customers. Design is also a useful instrument that could be harnessed to help the organisation realise and evaluate potential future business opportunities, in both the service and manufacturing sectors. At a strategic level, design can help maximise the company's potential to deliver desirable products and services to new markets whilst also defending existing markets from overseas competitors (see Table 3).

This illustrates the many different and diverse ways that design has contributed to business performance. Trueman (1998) classifies design strategies into four distinct areas, showing the differing benefits that design can provide through **added value**; manipulating image; enhancing process and improving production (see Table 4).

Percentage of all companies (ordered by employment size) saying design has contributed, at least to some extent, to the following issues:

Table 3

	0–19	20–49	50–249	250+
Increased competitiveness	25	75	82	80
Increased profits	22	79	78	76
Better communication with customers	26	80	83	87
Reduced costs	6	62	64	54
Improved quality of products and services	26	69	87	78
Increased market share	16	70	83	83

Source: Design Council National Survey, 2002

Brand
A name, term, design, symbol or any other feature that identifies one seller's goods or service as distinct from those of other sellers. The legal term for brand is *trademark*. A brand may identify one item, a family of items or all items of that seller.

PACEC
A well-established, specialist economic consultancy practice, with offices in Cambridge and London. It undertakes economic development and regeneration strategies, appraisal and feasibility studies.

Added value
The increase in worth of a product or service as a result of a particular activity; in the context of marketing, the activity might be packaging or branding.

**Vision and Values in
Design Management**

Design
directions

Design
transformations

Design
advocacy

Design
alliances

Levels of design strategy   Table 4

Design strategy	Design attributes	Company goals
Value	Product styling Aesthetics Quality Standards Added value	To add value for consumer and enhance company reputation
Image	Product differentiation Product diversification Product identity Brand identity Brand creation	Company image and strategy
Process	Generate new ideas Idea communication Interpret ideas Integrate ideas Promote products	Culture for new ideas, creativity and innovation
Production	Reduce complexity. Use new technology and materials Reduce production time	Improvement and reduce time to market

Source: Trueman, 1998

Added value

In increasingly competitive marketplaces the ultimate aim of the company is to offer their customers products and services that they want to buy and value in preference to what is on offer from competitors. Therefore, using design effectively will enable the company to increase the perceived value of their product offerings and maintain the competitive advantage. It is widely accepted that the successful organisation will no longer focus on lowest cost, but will strive to provide added-value products and services that are distinctive and appealing.

Customers are now far more demanding due to increased spending power and the proliferation of choice. Therefore, the company needs to anticipate, respond to and, more importantly, exceed the customer's expectations. Their rivals will overtake companies who fail to adapt and compete in this way. Geoff Hooker, Product and Market Development Director at British Steel, comments that: '...in their search to stand out from the crowd, more giant corporations will come to see design as a key source of competitive differentiation and added value. They will realise what we at British Steel have long known: good product design is crucial to commercial success.'

The value of
design

Quantifying the
benefits

Communicating
the vision

16|17

Figure 1
Apple fully leverages technology and service
offerings through design.

Figures 2 and 3
Bosch and Kodak constantly renew and
provide products that exceed their
customers' expectations.

Figures 4 and 5
Chanel and Clinique use design 'seductively'
to create strong and memorable advertising
campaigns.

Figures 6 and 7
Stella McCartney and Burberry remain
market leaders in the increasingly
competitive fashion industry by
transforming market intelligence into highly
desirable product lines.

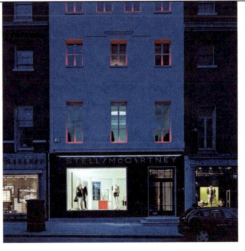

Figures 8 and 9
Lufthansa and Virgin create memorable
experiences of travel through the careful use
of product and service design.

Figures 10 and 11
Marks & Spencer and Sainsbury's use design
to convey the core philosophy of quality and
high-value service throughout every aspect
of customer engagement.

**Vision and Values in
Design Management**

Design
directions

Design
transformations

Design
advocacy

Design
alliances

Image

Utilised effectively, design can be an excellent means for managing and coordinating how the organisation looks to its customers, as well as the way in which it communicates with them. **Wally Olins** (1990) argues that, '…design is a major corporate resource, equal in significance just like other functions'. The organisation is continually producing designed material that conveys clear messages to both internal employees and their customers, so it is vital that a consistent and unambiguous statement of values is reflected in a coherent manner.

Failure to coordinate these messages effectively could result in poor company image and limited marketplace recognition. Organisations that have an enlightened understanding of design manage their company image very closely, benefiting from the impact of this positive image in many areas, such as recruitment and increased sales. Olins (1990) comments that design can offer emotional connections between the organisation and their customers as opposed to rational means: '…it is virtually impossible to detect quality differences between the products of major financial service companies, or petrol retailers, or the various chemical companies, for instance. This means that companies and their brands have increasingly to compete with each other on emotional rather than rational grounds. The company with the strongest, most consistent, most attractive, best implemented and manifested identity will emerge on top in this race.'

Design can be employed in the public service sector as much as in the business sector, playing a major role in the way services are developed and delivered more effectively. Design can:
— improve healthcare provision
— improve the quality of education through better environments and systems
— enable more effective and efficient recycling of waste products
— increase the effectiveness and image of public transport.

Research conducted for the Design Council in 2002 asked public sector organisations how they perceive the benefits of design to their organisation and ultimately to their customers (see Table 5).

What is design for?
Percentage of respondents (by service)

Table 5

	Total	Learning	Transport	Waste	Health
Design is about services working well to meet customer needs	76	79	80	75	68
Design is used to develop new products and services	65	57	73	73	64
Design is a creative thinking and envisioning process	61	60	63	68	53
Design is about how services look and are presented	54	52	54	67	47
Design is a strategic business tool	50	51	56	52	43
Design is used to provide a service that is tangible	40	38	45	38	39

Source: Trueman, 1998

Wally Olins
Olins co-founded Wolff Olins and was until 1997 its chairman. He is now chairman of Saffron Brand Consultants. He was awarded a CBE in 1999, has been nominated for the Prince Philip Designers Prize and received the Royal Society of Arts' Bicentenary Medal for his contribution to design and marketing.

The value of
design

Quantifying the
benefits

Communicating
the vision

18|19

Communicating core values
An ethically responsible organisation, such as the Co-operative Bank, should convey clear messages to both internal employees and its customers. It is vital that a consistent and unambiguous statement of values is communicated in a coherent manner.

Figure 1

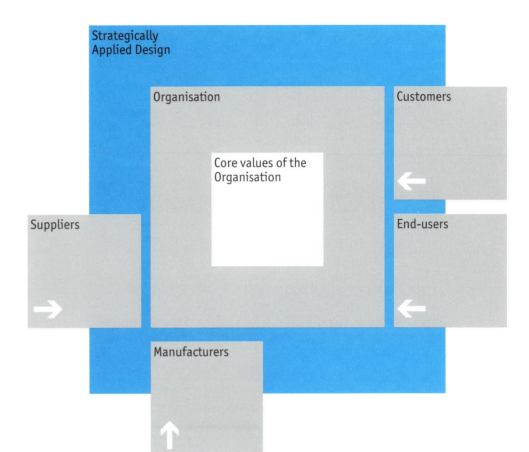

Strategically
Applied Design

Organisation

Customers

Core values of the
Organisation

Suppliers

End-users

Manufacturers

Figure 2
In the UK, the National Health Service (NHS) draws upon design expertise to ensure that both product and, more importantly, service offerings are consistently and effectively delivered through the use of systematic design 'thinking'.

Figure 3
Virgin has created a consistent and coordinated experience of elegant travel through the combination of experiential design and customer-centred thinking.

Figure 4
Through the careful design of 'learning environments', educational development becomes more effective in user-centred classrooms and lecture theatres.

The co-operative bank
good with money

The
Ethical
Consumerism
Report
2008

Part of The co-operative financial services

Figure 5
The Co-operative Bank has a firm commitment to ethically responsible behaviour in its business practice.

**Vision and Values in
Design Management**

Design
directions

Design
transformations

Design
advocacy

Design
alliances

Enhancing process

A well-defined and executed **NPD** process is a prerequisite to maintaining the competitive advantage in dynamic global markets. One frequently quoted statistic suggests that 85% of all future product costs are determined by the time a design project reaches the concept stage.

Therefore, investing in design at the initial stages of the product development is essential to achieving a successful outcome. Most production costs are already determined by the end of the design stage, even though only a small proportion of that is actually spent on design. However, achieving this requires an understanding of the discrete stages a project is likely to move through in its journey from idea to product commercialisation.

A major report for the Design Council, undertaken by the London Business School, estimated that the manufacturing sector in the UK spends £10bn a year on design and product development activities (1995 prices). This makes up 2.6% of manufacturing turnover, accounting for some 4.5% of the manufacturing sector workforce. A follow-up report (Sentence and Walters, 1997), which looked more closely at the link between design and performance, concluded that this operated primarily through the impact on export orientation; companies that were more design-intensive were able to grow faster because of higher sales in overseas markets.

Improving production

Design is key to enabling an organisation to remain competitive by lowering its production costs. Taking back product design to first principles can significantly increase production efficiency. Through design activity, design can reduce the complexity of component parts in a product, introduce new technology or materials and reduce production time. Design for manufacture encapsulates the conception, design, production and commercialisation of a product.

**Future product costs incurred
at the design stages**

Figure 1

%

Source: Design Council, 1998

The value of
design

Quantifying the
benefits

Communicating
the vision

20|21

A generic product development process
Key stages of development

Figure 2

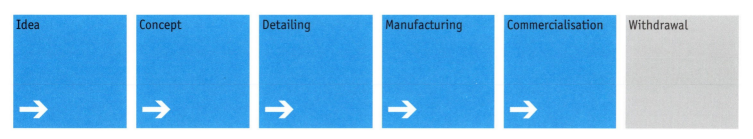

| Idea | Concept | Detailing | Manufacturing | Commercialisation | Withdrawal |

The idea or 'trigger' for a new product may come from the emergence of new technologies or feedback from market intelligence.

If viable, the trigger is developed into an initial product concept, then through detailed design development, the concept is taken further for manufacture (**DFM**).

After production the product is commercialised and enters the marketplace. Having gone through its natural product lifecycle (**PLC**), the product is either modified or withdrawn from the marketplace. In fast-moving technological industries the rate of product obsolescence is increased.

'. . . the benefits of good design are widely recognised . . . across the whole public sector, well-designed and attractive working environments can aid staff retention and recruitment while delivering real value for money.'
Tony Blair

New product development (NPD)
A disciplined and defined set of tasks and steps by which a company repetitively converts embryonic ideas into saleable products or services.

Design for manufacturability (DFM)
The systematic consideration of manufacturing issues in the design and development process, facilitating the fabrication of components and their assembly into the overall product.

Product life cycle (PLC)
The four stages that a new product is thought to go through from birth to death: introduction, growth, maturity and decline. Controversy surrounds whether products go through this cycle in any predictable way.

**Vision and Values in
Design Management**

Design
directions

Design
transformations

Design
advocacy

Design
alliances

Interview
Richelle Harun

Richelle Harun is senior design manager at London Development Agency. She trained as a textile designer before moving into design management. Her personal research field focused on the dynamics of small companies and their ability to assimilate design knowledge to catalyse innovation. Whilst working at the Design Council she developed Designing Demand, a nationwide design support programme for small business, which was launched in response to the Cox review of creativity in business (2005). Integrating design and business is still central to her role at the LDA where she is the development lead on design interventions including the London Design Festival, Manufacturing Advisory Service and Designing Demand.

Designing Demand is an exciting and challenging initiative. What is its core remit in terms of business engagement?
Designing Demand is part of a core portfolio of business support services which aim to improve regional economic performance. This programme helps small and medium enterprises understand how design can be integrated into their business to increase profit and competitiveness. By actively experiencing a successful design project, companies start to embed the management skills and processes needed to do it for themselves.

You are involved in raising awareness concerning the benefits and impact of design enhancement; from your own experience what percentage of businesses are still unfamiliar with design?
Design Council reported that on average in the UK 25% of business didn't believe that design played a role in their business and a third of companies surveyed do not use design services (Design Council 2006). From my experience most company owners/managers are very familiar with design, but only as a consumer and in terms of their personal lives and their purchasing decisions. Translating this to their business is more difficult, especially in non consumer facing goods and B2B markets where managers find it much more difficult to imagine themselves as the customer and going through the experience of buying a particular product or service. In many businesses, design is assigned to marketing and to one-off projects, such as websites and re-packaging. Taking such a narrow view of design can mean that brands, products and services are not consistent or in line with future aspirations.

Other than financial metrics, what metrics do you use to convince businesses of the value of design?
Bottom line impact is hard to argue with but it's also hard to claim credit for exclusively. Design is part of the mix of a successful organisation and increasingly seen as being important in bringing pride in an organisation to retain staff, reduce sick leave, increase brand loyalty and highlight corporate social responsibility strategies.

The value of
design

Quantifying the
benefits

Communicating
the vision

22|23

Designing Demand places great emphasis on workshops to discover the benefits of design. How do these work?
Workshops are designed to be an experience rather than a taught seminar, where managers can identify and discuss design opportunities in their business openly with experts and their peers. Workshop tools such as 'Matchbox' are used to encourage debate about issues in a specific business and involve peers in finding solutions. Underpinning Matchbox is the proposition that design can be used across the business and be used to help realise strategic goals or challenges.

You offer tools and techniques developed by the Design Council to generate and support strategic design decision making. Could you provide some detail on these?
At the core of the national Designing Demand programme model are Design Council developed tools which help aid the dialogue between design expert and client. Communication is key to any successful project and a designed approach developed this beyond the use of language to be experience-led. The Generate Framework, for instance, is the antithesis of the classic business audit tool; no check boxes, scales, scores or backward looking benchmarks. Although the aims were similar to identify, diagnose and prioritise action, a framework was much more flexible. A Generate workshop would typically take half a day; it is facilitated by a Design Associate and involves the owner and at least three senior managers. Loosely following the framework, the team is guided through a series of open-ended questions around product, service, brand, team and customers to identify the key business priorities for the business. Answers are stuck on post-it notes on an A1 chart and are left displayed and updated throughout the whole project. The process acts as a shortcut to relevant background information as well as providing an insight into personalities and team dynamics. Design opportunities are identified and prioritised and, as opposed to traditional methods, have senior management backing.

In terms of typical start-up businesses and in particular the ones on very tight budgets, what is the first thing you do regarding using design; where do you start?
For a start-up business, design is critical in the initial positioning of the product or service next to the competition, projecting the right values of the company and in some cases selling the concept to investors. Unfortunately at this stage in a business, the resources available don't often match the company's ambition. Prioritising is critical and looking at more creative ways of accessing design skills should be considered, i.e. designers who work on commission or royalty basis, working with design university students or looking out for grants and support provided by your local regional development agency. Always make sure you know exactly the costs up front but remember not to base your design decisions on whatever is cheapest. You'll end up paying for it in the end when the sales are slow.

When you work with businesses who are familiar with design, what other more sophisticated tools or interventions do you offer?
The more design savvy a client is, the more opportunity you have to focus their overall strategy instead of single projects. But this type of design is much less visible – i.e. redesigning processes, structures and strategies for new business. Bigger companies may be more familiar with design but face very particular challenges when decision making and coordinating the design process across different departments and levels. The immersion day was designed for a bigger business (this is a high impact, one-day immersion in design, facilitated by leading designers in their expert areas as a type of strategic design SWOT analysis).

Not only do you work with the private sector, you are now engaging with the public sector as well; what are the similarities and differences?
The Cox review brought design to the forefront of the business policy and the subsequent roll out of Designing Demand made it possible for small businesses nationwide to take action and to be shown how design can be integrated into everyday business strategy. Whilst think tanks and policy makers are clear on the need to re-design public services around the needs and lifestyles of people, the link with design is only made within discrete disciplines, i.e. architecture, product design, interiors. A broader view of design is needed to show real impact; for example, within the Building Schools for the Future to address the sustainability of the building and the curriculum as well as the community in which it resides.

Is there anything you would like to add that we haven't covered but you consider important to raise?
It's a very exciting time for design which brings new challenges for design management. The need for more creative approaches, particularly in the public sector, has brought a renewed focus on design methods. Try to embrace the opportunities without putting a label on it or unduly inflating expectations. Show how design can be part of the process and solution.

'The more design savvy a client is, the more opportunity you have to focus their overall strategy instead of single projects.'
Richelle Harun

Quantifying the benefits

The quantifiable benefits of design to the organisation are considerable and commonly understood. Continual research and collaboration with industrial partners by the Design Council and related organisations is raising awareness and significance of what design can offer to the organisation.

The value of design
The five key areas of organisational activity
where design can make a significant impact.

Figure 1

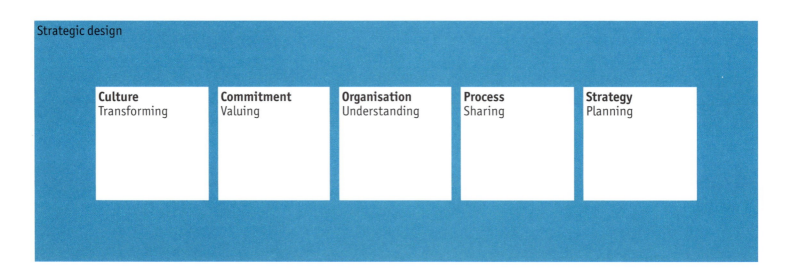

Strategic design

Culture	Commitment	Organisation	Process	Strategy
Transforming	Valuing	Understanding	Sharing	Planning

The value of
design

Quantifying the
benefits

Communicating
the vision

24|25

Trends indicate that design expertise may be especially critical for competitive and growth purposes within global markets. Designers may conceive, shape and communicate new innovative products and visualise brands, but design often needs to be coordinated and carefully aligned with the firm's strategy and core competencies.

Careful attention to design and its effective management can lead to the development of new and innovative products and services; stronger company image by the enhancement of brand values and corporate identity; and the ability to design and manufacture products utilising new technologies and innovative production techniques. However, design has equally stronger 'softer' benefits that are harder to measure and quantify; when viewed and understood within a wider organisational context, its intrinsic value and ability to transform is considerable.

Research for the Design Council by Brunel University and the University of Central England (1998) investigated the impact of design-led Teaching Company Schemes (known commonly as Knowledge Transfer Partnerships). They identified five key areas of organisational activity where design can significantly contribute:
— process: a shared journey
— organisation: rethinking understanding
— strategy: future planning
— culture: transforming behaviour
— commitment: valuing design

Through design enhancement and engagement, the research identified five key factors where design made considerable impact, often discretely. When viewed in entirety, the transformative nature of design changed the very complexion of the organisations.

'Management needs to ensure
that the fostering of creativity is
one of its specific goals.'
Cooper and Press

Key drivers on new product development
The initial idea or driver for developing a
new product could either come from external
sources or from within the organisation
itself.

Figure 2

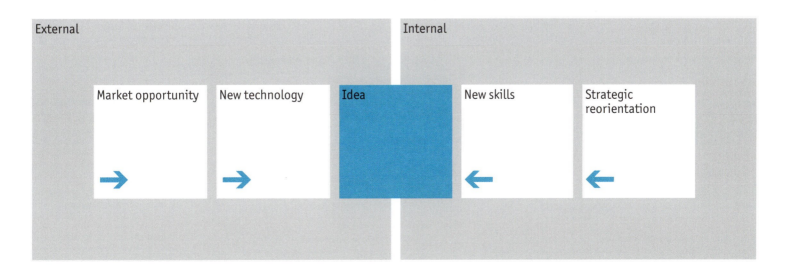

**Vision and Values in
Design Management**

Design
directions

Design
transformations

Design
advocacy

Design
alliances

Process: a shared journey

It is commonly agreed that firms and organisations of varying sizes, ranging from the small and medium sized enterprise to the large, multinational organisation employing thousands of employees, have typically neglected to embed and implement an organising design capability. Or, as is so often the case, organisations seem to have problems engaging with designers in order to harness their full creative and innovative potential. One perennial problem is concerned with the definition of 'design'. Design causes ambiguities because it has more than one common meaning. Often and sadly frequently, it tends to be viewed as merely style and appearance, or a very broad meaning is conveyed that is not well differentiated from planning or product development in general. However, a more suitable and broader meaning of design is that it is an activity as well as an aesthetic and interdisciplinary competence, which involves both the mental conception and visible projection of future form and configuration of human artefacts for industrial and/or welfare purposes (Walsh et al, 1992).

Professor **Birgit Jevnaker** (1995) comments further on this point, suggesting that '...design and innovation as drivers of value creation is thus a critical theme bringing forward the creative imagination made visible, whether the aim is incremental or more radical innovation, or both.'

The process of design could be compared to that of a journey. At its initial stages of inception, the journey has a rough direction and a particular emphasis is assigned to key considerations to ensure success. From the initial 'trigger' generating the idea – be it a gap in the market or new technological developments leading to **incremental modifications** to an existing product – through to the development of a radically new product, the process is fraught with risks and the possibility of total product failure. In this high-risk situation the process of developing a new product becomes a mutually interdependent exercise in sharing knowledge, expertise and vision. The design process is a complex, iterative and often frustrating journey of balancing stakeholder expectations, financial limitations, organisational competencies and mutual values.

It requires the input and expertise of diverse and often contradictory elements, each with their own unique perspectives and constraints. Central to this is the designer, who has to manage and balance expectations throughout each discrete stage of product development, often relying upon intuition and experience to drive the concept through to commercialisation. This has major implications for the way in which the organisation views design and its ultimate strategic importance. Professor **Lisbeth Svengren Holm** (1995) articulates this sentiment further, suggesting that design is more than a method. Design is also a view of practice that is risk-orientated, implying that actions are based on maximising experience rather than minimising risks.

In essence, this suggests that the management of design is a challenge to take responsibility for the environment and its physical objects. In applying techniques at a managerial level, there must be recognition of other factors influencing the design manager's ability to absorb and apply information throughout every aspect of organisational activity.

The role of design often transcends departmental boundaries within the organisation.

Figure 1

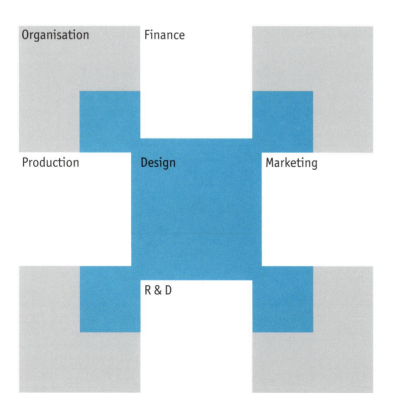

Organisation　　Finance

Production　　Design　　Marketing

R & D

The value of
design

Quantifying the
benefits

Communicating
the vision

26|27

As a consequence of design and its process crossing organisational boundaries, departmental functions and organisational domains become unified towards one common goal. It is through this shared ownership of the new product development process, that design has meaning and real value to the organisation.

Through value creation and raising awareness within the organisation, design becomes a strategic asset, a valuable tool in the armoury of competitive advantage and differentiation. As the level of sophistication and understanding of design increases, so does the ability to envision new futures and strategic horizons for long-term growth. Press and Cooper (2003) encapsulate this sentiment by adding that 'as our level of sophistication increases, so the demands increase on the designer to understand our relationship with the material world. However, the designer is not alone; organisations need to build the core skills around design thinking.'

'Design is what links creativity and innovation. It shapes ideas to become practical and attractive propositions for users or customers. Design may be described as creativity deployed to a specific end.'
Sir George Cox

The design and marketing interface – transferring market intelligence into the design process.

Figure 2

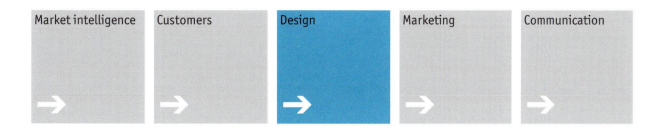

Market intelligence → Customers → Design → Marketing → Communication

Birgit Jevnaker
Jevnaker is Associate Professor in the Department of Innovation and Economic Organization at the Norwegian School of Management. She looks at how voices that champion design can influence and enhance corporate strategy.

Incremental modifications
A small change made to an existing product that serves to keep the product fresh in the eyes of customers.

Lisbeth Svengren Holm
Svengren Holm is Assistant Professor at Stockholm University School of Business. She also holds the Lise Meitner Professorship at Lund University, Department of Design Sciences.

**Vision and Values in
Design Management**

Design
directions

Design
transformations

Design
advocacy

Design
alliances

Organisation: rethinking understanding

Harnessing and utilising design at a strategic level can and indeed does lead to long-term benefits for the organisation. If we investigate more closely what design can offer, it provides:
— the ability to generate form to ideas
— to rethink business operation and process
— the development of new business strategies.

First, design can enable new and often radical ways of thinking and entering new areas of business activity. However, for this to be achieved, design needs to be properly organised and coordinated within the organisation. If so, it could offer long-term benefits and strategic opportunities to the development of innovative and novel products and increase the market attractiveness of existing products and services through redesign. At a process level, the role of design can help provide alternative methods of manufacturing through cost savings and the rationalisation of materials and suppliers. Also, if taken in entirety these combined interventions could lead to significant cost savings in both time and labour costs, thus ultimately ensuring increased profits for the organisation.

Lastly, through careful and continual dialogue with marketing, market information can be intelligently and creatively managed to enable the designer to focus upon designing products and services that appeal to specific **market segments** offering a sense of delight and value to end-users in often saturated marketplaces.

Through the transformative nature of design management and the way in which it is adapting to emergent and fluid economic and/or business demands, its influence on business strategy is increasingly gaining prominence. Professor Naomi Gornick (2006) wonderfully encapsulates the growing value of design management, suggesting that '...corporate design management is progressing steadily, increasing in personnel year by year. We can see the difficulties in progressing management thinking from a traditionally safe scientific framework to a more flexible culture of creativity and transformation.'

What if the organisation doesn't have a dedicated **in-house design** function? There has been lengthy and continual debate about the benefits of in-house design expertise versus external design consultancy. The debate will be explored further in subsequent sections of this book, but for now, let us investigate key factors surrounding the argument, and whether one route is more preferred and advantageous than the other. It is generally and commonly agreed that there are three main routes to design enhancement. The first is to establish an in-house design unit; second, to employ an external design consultant on a short-term basis; and third, a combination of both routes. All these routes are equally valid, yet choosing the most appropriate option is a complex and often bewildering process.

Let us focus upon the creation or expansion of an in-house design unit and the many benefits that it has to offer. In a small company environment (which is typical of many design-orientated businesses), in-house design can be of considerable benefit throughout all aspects of day-to-day business activity.

In-house design
A dedicated in-house design facility that is situated at the core of organisational activity, managing new product development and its ultimate success.

Figure 1

External consultancy
The external design consultant is predominantly engaged on a short-term project-by-project basis.

Figure 2

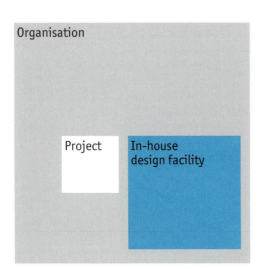

Market segments
The division of the market into groups based on factors such as age, gender and family size. Also known as 'demographic segmentation'.

In-house design
An established design team or department within an organisation.

The value of
design

Quantifying the
benefits

Communicating
the vision

28|29

Familiarity with the product or service and the very means of its production, technical development and marketing can provide financial benefits and cost-effectiveness to the business. With closer working relationships and effective communication between all departments in the company, the risk of project failure is minimised.

Now we will discuss the role and benefits of utilising external design. Outside consultants can offer direct and indirect benefits to the organisation; however, problems can occur in 'accessing' the most appropriate consultants and design brief formulation. Recent evidence suggests that external design consultants can add fresh and innovative ideas and solutions to long-standing or complex problems that an in-house design unit may have unwittingly overlooked through either familiarity or complacency, or a combination of both. In the short term, external consultants can be engaged on an 'as and when' basis, brought in to provide additional expertise and new ways of thinking to product development.

The combination of in-house and external design input is often described as 'the third way'. This route is perhaps the most appropriate when there is a knowledge and skill deficiency associated with a given project or when further assistance is needed in order to complete a project on time and within the agreed budget.

Regarding these difficulties of balancing the different and often complex routes to design engagement, Professor Margaret Bruce (1998) offers some interesting advice: a blend of in-house and external design expertise appears to overcome the problems and build on the positive aspects of each situation. However, the integration of the in-house and external professionals has to be managed carefully to ensure that they are truly working together. The potential fear of giving away commercially sensitive information and the need to build up an open and trusting relationship are both particularly acute.

It can be agreed that design offers a radical and often misunderstood source of opportunity, allowing the organisation to restructure and rethink its operational and business model, to forge strategic partnerships and alliances. Each route to design enhancement offers many strategic benefits to the organisation, and of course each route has its own inherent failings, but when viewed as a possible source of added value the risk becomes manageable when balanced against long-term aims. How does an organisation choose the preferred route to design enhancement? How do they balance short-term gains against long-term objectives? These are the long-term significant decisions that the organisation must make; however, we could agree that the route to success depends on how design is viewed, valued and understood. When all the factors of its very nature are taken into account, it is argued that design can add value, envision new opportunities and provide new radical avenues for organisational development.

The third way

The 'third' way is when the in-house design function requires the specialist expertise of an external design consultant for a complex or highly specialist design project. Usually, this relationship is short-term and ultimate project responsibility rests upon the internal design manager.

Figure 3

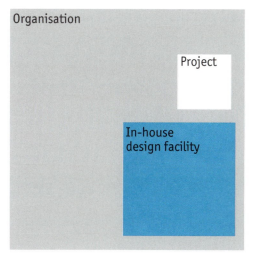

**Vision and Values in
Design Management**

Design
directions

Design
transformations

Design
advocacy

Design
alliances

Strategy: future planning

Strategy could be described 'as an underlying logic beneath the flow of decisions which create the future' and within the context of design strategy, this definition remains unsurpassed. Designers could be considered the 'unsung' heroes of strategy development; they probe, test and stretch what is possible in the understanding of product development. Designers have an inherent ability to explore form and function and stretch each possibility further, which in effect offers new avenues for market exploitation and eventual strategic product growth. Value can be added to existing or planned new products by drawing upon expertise from other organisational departments, identifying and sourcing knowledge from disparate and unconventional areas of wisdom, and incorporating this into **blue-sky thinking** and design concept development.

Designers must be, in essence, empathic and user-orientated in their understanding and approach to questioning the purpose and value of their ideas. Designers predominantly search for the context in which the product is used, using their intuitive skills and past experience to understand the problem at hand and establish creative solutions to overcome it.

Throughout this iterative and often lengthy process, the issue of balance and inclusivity becomes paramount. How does one balance the need of one **stakeholder** against the often conflicting demands of other stakeholders? It is this innate, intuitive and sensitive skill-set that the designer has to offer in understanding diverse opinions throughout the design development process. However, at the very core of this, is the ability to be flexible when valuing and considering the merits of every design solution. Each solution offers a rich seam of potential opportunity to be embraced and exploited; alternatively, each solution could be a missed opportunity for further growth. So, what do designers have to offer in the development of fluid and dynamic design strategies? The list could be considered endless; however, the significant points worthy of discussion include the following five aspects:

— Design 'antennae': designers and more importantly, design managers constantly 'scan' complex and highly segmented markets for new and innovative product introductions. Intuition and experience are the key ingredients to this unique and highly valued approach to strategy development.

— Design 'democracy': through embracing all key stakeholders and constituencies the risk of failure is minimised. Product failure can never be removed but it can be anticipated and overcome through an inclusive and empathic approach to new product development. Often this is through the delicate and sensitive process of communication, listening, understanding and observing.

— Design 'divergence': understanding problems from lateral and esoteric perspectives. Designers don't do anything as straightforward as seeing a problem from one dimension. They are multi-dimensional and panoptic in exploring tensions and boundaries through 360 degrees of objectivity and intuition. This highly valued and envied way of seeing and understanding a problem often leads to radical and challenging solutions that initiate new business opportunities.

Understanding design

At the heart of envisioning new products and furthermore, services, designers are in essence, empathic and user-orientated in their understanding and approach to design.

Figure 1

| Design understanding → | Context of use → | End-user → | Product/service |

Blue-sky thinking
Viewing a problem from a lateral perspective offering wildly innovative solutions.

Stakeholder
Any party (both inside and outside the company) who has a significant influence over the design, development, manufacture, distribution and use of a product.

The value of
design

Quantifying the
benefits

Communicating
the vision

30|31

— Design 'desire': passion and commitment to fulfilling a challenging design brief is essential in the problem-solving process. By crossing boundaries and sourcing specialist knowledge from other disciplines and departmental functions, this combined knowledge and experience is brought to bear upon a problem, leading to its overall resolution.

— Design 'disjunction': designers thrive on chaos, uncertainty and emergence; this, they argue, adds that creative inspiration and drive in the product creation process. However, middle-management demands order, certainty and conformity; this tension and creative dynamic establishes a creative equilibrium that enables a wider contextual framework for progression.

Figure 2
Nokia carefully integrates design and innovation to ensure its products and services remain at the forefront of technological developments.

Figure 3
IDEO, based in Palo Alto, USA, is one of the most respected and imitated design consultancies in the world. It is responsible for producing many household-name products in everyday use.

Figure 4
Orange has a sophisticated understanding of design and uses it to full effect in conveying the benefits of its products and services to customers.

Figure 5
Apple is synonymous with design excellence. Many of its products and services radically transform the industry on a continual basis.

Culture: transforming behaviour

Design, it can be argued, is a very subtle 'change-agent'; through every conversation, every gesture, it has the ability and power to change firmly rooted perceptions. Creativity and exchange of ideas are crucial when building up innovative activity within an organisation. Sutton and Kelly (1997) describe how culture and creative methods are used in the very successful American design agency IDEO.

Instead of doing creative work in isolation, designers work while clients, reporters, students and researchers visit the design studios. Normally, working with an audience increases anxiety and decreases creativity. At IDEO it works in the opposite way. IDEO has a specific company creative culture. Some companies even immerse their own designers in the IDEO culture for six weeks at a time to improve their product development skills (Gotzsch, 1999). So, how does an organisation approach this level of understanding where the designer's creativity remains free and unhindered?

Alvin Toffler (1991) carefully summarises this difficult and complex issue by suggesting '...that free workers tend to be more creative than those who work under tightly supervised, totalitarian conditions.' Thus the need for innovation encourages worker autonomy. It also implies a totally different power relationship between employer and employee. Cooper and Press (1995) synthesise these viewpoints, arguing that 'this certainly does not mean that creativity is inconsistent with the objectives of management; rather that management needs to ensure that the fostering of creativity is one of its specific goals.' Design management is indeed one of the methods used to attain this.

If we focus more carefully, it becomes more apparent that 'creativity' per se is not an individual spark of genius, but more an intelligently managed and choreographed environment for risk taking and intellectual freedom. Creative leadership is emphasised by Rickards and Moger (1999), who refer to four distinct features of creative leaders: they believe in 'win-win'; having a leadership style that is both empowering and motivating; developing strategies and techniques which encourage members of the team to solve problems; and align individual needs to the task in hand and responsibilities of the team.

To summarise, it could be argued that design is at the very core of innovative activity. The designer brings together all the disparate strands of organisational activity, to form a unified consciousness of focus in the product development process. To achieve this, designers have innate skills to visualise and communicate different professional languages, interweaving this knowledge into a creative fusion of innovative activity. Design is a core competence constantly challenging the worth of existing product offerings, striving for renewed and revitalised solutions to existing problems.

'Design has a role to play not only in creating a successful user experience, especially in service areas such as public transport, but also by influencing user behaviour in order to assist the operations and delivery of the service.'
Dr Alison Prendiville

The value of
design

Quantifying the
benefits

Communicating
the vision

32|33

Commitment: valuing design

Even with strategy, process, organisation and culture, ultimately without commitment from boardroom level, design remains impotent, if not redundant, as a strategic asset. The Design Council has for many years promoted the value of design to key decision makers and senior company staff through many facets of measurement. If we look at incredibly successful global brands and products, it is commonplace to see directors and senior CEOs who truly value design, such as Jonathan Ive, Vice President of Industrial Design at Apple; Clive Grinyer, Director of Design, Orange France Telecom; and Bill Sermon, Vice President of Design, Nokia Multimedia.

Without these leading figures promoting design, who could have predicted the long-term success and profitability of these organisations, considering the immense competition that they face?

However, moving aside from the harder financial benefits that these organisations have gained, let's focus more closely on the other, softer benefits to which design enhancement has contributed. Apple has an incredibly strong customer loyalty base. The brand and its core values communicate the very essence of its ultimate vision – producing and manufacturing technology-led products and services that remain at the cutting edge. Design is at the core of every aspect of company activity and thought, almost at a molecular level of consciousness. Through this commitment to the consistent and intelligent use of design – not just in terms of products and services, but also thinking, communication and behaviour – the organisation constantly achieves market superiority and widely held respect. If we look at the other end of organisational operation and size, Hope Technology, based in Yorkshire, UK, places an equal emphasis on value-added design. It designs, produces and manufactures specialist bespoke parts for bicycles that are respected throughout the professional cycling world.

Used intelligently, design can reduce production and manufacturing costs by rethinking production methods by drawing upon specialist expertise through the supply chain and extended networks. Design can increase and maintain customer loyalty as shown by Apple, where the organisation constantly strives for differentiation by designing-in features that offer real tangible benefits to its customers. On a much softer aspect of design and communication of company values, the Co-operative Bank is committed to ensuring that investors' money is invested wisely and most importantly, responsibly. Their values are historically deep-rooted, but it is through the medium of design and the way design is sensitively harnessed that these ethically driven values are communicated.

The evidence is conclusive: it is those companies that harness design which survive and prosper in turbulent and highly competitive marketplaces. The message is clear: design does make a significant difference; it is a low risk investment and, if used effectively, it will yield substantial rewards.

'Organisations need to build the core skills around design thinking.'
Cooper and Press

**Vision and Values in
Design Management**

Design
directions

Design
transformations

Design
advocacy

Design
alliances

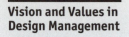

Interview
Dr Alison Prendiville

Dr Alison Prendiville is senior lecturer in
Contextual and Business Studies on the
Product Design degree at the University of
East London. She is interested in improving
awareness of contextual issues for students
in today's rapidly evolving economy. In
addition to the teaching she is also an active
member of the research team in the
Industrial Design Centre. Her research
activity has focused on service design
relating to urban mass transit (and the role
of contextual issues in shaping these);
and an EU-funded project Modality,
Intermodality and Interchange (MIMIC),
examining barriers relative and absolute at
transport interchanges.

**One of the reasons why many
organisations fail to fully utilise design is
because they are unclear as to its value.
What would you say to them to convince
them of its importance?**
From my experience, in certain situations
the value of design can be difficult to
quantify, especially in areas which may be
engineering led. Here, as in many other
business areas, design is perceived as
something superficial that is added at key
stages of the business management process.
Treated in this way, design is nothing more
than 'icing on a cake', a stylistic approach,
that is only seen as an isolated activity.
Design needs to be integrated into the
culture of an organisation not only to help
in the day-to-day decision making such as
assisting marketing or coordinating brand
values, but more fundamentally in a wider
strategic role. In this more embedded
capacity design assists organisations to
insert design thinking into the company
strategy, whether it's about identifying
future trends and directing corporate
objectives or assisting in organisational
change. The nature of design, which often
involves balancing decision making with
conflicting requirements, and its ability to
deal with complexity, involving different
disciplines, means it has wide application
for business practice.

**You could say the process of design is
similar to that of a journey; what would
you consider the most important part of
that journey to be?**
My first impression when answering this
question was to place the emphasis on the
investigatory and research phase of any
creative process in terms of identifying a
problem, rationalising whether it can be
solved by design, the design brief, costs,
time frames; the logistics of getting
'somewhere'. On reflection, however, when
considering the design process the most
important part is the on-going exploration,
refinement, development of ideas and the
opening up of new possibilities; the journey
has many stops with lots of exchange
between a variety of expertise. Equally all
the best journeys conclude with an arrival,
an end point, which in itself comes to
represent the journey and also a point of
evaluation in which appropriateness of
decision making and outcomes can be
assessed. Design is an iterative process
which is inter-dependent on the importance
of each phase of the journey. One cannot
identify any one aspect in isolation; like a
journey there will be interesting events en
route, but getting there is the main purpose.

The value of
design

Quantifying the
benefits

Communicating
the vision

34|35

What would you consider to be the long-term benefits of design, especially in today's ultra competitive marketplace?
Design offers the tangible and intangible evidence of an organisation, creates brand attributes and offers product and service differentiation for customers. The integration of design, long term, creates brand values which become central to a company's market position; the design and innovation of a product or service is representative of the quality of the company. For example, new products from Fritz Hansen are expected and required to reflect the company culture based on the quality and reputation of their design classics, such as the Egg and Swan chairs, designs that are timeless and historically significant because of their materials, proportion and form. Increasingly, organisations are also using design to achieve greener and more responsible business practices, which also serve as useful marketing tools. Marks and Spencer and their 'Plan A' that aims to make the business carbon neutral by 2012, is using design to set the benchmark for sustainability in retailing. In all instances when an organisation creates and establishes a unique design culture, as part of its corporate objectives, that organisation is giving itself greater leverage to compete and maintain its competitive advantage rather than relying on price and cost cutting.

It has been said design management has the ability to enable organisations to radically change and rethink business practice; do you have any particular thoughts on this?
Yes, design management can play a huge and critical role in enabling a company to rethink its business, as long as it has boardroom support and is positively incorporated throughout an organisation. Design management is the bridge between business and design and ultimately the corporate objectives. This has been demonstrated historically from early examples such as Wedgwood using branding and product innovation for competitive advantage, to contemporary companies such as McDonalds with its shift from fast food to modern 'healthier' lounge-cafes and the AA, which has re-positioned itself as the Fourth Emergency Service.

How do you think designers could contribute to business strategy; would you say their contribution is valuable?
Designers are fundamental to a business's strategic thinking. This is because they have the potential to identify problems and recognise opportunities across different disciplines. Designers think and work in a holistic way that joins up areas of business practice that are often compartmentalised. For example, designers link up financial aspects and interests in a business via return on investment and cost savings in the design of a product or service but equally are comfortable collaborating with marketing in order to enter new markets or respond to changing consumer needs. However, it is necessary for the designer to understand and appreciate the wider role that they can play within a business, as catalysts for change. Unfortunately many design courses focus on the design process as an individualistic creative exercise and fail to place it in the wider business or social context. Consequently, some designers have a narrow view of their role and influence within an organisation.

Designers often see problems and potential opportunities from different perspectives; do you think this is a unique skill in strategy development?
Design training ideally centres on a multi-disciplinary approach that encourages creative thinking as well as problem solving. The fact that design is a wide ranging activity which draws on different disciplines and experts means that designers are often required to embrace and work with ideas which may sit less comfortably or may come into conflict with other areas of business management. However, although I think this skill is more common to designers, I don't think it is unique to them. Design is the means by which a company articulates its position, brand values and corporate goals but through a design manager it should also create a culture that embraces, through collaboration, opportunities and input to company strategy from other business management disciplines within the organisation.

IDEO in Palo Alto is well-recognised for fostering a creative environment to support innovative activity; could you offer any other celebrated examples?
To me Hilary Cottam is an example of someone fostering a creative environment through her consultancy work, which applies design to the macro context of the public sector such as schools, local government, transport, health care and prisons. Methods commonly used to problem solve, explore user behaviour and prototype in a design process are applied to a wider social context to understand and engage citizens and users in the process of addressing society's problems. The approach is multi-disciplinary, relying on designers, policy makers and social scientists. Moving design away from the notion of an output and commodity into one of designing and influencing social relationships and networks, yet at the same time offering prototyping and testing of such models, is unique.

Many globally successful brands have full boardroom commitment to support design; have you any other good examples that you would like to praise?
Although not often immediately considered to be a global brand, I feel Transport for London (TfL) has many of the prerequisites for this title. Set up in July 2000 as a strategic authority, it oversees the provision of transport in London. The coordination of all the different transport elements that make up London's transport network from the Oyster card through to signage and station design, into a coherent and integrated service, together with it being the custodian of some of the most iconic design symbols of the 20th century, makes London's transport one of the most instantly recognisable systems in the world. Frank Pick, head of the London Passenger Transport Board in the 1920s, was faced with delivering design in a very complicated organisation, which was also required to meet commercial ends and win managerial approval (Forty 1995). In the same way, Innes Ferguson, TfL's Group Design Manager, today demonstrates how design, when used strategically and with support from the Greater London Authority, can create cohesion and assist in the operation of one of the world's oldest and largest transport systems and similarly meet very challenging commercial ends.

Vision and Values in Design Management

Design
directions

Design
transformations

Design
advocacy

Design
alliances

Communicating the vision

For design to be widely understood and accepted by the organisation, it often requires a key individual or 'champion' to drive forward. Some organisations have a champion to promote its worth both inside and outside of the company; others have such a strong and well-established design legacy that their entire business model is communicated through the vision of design. This section examines the characteristics of a design champion.

Figures 1 and 2
Stefano Marzano, CEO and Chief Creative Director at Philips Design, has championed design at Philips, producing some of the most innovative and recognisable household products in use today.

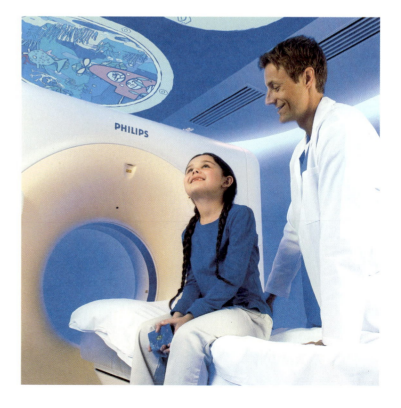

The value of
design

Quantifying the
benefits

Communicating
the vision

36|37

Design champions

It is commonly understood that most successful business processes require good, if not visionary leadership, and design is no exception to this rule. Two issues quickly come to the fore when trying to ascertain key characteristics of visionary design champions; the first one is 'influence' and the other is 'intent'. Extending design influence throughout all areas of business activity is a key priority for the champion, whereby the value and benefits of design are constantly and persuasively communicated to often a wide and disparate set of audiences. This could involve speaking to supply chain partners in the potential development of innovative new-to-world products, through to top-level brand development. Secondly, 'intent' is constantly ensuring that the integrity or the key essence of the core concept is not diluted throughout subsequent stages of design development. In a way, it is more akin to a protective parent ensuring that their child doesn't get bullied in the playground. If one considers the numerous and intensely problematic phases of manufacturing and production alone, the issue of maintaining design intent becomes paramount.

Individuals and design

Trying to understand the nature of design champions presents a conundrum; often these individuals are sources of innovative activity in both processes and subsequent products, yet organisational structures stress order and adherence to prescribed methods of day-to-day operation. The magic moments of innovation arise when design champions assert their individuality, breaking free from common organisational orthodoxies, synthesising novel interpretations that move design projects into new horizons. What we are seeing in contemporary business practice is the emergence of the importance of individuals to design and innovation. Design champions need power and prestige to overcome organisational resistance to risk taking and conformity. Some organisations identify a role for design champions to drive new projects through organisational or procedural boundaries which may be encountered. In such companies, an elite 'task-force' approach is quite commonplace with a small select group of engineers, designers, marketers and others assigned to specific projects. Other organisations may prefer to use a more broadly based method, perhaps built on one or more large units within which there are a number of projects. Individuals may then move in or out of these projects depending upon the need for their particular skills.

However, whatever organisational structure is adopted, strong leadership and management will be required. We can agree that all managers are confronted by change, none more so than design managers; however if no change ever occurred then there would be no need for a design manager at all. If markets were static, or totally predictable, no one would need to take bold decisions about the development of new products or services. If we take this thinking further, if customers' tastes and loyalties never changed then no new products would be required. However, moving back to the real world of today's globalised marketplace, change is an ever present fact of life. For a combination of differing reasons, all companies must continually adjust their practices and activities to compensate for changes which are taking place. In the same manner of thinking, changes in the marketplace are constantly dictating a need for the design of new products or improving old ones, giving rise to some degree of change within the organisation. Regardless of its extent, many organisations will try to resist change right up to the point where business survival is seen to be at stake.

'In UK businesses where design is integral to operations, 84% say they've increased their competitiveness through design; and 79% think that design's importance to competitiveness has risen over the past decade.'
Design Council

Design
directions

Design
transformations

Design
advocacy

Design
alliances

Championing change

Organisational change has become a way of life – change in industry is now commonplace. By and large the three forces of change include globalisation, information technology and processing and **industry consolidation**. The first two forces for change – globalisation and technology – will inevitably grow. However, it's not just enough for organisations to simply 'go international' or acquire 'fully networked' status. In today's business environment organisations need to be more fluid, inclusive and agile. They need to manage complex information flows, embrace new ways of operation and 'thinking' quickly, and communicate this new ethos throughout every aspect of operation – communicating the vision. The third driving factor – industry consolidation – continually grows in importance. The rising trend of mergers and acquisitions and strategic alliances brings both dangers and unique benefits to the organisation.

Partnerships, international joint ventures and strategic alliances can be less dramatic but more highly evolved vehicles for innovation. However, many alliances often fail because, whilst there is strong support at the top of the organisation, departments at lower levels are left to resolve tensions and conflict.

Change occurs constantly and at many levels in an organisation. There may be an occasional seismic event within the organisation, often induced by external forces; there are also the everyday actions of people engaged in their work. In 'change-adept' companies, people simply respond to clients and customers and move on to the next design development project. They do not necessarily change their assumptions about how organisations operate, but they continuously learn and adapt.

Innovative, change-adept organisations predominantly share three key characteristics, each associated with a particular role for design champions.

1 Championing innovation – to encourage innovative activity; effective design leaders nurture and help develop new concepts, ideas and novel applications of technology that differentiate organisations.

2 Championing performance – providing organisational and personal competence, supported by continual professional development and training, to execute and deliver added value to more demanding clients.

3 Championing collaboration – making cross-organisational and cross-cultural boundaries with partners who can extend and leverage the organisation's reach.

These distinct but valuable 'soft' assets accrue naturally to design-aware organisations, just as they do to successful individuals. They reflect habits, personal skills, behaviour and relationships. When they are deeply engrained in an organisation, change is commonplace and resistance is nominally low. Change driven by crisis is usually viewed as a threat – not an opportunity.

'Designers think and work in a holistic way which joins up areas of business practice that are often compartmentalised.'
Dr Alison Prendiville

Industry consolidation
Technological change and innovation are radically transforming established business models and practice, leading to the emergence of new collaborative partnerships across the globe.

The value of
design

Quantifying the
benefits

Communicating
the vision

38|39

Figures 1 and 2
Sir Norman Foster has produced some of the
most recognisable feats of architecture and
engineering around the world through
visionary leadership.

Figures 3 and 4
Morgan has taken its highly distinctive
vehicles into the 21st century without
sacrificing the company's long association
with tradition.

Design
directions

Design
transformations

Design
advocacy

Design
alliances

Characteristics of design champions

The key attributes a design champion can offer an organisation are passion, conviction and the ability to instil confidence in others. Some of the most important characteristics of design champions are as follows:

— Antennae for change: actively scanning both the internal and external business environment for movements and trends in technology and the marketplace. Partnerships, collaborative agreements and working closely with suppliers can all provide a rich source of knowledge that can be harnessed within the company.

— Panoptic vision: champions view data and information from a kaleidoscopic range of sources. They constantly question their assumptions about how pieces of the organisation and marketplace fit together. Champions remember that there are many solutions to a given problem and that by looking through a kaleidoscopic lens they can envision new solutions and sustainable futures.

— Advocates for aspiration: in order to foster a climate of risk-taking and innovative activity, conviction of purpose is fundamental. Often design champions talk about communicating a vision as an instrument of change, but you could also interchange the term vision with aspiration.

— Coalition developers: champions need the involvement of people who have access to resources, knowledge and political influence to make change happen. Coalition building and fostering is arguably the most neglected factor in the change process. In the initial stages of planning change, champions must identify key advocates and extol the benefits of their idea with the same passion and deliberation as the entrepreneur. Coalition building requires an understanding of the politics of change, and in any organisation those politics are formidable.

— Vision transfer: once a coalition has been established, the champion needs to constantly ensure that the design project team are fully supported throughout the duration of the project. Rather than handing over an idea for implementation, the team needs to take ownership and embrace the merits of the concept – in essence transferring the vision throughout the organisation.

— Ensuring intent: one of the major failing points of developing new, challenging products is the middle stages of development – manifesting the idea from concept to reality. There have been many examples of an idea created by senior management, then left to others to take it through to commercialisation. Most people get excited by the initial idea and the many rewards that it has to offer, and everybody loves endings, especially happy endings; it's the hard work in between that demands the attention of true design champions.

— Recognition reward: remembering to reward the design team or key individuals is a critical skill. Design is a team-based multidisciplinary activity and celebrating team accomplishments is a critical leadership skill; arguably it is one of the most under-utilised motivational tools in organisations today. Many people are involved in changing the way an organisation views and utilises design and it is important to share the credit. Never has the old adage been so true: 'Success has many parents but failure is an orphan.'

Figure 1
Peter Saville created a strong identity to the emergent music scene of Manchester in the 1980s. Saville's album design for Joy Division's last album, *Closer,* was controversial in its depiction of Christ's body entombed.

The value of
design

Quantifying the
benefits

Communicating
the vision

40|41

Championing and driving change through inspirational leadership has become a major theme of focus of commentary for good reason and this book embraces the issue throughout subsequent sections. Design champions, leaders and managers set the direction, define the context and help maintain coherence for their respective organisations. Champions manage the culture, or at least the vehicles through which that culture is expressed. They set the boundaries for mutual collaboration, autonomy and the sharing of ideas and knowledge, affording meaning to and understanding of events that would otherwise appear random, chaotic and spontaneous. Increasingly, the intangible assets cannot be planned and ruled yet they are critical to design success. Design champions' ideas or concepts, their commitment to high standards of competence and their placement of trust with strategic partners are what set apart design-aware organisations. All these inherent requirements can be enhanced by design leaders, but none can be mandated.

Summary

Design champions: leaders or managers? That is the primary question of this book. Who is best placed to drive the vision of design throughout every aspect of organisational activity? Are they all equally different with different skillsets and responsibilities within the organisation or do they each have their own intrinsic role to play in the initiation, implementation and delivery of design vision? Design needs a voice and presence within the company, and none more so than within the higher echelons of corporate decision making – the boardroom. However, once the strategic decision has been made, who then is most suited to communicate the vision? Taking an idea from a fledgling concept through to commercialisation involves overcoming many obstacles and tensions – often these barriers are institutionalised within the company itself. How can design overcome these obstacles?

Design is a proactive force for change, requiring immense vision, passion and political skills in order to succeed; design should no longer be regarded as a 'silent' activity as its importance has been neglected for far too long. The position and responsibilities of the design champion are becoming increasingly complex. Design development is no longer a localised activity, positioned neatly and comfortably within company boundaries; the boundaries of the company are increasingly shifting and becoming blurred, dissolving at the interface between supplier, organisation and consumer. To transcend these malleable boundaries of operation and responsibility, there is growing recognition and demand for design champions to communicate the vision of design and the rewards that it has to offer.

'A recent CBI survey showed that 55% of manufacturing firms see design and development as one of their most important sources of competitive advantage in five years' time.'
Confederation of British Industry (CBI)

Case study
Transcending organisational boundaries

This case study illustrates how the active involvement of a lead design consultant radically transformed a straightforward design brief into a radical new product introduction, providing huge rewards for the client company. By adopting a central role within the design development process, the design team were able to take a more holistic approach to the development and testing of initial ideas through to commercialisation. Drawing upon expertise from within the supply chain, this specialist knowledge was used to inform and shape the development of an ambitious concept that allowed the company to enter into highly competitive markets in both Europe and the USA. To drive this vision, proactive design leadership was required to ensure the manifestation of strategic intent.

'A quarter of manufacturers rank design as the most crucial factor in their business success (UK average 15%). And over half (56%) feel design has become more important in the past decade.'
Design Council

The value of
design

Quantifying the
benefits

Communicating
the vision

42|43

The company

Ideal Standard, based in the UK, is primarily involved with the manufacturing and marketing of bathroom and sanitary equipment. Its parent company is based in North America. Total sales (which include bathrooms) has exceeded $1.8 billion. The company has been significantly affected by stagnant market conditions and increased competition in what is considered a mature marketplace. However, by restructuring their existing product ranges, Ideal Standard remains competitive and financially secure in difficult economic conditions.

The designers

Evoke Creative (formerly called David Raffo Design) was first established in Cheshire, in 1980. After 21 years in practice, it is considered one of the leading design agencies in the UK, with a history of successful projects that include medical equipment, toys and fitness equipment.

Product development

The trigger

In 1998 Ideal Standard identified a suitable opportunity in the complex shower market to introduce a new and progressive shower range that could be developed and marketed throughout Europe and North America. At the time, the shower market was in a period of stagnation and slow growth; therefore, the new product range had to offer unique benefits to the customer in order to gain an established position in what was already a crowded marketplace.

At the time, Ideal Standard did not have an existing product range suitable for the identified target audience and its nearest rivals already had an established presence in the market. Through the combination of these factors, it was clearly apparent that there was a high degree of risk involved in the development of any potential shower range system. Trevi, a major brand under the Ideal Standard umbrella, was neither operating nor recognised in that specialist marketplace, but they had the elements required to enter the marketplace including a very strong and agile manufacturing capability.

The brief

The design consultants were initially identified and selected to work on the new product development programme. They already had worked with Ideal Standard on other unrelated projects and had a good relationship with the company. The director of new product development at Ideal Standard was instrumental in developing the design brief. This was then further refined and developed with the design team. Two main factors were crucial in the formulation of the brief; first, that Ideal Standard were entering a highly competitive and mature marketplace, so it had to have a clear direction and focus on a sustainable strategic future within that marketplace. Secondly, Ideal Standard did not have an existing product range to either work with or further refine. However, it did have a large 'inventory' of component parts, valves and screens that could be consolidated into a new and innovative product range. During this early and critical stage, Trevi and Ideal Standard suppliers joined the product development team to establish a full working partnership to enable the designers to progress the concept through to commercialisation.

Figure 1
Initial feedback on Trevi's new showering range was extremely favourable.

**Vision and Values in
Design Management**

Design
directions

Design
transformations

Design
advocacy

Design
alliances

The role of innovation

The design team were highly instrumental in providing innovative approaches to the project during the initial stages. The designers had a long and well proven track record of working with complex medical products and related technologies which greatly informed their strategic approach to the user interface and controls for the shower units. In particular, the design team were keen to explore and investigate pure technology and then tailor it to the development programme. Following an exhaustive analysis of rival product offerings and having developed an enhanced understanding of Ideal Standard's manufacturing capabilities, the designers were confident from the very outset that the company had the appropriate expertise to successfully develop the ambitious design concept. Very early on during the conceptual stages, the design team decided to further explore the idea of a pre-programmed user control panel that featured pre-set showering options. This was a significant departure from competing products in the marketplace, thus offering Trevi a key source of differentiation. By investigating competing products within the marketplace, the designers were quickly able to identify design-led opportunities with which it could enable the new product range to offer clear and value added benefits to the customer. The extended project team were in full agreement on the robustness and worth of the design concept and its viability for full scale development and commercialisation. Plus, they had established a common consensus on marketing the product range not as a shower, but more of a showering 'experience'.

Multidisciplinary team involvement

A key factor contributing to the success of the project was the involvement of primary stakeholders during the design and production of the concept. The product manager for Ideal Standard worked very closely with the design team, offering invaluable specialist expertise regarding manufacturing and supply chain involvement. Over an intense period of two to three months, the project team developed, tested and at times rejected ideas time and time again in a bid to select the most appropriate concept for refinement. Of primary concern was how the development team could assemble the core functional features of the showering system to create a series of specific showering 'moods' and then to refine this strategy through the design development process.

Design leadership

At the early stages of the design project, the design team were very much regarded and engaged as consultants on a short-term basis. However, over time, the designers moved further into the company, attending strategy meetings and playing a significant role in specialist negotiations regarding product development and manufacturing options. By forging a more intimate understanding of the complexities of production and potential problem areas that may arise further down the line, the lead designer was invited to attend weekly meetings representing strategic design direction as opposed to just a short-term design consultant.

Also, by creating a greater sense of partnership with Ideal Standard, the designer had an increased understanding of how the company functioned, which included looking at their constraints and strengths – in particular their manufacturing capacity. As the project developed, reaching the critical production stages, the design team began to work 'within' the organisation, enjoying direct access to all the key suppliers, benefiting from their knowledge and expertise. Arising from this centralised position, the design team had a broader understanding of what expertise they could draw upon to provide highly technical involvement in the development of the product. As a consequence of this central role, they could then communicate the essence and vision of the strategic vision to the marketing, finance and management departments who all had an active stake in its overall success.

What was crucial to maintaining strategic design vision of the core concept was the design team's proactive involvement throughout all stages of its development. This was particularly acute when devising all point of sales advertising imagery and brochures to two different international markets – the USA and UK. Plus, the lead designer had an active role in establishing a strong and robust brand identity for the moods concept that was critical in raising its visibility in crowded marketplaces at home and overseas.

'In a challenging economic climate, the need to stand out from the competition by adding value becomes more acute. Using design is a great way to achieve that.'
Design Council

The value of
design

Quantifying the
benefits

Communicating
the vision

44|45

Summary

The new showering and bathing range was launched to critical acclaim throughout the USA and mainland Europe. Initial feedback was extremely favourable, with the market fully accepting the product range and all the unique user benefits that it offered. As a result of strategic design investment and, in particular the vision of the design team, Ideal Standard managed to successfully consolidate its vast inventory of valves, screens, and panels into a successful and highly innovative product offering. The design team undertook an extensive audit of the inventory of parts and realised very quickly that they could be combined to form a cost-effective basis for the new showering concept. In order to achieve this, however, lengthy consultation and negotiation was required between all the core constituencies within the company and supply chain partners outside of it.

By forming a strategic mutual alliance between the design manager and key decision makers at Ideal Standard, the concept vision was driven through critical stages of decision making at boardroom level and on the shop floor. The moods concept was testament to the ingenuity of the design team and taking this abstract idea successfully through production was remarkable, considering the complexities of combining the disparate elements into one product system. Inevitably there were technical problems in assembly, but by drawing upon expertise from supply chain partners, these problems were overcome.

'In our modern world, teamwork and problem solving are what's going to take us forward.'
Paul Saunders

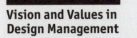
Revision questions

Afterword

Two clear themes have emerged from this study: first, the importance of key individuals within the design development process; and secondly, how visionary design leadership can take an initial idea right through the critical stages of development to the marketplace. Ultimately the case study has illustrated how design, which has a potent presence within an organisation, can be used to reach out and forge connections with external organisations and help ensure project success.

1 A large percentage of the success of this concept was attributed to the involvement of key individuals within the client organisation. Why was their involvement so important?

2 The supply chain partners contributed invaluable expertise within design development; at what stage would you consider their involvement crucially important?

3 At what stage of the design process would you start considering the issue of branding when developing a new to the market product?

4 In mature and often crowded marketplaces, what can design offer the organisation in order for them to be profitable?

5 Multidisciplinary project teams are vital to developing new products, but what could be the potential problems with a team of members drawn from often disparate professional backgrounds?

'Design is the thread that connects ideas and discovery to people and markets.'
Design Council

Further recommended reading

Author	Title	Publisher	Date	Comments
—	*Harvard Business Review on Supply Chain Management*	Harvard Business School Press	2006	As you would expect from Harvard Business School – a thorough account of supply chain dynamics and the value of collaborative partnerships in industry.
Buckingham, M. and Coffman, C.	*First, Break all the Rules*	Pocket Books	New edition 2005	A gem of a book, discussing how successful managers ignore conventional thinking to get the best out of their employees.
Lean Martin, J.W.	*Six Sigma for Supply Chain Management: The 10-step Solution Process*	McGraw-Hill Professional	2006	This book teaches business managers and students how to apply the tenets of lean operations and six sigma management principles to supply chain management.
Liker, J.	*The Toyota Way: 14 Management Principles from the World's Greatest Manufacturer*	McGraw-Hill Professional	Reissue edition 2004	A unique insight into Toyota and how they create and value a culture of continuous learning – invaluable to anyone interested in either the Toyota success story or the subject itself.
Sloane, P.	*The Leader's Guide to Lateral Thinking Skills: Unlocking the Creativity and Innovation in You and Your Team*	Kogan Page Ltd	Second revised edition 2006	The author makes a strong case for innovation and lateral thinking in business, where doing new, different things in new, different ways is more important than doing the same things more efficiently.

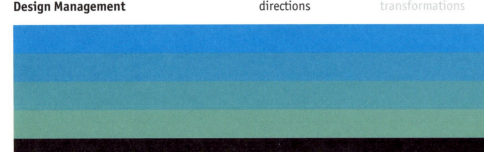

Chapter summary

The value of design is immense to the organisation, offering many different and diverse benefits providing strategic growth and direction. The chapter began by offering strong evidence that design can boost a company's operating performance and long-term economic growth. We talked about how design can be classified into four distinct areas: added value; image; enhancing process; and its ability to improve production and manufacturing effectiveness. We then discussed the business imperative for the need for intelligent design management and the 'softer' benefits that it can provide, not only through value creation but by adding meaning and real value to the organisation. Having provided a broad discussion of the many benefits of design, we talked about design champions and how key individuals often put strategic design management firmly on the corporate agenda.

Revision questions

Based on what has been discussed, you should now be able to answer the following five questions.

1 The Design Council provides a strong case for the role and value of design to industry; however, many organisations are still reticent to invest in design. How would you convince an organisation to adopt a higher awareness of design?

2 What are the pros and cons of using an external design consultant?

3 How can the designer contribute to business strategy formulation and planning?

4 Can creativity be learned? If so, provide some tools and techniques that can help the user to unlock their full creative potential.

5 Can you provide examples of both large and small innovative organisations that use design to its fullest effect?

The value of
design

Quantifying the
benefits

Communicating
the vision

48|49

Further recommended reading

Author	Title	Publisher	Date	Comments
Cox, G.	*Cox Review of Creativity in Business: building on the UK's strengths*	UK Treasury	2005	Excellent and highly informative report that passionately argues the value and importance of design to industry and the UK economy.
Design Council	*The Business of Design: design industry research*	Design Council	2007	Design Council is an invaluable source of facts, information and advice for all aspects of design. Every year it releases research findings on the business and value of design – its excellent website makes accessing the information straightforward and manageable.
Gorb, P. (editor)	*Design Talks. London Business School Design Management Seminars*	Design Council	1988	Don't be put off by the date, this book is as important and worthwhile now as when it was first published. The varied and highly respected contributors offer critical commentary from diverse industrial backgrounds.
Lawson, B	*How Designers Think: the design process demystified*	Architecture Press	2005	This book is a true classic. It covers every aspect of the design process and designing, written in a straightforward manner, but highly authoritative and detailed in presentation.
Philips, P.	*Creating the Perfect Design Brief*	Allworth Press	2004	Peter Philips offers a broad and varied account of design strategy and its implementation based on his extensive industry experience and expertise.

**Vision and Values in
Design Management**

Design
directions

Design
transformations

Design
advocacy

Design
alliances

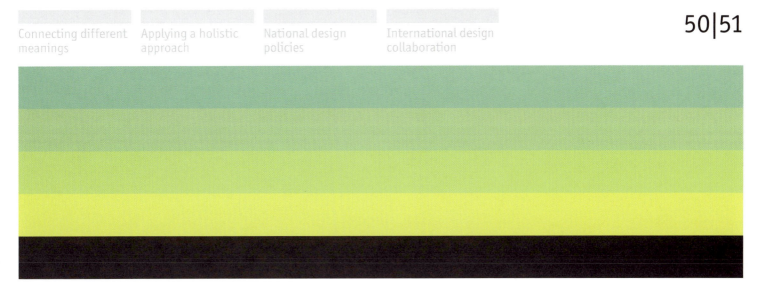

Chapter two
Design transformations

Design and design management has many different interpretations and methods of strategic application. Used in a visionary manner, it has the power to transform the way an organisation views itself, leading to endless possibilities of value-added change and corporate success.

**Vision and Values in
Design Management**

Design
directions

Design
transformations

Design
advocacy

Design
alliances

Connecting different meanings

Design management means many different
things to many people and yet it still
demands a definitive description in order for
it to be fully understood. As its true nature
and latent value remains explicitly undefined
and unclear, this perhaps could be viewed as
a strength as opposed to a weakness. By
requiring clarification and commercial
application, organisations have adopted,
adapted and applied the key tenets of design
management principles within very specific
industrial and commercial contexts to suit
strategic corporate aims and objectives.

'Every body continues in its state of rest, or of
uniform motion in a right line, unless it is
compelled to change that state by forces
impressed upon it.'
Principia Mathematica

The five stages of design

The role and nature of design has changed considerably over the last 20 years. First, let us investigate the five stages of design 'thinking' within the organisation, starting from a base level of minimal engagement.

Level 1 is the stage at which the organisation has minimal understanding of design; its use is alien and its value is regarded as negligible. Anecdotal evidence suggests that the majority of these companies often compete on the unsustainable business model of low-value pricing strategies, producing goods and services at the least cost with no design considerations. One could rightfully ask that if design is so important, why don't companies use it more often and in particular at a strategic level? Attempts to raise the profile of design at level 1 frequently run into two problems: first managers have different perceptions of design; and secondly, it is notoriously difficult to quantify the impact of design on profitability.

Level 2 of the design ladder is the stage at which organisations use design superficially to 'restyle' or slightly modify existing or new products, mostly on a day-to-day basis. They view design as an operational resource to achieve competitive advantage through product differentiation and incremental innovation. Managers of small businesses often do not see the point in strategic planning; perhaps they do not have the time or resources to formulate such plans.

Level 3 is where design as an integrated process begins to emerge. Design by its very nature overlaps and touches upon every aspect of business culture. Due to the iterative process of designing and the tangible outcomes of that complex process, it requires representatives from the various business functions to articulate their views into the product development process. As a consequence, the value and role of design management begins to emerge, frequently serving as a conduit between the disparate groups. With design now at the core of the organisation, its unifying nature offers a dynamic platform for innovative ideas and blue-sky thinking to contribute to business strategy.

Level 4 is the stage at which design is regarded as a core strategic competence. Here it is a vital source of sustainable competitive advantage, offering the organisation opportunities to envision, shape and transform its overall scope and long-term direction. Design will never be at the top of the business agenda; however, it can be one of the most pervasive and creative elements of boardroom influence.

Level 5, 'design as innovation', marks the zenith of design understanding and deployment. This level of design influence could be also regarded as 'design leadership', a term coined by two of its leading advocates – Raymond Turner, group designer at BAA, and Alan Topalian, director of Alto Design Management. Design at this level of operation, along with sophisticated management, enables long-term new business horizons whilst ensuring and maintaining strategic intent. Organisations that have achieved this level of design consciousness include the British Airways Authority (BAA), Braun, Honda and Oakley.

At each level of the design ladder, design and its management takes a different form of deployment and application. By moving up the ladder, it moves further into the heart of business activity, becoming more explicit on the business agenda: companies that reach level 5 of design thinking fully understand its worth. By reaching this stage, they have also defined and implemented a design management function and/or system to carefully leverage its influence. The form, nature and operation of its character has carefully matured and shaped its identity to reflect and embrace its surrounding organisational 'complexion'. This varied understanding and configuration of design management frequently differs from organisation to organisation; between public and private sector activity and further beyond, to regional and international arenas of operation.

The five stages of design thinking

Figure 1

Level 1 **Awareness**	Level 2 **Restyling**	Level 3 **Integration**	Level 4 **Strategy**	Level 5 **Innovation**

'Stimulating exports: 51% of Queen's Award for Export Achievement winners in 2002 directly attributed overseas sales success to their investment in design. Over 90% found that design was valued by their international customers and 86% indicated that design helps them to compete internationally.'
Whyte, Salter, Gann and Davies

Figures 1, 2 and 3
Level 5, Design as Innovation, marks the zenith of design understanding and deployment. Companies that have reached this level of design consciousness include Braun, Honda and Oakley.

Connecting different meanings | Applying a holistic approach | National design policies | International design collaboration

54|55

Design alliances – a collaborative partnership

The erosion of market tariffs and trade restrictions creates significant market opportunities as well as ways to increase profitability and commercial success. However, for an organisation to capitalise on these fertile grounds of exploitation, they must have a framework for design management firmly in place to manage and leverage design to its fullest potential. **International joint ventures** (IJV) are increasingly commonplace and it could be argued that they pose the least risk in terms of entering new overseas marketplaces.

In essence, an international joint venture is the collaboration between two or more overseas organisations. This enables development of new and innovative product or service offerings in existing or mature marketplaces, providing the customer with a richer and more 'meaningful' experience of engagement with the product or service. The opportunities to take and transfer company offerings from one national context to another are significant, but equally so are the pitfalls and traps of commercial failure.

To overcome these dangers, the design manager has to adopt new and innovative ways of working, initiating and developing new products and services that transcend geographic and cultural differences. In theory this sounds rather straightforward and manageable, but in practice it requires all the intellectual and financial resources of a large organisation to coordinate and carefully balance the inherent risk of failure.

Design alliances – a brief example

To provide a simple example of an international joint venture, let us suppose a major UK-based mobile phone handset provider wants to enter into the Chinese marketplace. Over the duration of its long-term development, the handset provider has developed intimate market knowledge of the 'wants' and 'needs' of its UK-based customer audience. Through ambitious expansion plans, the company has now adopted a strategic focus on penetrating the dynamic and potentially lucrative Chinese mobile phone marketplace.

However, they have reluctantly recognised that they do not have sufficient information-rich and intimate knowledge of the local marketplace and consumer needs required to launch a significantly modified handset. In order to overcome this failing, they have identified and successfully negotiated a collaborative partnership agreement with a comparable organisation based in Beijing. Through the combination of technological expertise and a sophisticated new product development framework, their partners in Beijing incorporated these strengths into the market positioning and branding of an innovative and novel product / service offering. Through this mutually rewarding partnership where both organisations concentrate their strengths towards one common business objective, the collaborative arrangement has managed to reduce the risk of failure in developing a new product offering in a potentially rewarding and long-term strategic niche marketplace. Through the careful use of integrated design, a series of complex interactions between end-users, designers and marketers has translated an ambitious blue-sky concept into reality.

'The Design Council found that 32% of firms with 250 or more employees see design as integral to their operations. The research also found a higher intensity of design activity among rapidly growing businesses, which were six times more likely than static ones to see design as integral to their operation.'
Design Council

International joint ventures
In a joint venture, two or more companies agree to share capital, technology, human resources, risks and rewards in a formation of a new product or service under shared control.

Case study
Transforming perception through design

Professor David Sanderson discusses his close involvement with Aynsley China to establish an in-house design facility to revitalise its product offerings. An in-house design team was developed over a two-year period, which raised the profile of design both within and outside the company. By the utilisation of sophisticated new technologies, innovative 3D forms and surface pattern designs were created to enhance existing product lines, whilst also leading to the development of new market opportunities. As a result, Aynsley enhanced its current brand values to those of an organisation committed to providing high-quality, innovative design-led products.

Figure 1
Aynsley China has been producing and marketing chinaware since 1775.

The company

Aynsley China is based in Stoke-on-Trent, UK. It is a long-established company, well respected for its extensive product lines. Since 1775 it has been producing and marketing chinaware that includes fine bone chinaware, boxed gift items and china florals. The brand is synonymous with traditional, quality English bone china.

The need for change

The global marketplace for traditional bone china gifts and tableware has become increasingly competitive for many UK-based organisations. Low value imported products have become commonplace in high street retail outlets, with the majority of the products arriving from China, India and Pacific Rim countries. In the past, Aynsley China has relied heavily upon its 'heritage' lines and not really addressed the issue of design in terms of developing value added products. Having recognised strong competition arriving from overseas, and its perceived weakness in the marketplace for being dated and out of touch with contemporary tastes, the company decided to establish an in-house design facility.

Aynsley planned to grow design from within the company, firmly establishing a visible design function that would be central in achieving its strategic aim of being associated with high value contemporary chinaware. Also, Aynsley wanted to defend its existing UK market share whilst also competing with other strong brands internationally. However, for this to be viable, Aynsley had to overcome key structural weaknesses within its existing form; notably that the value and application of design was virtually non-existent and it had no recognition within the company. In order to increase the product ranges to accommodate contemporary design-led chinaware and to continually produce products appealing to market tastes, the company had to adopt a strong design awareness and orientation across the board. Aynsley lacked knowledge and expertise about how to identify market trends and how to transform this rich seam of inspiration and opportunity into creating innovative, design-led products.

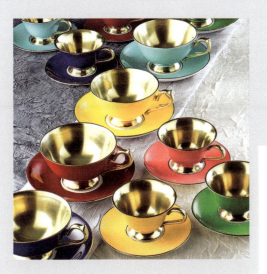

Figures 2 and 3
The Aynsley China brand is synonymous with style, elegance and quality.

'To survive in challenging economic conditions and stay ahead of overseas competition, UK businesses must add value by designing innovative products and services instead of cutting prices.'
Design Council

Vision and Values in Design Management

Design strategy: adopting an organisational design consciousness

To embark upon this significant journey of design transformation Aynsley entered into an Associate **Knowledge Transfer Partnership** with Staffordshire University, working predominantly with the Award Leader from the MA Ceramics Award and his colleagues within the Faculty of Arts, Media and Design. Two design graduates were employed as Associates, working within the company but guided under the supervision of the academic partner **Professor David Sanderson**.

Through close dialogue between the university and Aynsley, the Associates implemented the key aims and objectives of the KTP programme. The first key task was to conduct a feasibility study, identifying strengths and weaknesses within existing design procedures at Aynsley. To fully establish a new design focus, it was paramount to understand how the company valued design; how it used design; and its understanding between the different organisational departments. This was quite a comprehensive task, but essential in order to develop a new design focus. In conjunction with an internal audit, the second key aim was to look beyond the company and understand its perception by both existing customers and competing brands.

One way of achieving this was to visit international trade fairs, which included visiting the Frankfurt 'Ambiente' and the Paris 'Maison & Objet' exhibitions. However it was also considered pertinent to investigate the brand values of Aynsley: did the brand identity of the company truly reflect its position within the marketplace; were its existing product ranges perceived as being in unison with what the company stood for? The only way of solving these complex problems and critical factors for further development was to conduct a thorough and extensive design audit.

'Research found that designers are increasingly being asked by clients for intelligence on future market trends. As a result, "front-end research" (e.g. materials development, market evolution), which helps to inform innovation processes and activities, is becoming seen as a staple activity for designers.'
NESTA

Knowledge Transfer Partnership (KTP)
A UK Government-funded programme helping businesses to improve their competitiveness and productivity through the better use of knowledge, technology and skills. Each partnership employs one or more high calibre 'Associate' design graduates, transferring the knowledge from the university partner to the company.

Professor David Sanderson
Sanderson is the Award Leader for the MA Ceramic Design course at Staffordshire University. He has been an active design consultant with clients both in the UK and overseas. In 1992 he was shortlisted 'Highly Commended' for the Prince Philip Designer of the Year Award. In 2001 he was invited by the British Ceramic Confederation Executive to design the Queen's Golden Jubilee 'Gift' on behalf of the British Ceramic Industry. In 2008 David was awarded a Professorship by Staffordshire University for his extensive work with both industry and academia.

Connecting different
meanings

Applying a holistic
approach

National design
policies

International design
collaboration

58|59

Design development:
adding value through style

Building upon this extensive 'self reflection' and critical analysis, Aynsley had a clearer, more detailed understanding of how the company was perceived in the marketplace, and identified radical opportunities for new product development. With a reinvigorated focus and desire to develop cutting-edge chinaware concepts, the company generated numerous proposals exploring 2D and 3D forms that were a radical departure away from existing heritage product lines. To facilitate this exploration, new CAD and visualisation software was purchased, enabling the designers to generate and test conceptual ideas against the re-energised brand values of the company. Through constant communication between the designers and other business functions, the role and value of design gained prominence and importance within Aynsley.

In a way, it was a process of fostering a 'design appreciative environment' where everyone within the company could see what the benefits of design could offer. Taking this further, potential designs were approved for development, based on a new focused design strategy, but most importantly, the designs were intimately aligned to an ambitious marketing strategy that aimed to appeal to new markets and customers alike. Through the radical reappraisal of form, shape and packaging, novel chinaware products progressed into production with the eventual aim of attracting new business opportunities and customers. At this point it is worth raising the fundamental issue of 'costings' and the investment required for producing the new designs. In essence, to generate novel concepts costs only 15% of resources, mostly financial in terms of the designer's time. However, when these concepts are taken through detailing, manufacture, testing and refinement, the other 85% is locked into financing each aspect of development. Vital feedback of initial concepts was obtained by talking to clients, suppliers and ultimately customers.

The process was quite lengthy and at times tortuous, but it did prove valuable as customer feedback was crucial in the way Aynsley developed new product ranges in conjunction with brand aspirations. After completion of all these activities, a sample batch of product ranges was exhibited at international exhibitions and trade fairs to obtain crucial final feedback from customers. Once Aynsley was confident of the integrity and value of the new product ranges, the small product samples went into full scale manufacture and production. Very quickly, the new product ranges that were offered to the market were well received and valued. As the volume of sales increased, the company had to evaluate existing procedures on ensuring continuous quality of all final products. Feedback was good from customers, but to improve production standards and overall quality, slight modifications were implemented, addressing any potential flaws in the end product.

Figures 1, 2 and 3
Aynsley developed cutting-edge chinaware concepts through exploring both 2D and 3D forms that were a radical departure away from existing heritage product lines.

'Design enables the creation of innovative products and services, allowing companies to open new income streams and compete overseas.'
The Cox Review

**Vision and Values in
Design Management**

Design
directions

Design
transformations

Design
advocacy

Design
alliances

Design futures: planning for growth

Since completion of the two-year KTP programme, Aynsley is already beginning to see the benefits of the collaborative partnership. First, the two design Associates are slowly raising the profile of design within the company, having close involvement with other business functions. They liaise frequently with the marketing department in monitoring and identifying possible market trends that could be taken forward for development. Through this iterative relationship, ideas could be tested for feasibility, generating new market opportunities. Secondly, with the installation of new rapid prototyping and print technology, Aynsley has the ability to quickly test new 3D forms and surface pattern concepts, which often form the basis for research and development within the company. So what we are witnessing is the seamless relationship between market activities being captured by the marketing department and this knowledge being quickly transferred into product concepts, which are tested through new technologies. Over time, this framework for new product development will increase, forming a major part of Aynsley's design-led culture where design becomes a central resource to everyday business operation. With the ability to produce numerous product ranges that are in accordance with contemporary tastes and trends, the Aynsley brand will become synonymous with style, elegance and quality – one of the key objectives of the KTP partnership.

Summary

Using design effectively will enable a company to increase the perceived value of its product offerings and maintain strategic advantage. In today's highly complex and segmented markets customers are now far more demanding than they have ever been – mostly due to increased spending power and the proliferation of choice – especially in the chinaware and giftware marketplace. Aynsley has had to embrace design and new technologies in a response to globalisation and fierce overseas competition. It has also used design in a very strategic manner to control how the company is perceived by its customers. It has enhanced the brand values and identity to create a stronger and more positive image that reflects its true commitment to producing design-led, quality contemporary products.

Routes to design enhancement are often fraught with the need to balance many complex decisions, with certain options offering great benefits but inherent problems of implementation. Each company has to assess and reflect inwards, taking time to understand exactly what it wants to achieve through design and available resources to establish a stronger design presence within the company. So what are the commonplace routes to design success?

First, if design expertise is required on a short-term basis, perhaps for the duration of one project, then maybe the use of a design consultant could be the best option. If successful, then the design consultant could be retained on a longer basis, providing expertise on an 'as-and-when-basis'; however, this level of partnership and commitment is limited and short-term. Secondly, if the company is committed to establishing an in-house design facility, how could this route be pursued? Let's say a design team is assembled and established within the company. There could potentially be problems with complacency whereby design is compromised by internal politics, which the external design consultant doesn't have to face. However, an in-house design team understands core competencies, and has the skills and knowledge to draw upon if faced with technical or manufacturing difficulties further on in the design development programme. Finally, the company could pursue a combination of routes one and two, drawing upon 'fresh thinking' from beyond organisational boundaries, with the security of a strong visible design presence within the company to drive the design concept through to commercialisation.

'New and accurate data on the economic impact of design will contribute to current work on the knowledge economy, which has shown that design makes contributions that are not picked up by traditional metrics. For example, research by NESTA has shown that traditional innovation measures do not capture "hidden" innovations around the workplace, which often include the use of design processes.'
NESTA

Figure 1
Aynsley has fostered a design-led culture where design becomes a central resource to everyday business operation.

Figure 3
Once Aynsley was confident of the integrity and value of the new product ranges, the small product samples went into full scale production.

Figure 2
By installing new rapid prototyping and print technology, Aynsley has the ability to quickly test new 3D forms and surface pattern concepts.

**Vision and Values in
Design Management**

Design
directions

Design
transformations

Design
advocacy

Design
alliances

Revision questions

Afterword

Aynsley recognised the need to change, mostly brought about by overseas competition and the rise of increasingly tough market conditions. Having taken the bold step to embrace design and firmly place it within daily operation, Aynsley was faced with the next big issue: how to embed design within the organisation. Many companies have equally faced this task, but one route of action for company A may not be necessarily appropriate for company B. The route to design enhancement is a commonplace issue facing numerous design managers and companies today. But if this is conducted thoughtfully and intelligently, the benefits are immense.

1 In order to choose the preferred option for design enhancement, what issues would you investigate to inform your choice of appropriate route?

2 What are the pros and cons of selecting an external design consultant?

3 Conversely, what are the pros and cons of establishing an in-house design facility?

4 Is the third route the best option? If not, why not?

5 Can you identify any successful examples of a company that has tackled this issue? What did it achieve and how?

Connecting different
meanings

Applying a holistic
approach

National design
policies

International design
collaboration

62|63

Further recommended reading

Author	Title	Publisher	Date	Comments
Best, K.	*Design Management: Managing Design Strategy, Process and Implementation*	AVA Publishing	2006	Excellent book discussing in great detail all aspects of design strategy and its successful implementation.
Davenport, T.H. and Prusak, L.	*Working Knowledge: How Organizations Manage What They Know*	Harvard Business School Press	Second revised edition 2000	A great introduction as to how managing knowledge within the organisation can lead to sustainable advantage in fast moving industries.
Laurel, B.	*Design Research: Methods and Perspectives*	MIT Press	2004	A highly detailed view of research methods that can be used to inform the design development process.
McCormack, L.	*Designers are W*******	About Face Publishing	Second revised edition 2006	Don't be put off by the title, the book provides an honest and thought-provoking account of design practice in industry.
Senge, P.	*The Fifth Discipline*	Random House Business Books	2nd revised edition 2006	A true classic in management thinking – one book that should not be ignored.

Applying a holistic approach

Since its origins, design management has emerged and matured as a discipline, taking on more responsibility to engage with complex issues within an organisation, such as change management or stock market performance. With the advent of corporate social responsibility and green thinking, design management has to propose new strategies for product and service design, taking into account its social and environmental impacts.

As we have seen, design management by its very nature is a multi-disciplinary broad church of activity. At its core it is concerned with the management and coordination of the value creation process. This sounds rather simple and straightforward; however, if we deconstruct and analyse the value creation process, things start to become increasingly difficult to define and discuss. To clarify this aspect, let's draw upon a point raised by Mike Press and Rachel Cooper in their popular book **The Design Experience**. They passionately argue that 'design management now not only means managing the people and the process, but deconstructing and analysing the total product experience to enable the designer to work with the organisation team to understand and contribute to that experience.'

Quantifying the unquantifiable
Intangible factors are difficult to quantify. However, these are some of the critical sources of value that can be utilised by companies to improve their competitive advantage.

Figure 1

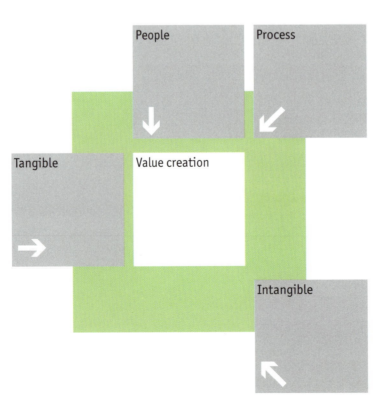

Connecting different meanings | Applying a holistic approach | National design policies | International design collaboration

64|65

Value creation – a brief discussion

Let us analyse and discuss 'value creation'. There are some common elements that are worthy of highlighting within this section. First, what is 'value'? Value is how we make sense of the world through meaningful experiences and emotional connections. Secondly, value is a constantly changing and fluid set of beliefs and aspirations constructed through two and three dimensions reflecting the individual's relationship with both 'others' and their sense of 'self'.

Now, if we move to 'creation', it is how the designer must manifest these intangible and kaleidoscopic sets of beliefs into a physical product or service. To achieve this complex task would involve drawing upon and understanding all these conflicting and contradictory variables into a cohesive concept proposition. So connecting and engaging with both 'value' and 'creation' involves crossing many organisational and departmental boundaries in the pursuit of resolving this complex issue. If we focus more closely, value could be embedded within the following aspects of design activity: market value; performance value; organisational value and social value.

Market value

Enhancing market value involves creating a perceived difference or advantage through the ability to develop a new or modified product that offers distinct benefits to its users. Within a Western context (mostly North America and Europe), the cost of manufacture of goods is relatively high compared to south-east Asia. Therefore the emphasis is placed more on quality (as perceived by the consumer) than low cost positioning. As a consequence, many organisations invest more heavily in design to add value and make their product offerings more desirable than just by price alone. Design also has the ability to provide innovative interpretations and new ways of seeing an existing product through the eyes of its users or customers. Design offers a creative impetus to reconfigure or re-evaluate a problem from a non-linear perspective; to provide new solutions or opportunities by way of a conceptual leap in understanding. Innovations by design can play a significant role in forging and establishing customer loyalty and encouraging them to pay more than they might otherwise for what is essentially the same product or service.

Creating value through design is particularly acute within the consumer goods sector. Here, the symbolic or perceived value of goods and services is increasingly important to consumers who are, in essence, paying price premiums for comparable products in terms of their functionality.

'Research by the Design Council discovered that environmental pressures would have an influence over the running of a company. 40% of businesses felt design would help them respond to this.'
Design Council

The Design Experience
Mike Press and Rachel Cooper, *The Design Experience: the role of design and designers in the twenty-first century*, Ashgate, Hampshire, 2003. An excellent student handbook introducing the reader to a variety of emergent design management issues and topics.

**Vision and Values in
Design Management**

Design
directions

Design
transformations

Design
advocacy

Design
alliances

Performance value

Performance value is often increased as a result of designers' inherent creativity and art and design education. Creative problem solving skills combined with the ability to communicate to a wide range of audiences brings real value throughout the design process. It is commonly agreed that creativity is the seed from which innovative ideas and solutions emerge and indeed flourish. However, all said and done, managing creative teams and the process of creativity is a considerable challenge for the organisation. A commonly held view is that a creative climate or creative culture is the single most important influence on the innovative potential of the organisation, where the collective force of the employees far exceeds that of individuals directly assigned to design.

This can be taken a step further, whereupon a strong organisational creative culture can ultimately be a unique selling point for the organisation, more so than its product offerings. The inherent implication is that such creative organisations benefit not only from their innovative products and services, but also because the creative culture is a strong selling point in its own right. Arguably, it may be suggested that the enlightened consumer looks beyond a company's products and services to the company itself and takes this into account in a decision making process. Design management is seen as one of the main routes through which ideas are transformed into business realities, unifying and funnelling the creative energy of the organisation into a directed and potent source of competitive advantage.

Organisational value

Organisational value offers the opportunity to rethink business strategy and operation. Through subtle influence and vision-sharing, design can empower the organisation to reinvent current business activity in light of commercial opportunities. Design management can add meaningful value through its focus on both the process of design and on design outcomes of that process – quality, cost and documentation (information) and by its emphasis on facilitating the members of the design team. Continual evaluation of the process will help improve effectiveness and efficiency within the entire business operation. As the organisation develops a greater appreciation of design, its value as a mechanism to envision new futures and 'experiences' takes on a deeper level of influence, providing a dynamic foundation for catalysing a common shared vision.

Value creation and design   Figure 1

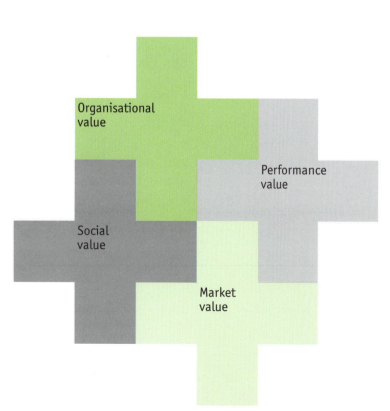

Connecting different meanings | **Applying a holistic approach** | National design policies | International design collaboration

66|67

Social value

This is particularly more acute when developing eco-friendly products and services and fostering a climate for corporate social responsibility in order to engage with wider environmental and social issues. Adopting a strong commitment to understanding and valuing the social dimension and impact of design can bring diverse and highly rewarding benefits. An increasing number of business sectors (motor vehicles, retail, offshore oil and gas operators and most recently engineering) are developing forward thinking design policies identifying how they can improve their contribution to enhancing social value and responsibility to all their stakeholders. Chapter four (Design alliances) explores this emergent issue in greater detail, discussing how fostering a strong social commitment does indeed offer significant rewards for the organisation and the wider environment far beyond business practice.

'The more serious a company is about using design, the likelier it is to see innovation as the best route to success and the less it has to rely on keeping prices low. Businesses where design plays an integral or significant role take a more balanced view of their competitive options.'
Design Council

Figure 2
UK company PG Tips has joined forces with the Rainforest Alliance to ensure that by 2010, all PG Tips tea suppliers meet their high sustainability standards.

Interview
Andy Cripps

Andy Cripps is a design management consultant. After graduating in industrial design in 1987, Andy spent the early part of his career as an in-house product designer – contributing to and managing projects for clients such as Shell, BP, Coopers & Lybrand, BMW and Volvo Cars. Having completed an MA in 1999, he has worked as a senior design manager in a number of UK manufacturing companies. He has designed and managed prize winning projects in the Marketing Week, Design Week and FX Awards. Andy is at home leading or managing manufacturing projects. He has 20 years' experience in bridging between the design and business communities and is equally able to address either party on their own terms. He aims to combine the best of the design and business worlds for market and financial success.

For the benefit of our readers who are unfamiliar with your area of activity, can you provide a brief overview of your consultancy work?
I work with manufacturing companies helping them to uncover where strategic design utilisation can add the most value to their business. This typically resolves into a number of agreed and identified tactical design projects in brand and NPD which I would scope and potentially manage to completion.

What do you consider the role of design management within an organisation?
It is the glue that bonds together the company's strategy for growth and development; its customers, whether existing or desired; its brand and its product or service delivery. It needs to have responsibility at the highest level within the organisation where it can exert real influence over these key areas – core to any business.

In what way can designers and design managers work together to gain more influence for design within an organisation?
By being excellent communicators! Whilst it is improving, business people have little exposure to design whilst in education – likewise with designers and business practice at art school. Understanding the realistic requirements and limitations each party has, together with a shared vision of what can be created as a team of equals – not clones of one another but celebrating different approaches – makes a huge impact. Without that trust and understanding, designers do not have the opportunity to meaningfully deliver their creativity and their tactical and practical skills.

Connecting different
meanings

Applying a holistic
approach

National design
policies

International design
collaboration

68|69

Do you think there is a difference between design management and design leadership?
Yes – in my view, design leadership is about design playing an active role in setting the strategic goals and vision for the business – literally helping the business to truly become 'design-led'. In tandem with this strategic input, design leadership should then embed design and creative thinking into the DNA of the business. Design management is equally important but is more usually involved in the precise shaping and scope of tactical, practical delivery of creative projects across the business.

According to your experience, how can design leadership drive creativity into business?
I think participation is a hugely powerful learning process. Imagine a design leader running a creative session, or brainstorm, with a team of directors. This uncovers thinking or outputs which are 'new' to the business, not all solely design focused but all potentially valuable. This is both an enjoyable and new experience to many directors. Demonstrating value in circumstances like this and others, design leadership can then make a powerful case for its existence and strategic influence over the whole business.

As a design leader, how do you work with the design manager and design team to harness their abilities to ensure project success?
Back to communication! Once the strategy is established, it needs to be made visible and communicated to the whole business including the design team. Individual roles, projects and research can then be related to the needs and timing of the bigger picture, openly discussed and agreed. Listening is a key attribute of a design leader to enable all contributors to be offered the opportunity to form the plan for the project(s). This can then be reviewed together going forward. Shared responsibility, teamworking, creativity and enjoyment are all key to delivering success.

In terms of creativity and innovation, how do you think it can influence business operation?
In today's crowded and pressured marketplaces businesses need to both differentiate themselves and deliver a clear and consistent offer to their customers. In my view, without creativity and innovation acting across the business, this becomes increasingly difficult, if not impossible to achieve. The pace of change is ever increasing to the point now where, as an individual, one cannot keep up! We therefore need to tap into other people's views and constantly need to look for new ways of 'doing' or understanding to provide increased customer benefits and efficient delivery. Unique offers brought to the market in a timely way do, of course, allow for higher margins too.

Do you think innovation is very important for company development, in other words do you think innovation can be considered as an engine to drive business development?
It's absolutely critical. It may not be about a business creating something new in terms of product or service but developing an innovative delivery mechanism, for instance.

Let's say if we fast-forward 10–15 years, what do you think would be the greatest challenges that we in the design community need to counter?
Keeping it human! Ensuring that technology worship and the pace of change doesn't steamroller people but fits as an efficient enabler between insights and innovation – with design as the delivery mechanism. Ensuring that manufacturing is truly globally sustainable in terms of people, materials, finances and benefits.

Andy, to conclude, is there anything else that you would like to add or raise or stress that you consider of great importance to the design profession in terms of future critical engagement?
Design is not the answer – but it's unlikely one will find the answer without it. Most powerful when engaged as a core skill with a team of complementary skillsets around it, design has the ability to deliver real improvements, not just change.

'In today's crowded and pressured marketplaces businesses need to both differentiate themselves and deliver a clear and consistent offer to their customers.'
Andy Cripps

National design policies

Increasing and developing an infrastructure for design advantage is fast becoming core to national design policy creation, where countries throughout the world are focusing their attentions on design as a source for maximising profitability within commercial operation. With ever-increasing levels of competition to attract overseas investment and global market share, countries are now positioning themselves as 'creative innovators' through the use of design. This section takes a look at a number of different countries and how they are establishing an infrastructure for design enhancement.

The world market

The potential of the world market is highly attractive to all organisations. In order to generate higher exports and more inward investment, governments are being forced to develop national policies to promote design. At the same time, other new, fast-moving opportunities are emerging. Information and communications technology and growing trade in intellectual property allow businesses to work with producers based elsewhere in the world, giving them access to dynamic parts of the world economy. The appropriate strategy will vary from business to business, but strong commercial, historical and cultural links with many other countries will provide sustainable advantages as potential areas of growth for national design activity. So, how does a country organise itself to promote its design strengths overseas and gain economic advantage? First, it requires a long-term strategic focus, based on multi-agency involvement, drawn from policy makers, educational institutions, industry and commerce. Also, on a more macro-level, a country needs to be 'seen' internationally as having a positive image of producing design and innovative products / services that attract and foster economic growth. Two simple examples are Finland, which is synonymous with producing highly attractive technology-led products and services in the telecommunications industry; and the UK, which has a worldwide reputation for being at the forefront of cutting-edge research and development in the pharmaceutical industry.

Connecting different
meanings

Applying a holistic
approach

National design
policies

International design
collaboration

70|71

Danish Design Council

In Denmark, the Danish Design Council (DDC) has been established to provide businesses both large and small with knowledge and expertise concerning all facets of design and its value to commercial growth. It is an independent institution that has a strategic focus to build an enhanced awareness of design and the distinct economic benefits design has to offer to the organisation. Secondly, it proactively engages with businesses to develop their skills and understanding of utilising design, not only at a project level but also at a strategic level to increase their market visibility, aiding sustainable growth. Lastly, and arguably most importantly, the DDC is committed to increasing Danish design on an international and national level. Every year, the DDC stages a variety of exhibitions showcasing all aspects of design with the long-term vision of establishing the country as a leading design-aware nation.

Design Council

The UK's Design Council is comparable to the DDC. It has five main areas of focus based on the use of design – business, government, media, education and design professionals. Over its history, the Design Council has promoted design both nationally and internationally. Activities range from the development of new tools for design and innovation through to supporting and giving advice to organisations to enable them to improve their in-house design capabilities. Building upon this activity, the Design Council released their strategy document 'The Good Design Plan: 2008-11' outlining five key objectives to enable UK organisations to fully utilise design at a higher level of application. The objectives include first supporting organisations in both the public and private sectors to continually innovate and build successful brands; secondly, to engage at a national and local level in involving communities in the creation of local services; thirdly, to support and augment skills within the creative industries through partnerships with schools and higher education institutions; fourth, to champion design in relation to the ever changing and dynamic current economic and social climate; and finally, to position the Design Council as a world-renowned institution, driving the fast-moving design agenda throughout the world.

Korean Institute of Design Promotion

The Korean Institute of Design Promotion (KIDP) has developed a series of strategic five-year plans to develop and promote industrial effectiveness in unison with its changing industrial infrastructure. Korea had a small light industry base in the 1960s and over subsequent decades it has gradually evolved into a world leader for producing intelligent home application networks and technology-led consumer durables. To assist in this industrial transformation a series of national design policies has been created, enabling organisations to strengthen their research and development activities, establishing regional design centres and rebranding Korea as 'Design Korea'.

Figure 1
Arne Jacobsen's Egg
Chair embodies Danish design.

'Designed and Made in China'

The Beijing Industrial Design Centre was founded in 1995. It is beginning to firmly establish itself as a one-stop source of design expertise and consultancy to regional industry. The Centre has two major remits: first, to promote the importance of developing new and innovative products; and secondly to provide guidance, enabling organisations to achieve this. China is slowly moving away from the perception of 'Made in China' to the more ambitious 'Designed and Made in China'. The country wants to distance itself from the restrictive image of high-volume, low-value manufacturing in sweated factory conditions. Through this continual process, a series of governmental initiatives has been implemented to promote the value of design in industry; to build up the state design education system to accommodate an increasingly sophisticated Chinese marketplace; and to attract investment from overseas through collaborative partnerships.

Later on in this chapter we discuss the emergence and development of design management in China (see pages 80–83).

Design Forum Finland

Similar to the Danish Design Council, Design Forum Finland (DFF) is an independent body promoting Finnish crafts, the industrial arts and industrial design in Finland and abroad. To underpin this mission, DFF centres most of its activities through a dedicated exhibition venue based in Helsinki, which on average attracts over 70,000 visitors annually. To complement this approach, DFF offers an extensive range of communication services and publications to disseminate the value of Finnish design. Currently, Design Forum Finland is working in partnership with the Fennia Insurance Group to host the Fennia Prize, which has quickly established itself as Finland's biggest design award, attracting entries from leading design orientated organisations in the country. Through this high-profile strategy, DFF aims to encourage companies to use design and value its importance in everyday practice.

The National Institute of Design, India

With the ambition to firmly establish itself as a regional superpower, India is looking to design as a key driver in developing their national export capacity. The nation also aims to be a leading 'influencer' of global design, especially Asian design, developing its core strengths and capabilities in intellectual and strategic design development to underpin its huge manufacturing capabilities. To achieve this long-term vision, the Indian Government conducted a multi-agency consultation process to establish a comprehensive and ambitious national design policy. The expansive policy document provided a 10-point plan to achieve global success through design engagement and intervention. Two key points forming the central vision were: 1) to position 'Designed in India' as a byword for quality and utility in conjunction with 'Made in India' and 'Served from India'; secondly, to establish itself as a leading 'Design-Hub' within the region.

Figure 1
Finland's Fennia Prize in 2007 was awarded to the Humanic reach truck by Rocla Plc. According to Rocla's in-house designer, Petteri Masalin, 'the prime considerations of design are usability, dependability, simplicity and functionality'.

Connecting different
meanings

Applying a holistic
approach

National design
policies

International design
collaboration

72|73

DesignSingapore

As a national initiative, DesignSingapore aims to place Singapore on the world map for design and creativity. It looks to develop a thriving, multi-disciplinary design cluster of industries and activities in Singapore that has relevance and value to a global audience. The initiative also aims to welcome design to business boardrooms, new audiences and new markets. The DesignSingapore Council, established in 2003 as a department within the Ministry of Information, Communications and the Arts, is the leading public organisation for the promotion and development of Singapore design. The Council is dedicated to enhancing Singapore's design capabilities and growing the appeal of design in everyday life through design scholarships within Singapore. The Council continually supports designers to raise their profile by showcasing their works at international platforms through the Overseas Promotion Partnership Programme, high-profile events and design competitions. The 'President's Design Award' is one such notable competition providing an opportunity for design-led organisations and individuals to promote their work to a wider international audience.

The Japan Design Foundation

The Japan Design Foundation (JDF) was established in the early 1980s to promote and foster international initiatives centred on design. Strongly endorsed and supported by the Ministry of Economy, Trade and Industry, the Foundation takes a holistic view in the way it presents and showcases Japanese design. Japan has fierce rivals in the region, in particular China, so to continually maintain national competitiveness and support to industry, the Japan Design Foundation provides a wide variety of business support initiatives to drive and create innovative products and services. Adopting a strategic and collaborative approach, the JDF plays a leading role in the 'Asian Design Network' to share and exchange knowledge and understanding through design activity.

Design Institute of Australia

The Design Institute of Australia (DIA) is the leading professional membership body for designers and design-led organisations in the country. Established in 1947, the DIA represents all designers in the country, providing strong representation of the design industry to the government. Based on a similar model to the UK Design Council, it provides designers with a valuable networking base at local, national and international levels. The DIA organises its activities into six areas of strategic activity: 1) endorsing and promoting design leadership at the highest level, both in commerce and industry; 2) offering designers membership to a professional body with a strong code of ethics and business practice; 3) disseminating information and membership services by the way of research publications, journals and other forms of knowledge-sharing media; 4) representation of the design industry and the profession to government and other influential decision-making bodies; 5) policy making in terms of ethical practice and governance / compliance legislation; and 6) membership networks and events management. Embracing all these complementary spheres of activity is the vision and mission to promote design excellence and practice throughout every aspect of national and international activity.

**Vision and Values in
Design Management**

Design
directions

**Design
transformations**

Design
advocacy

Design
alliances

Interview
Gavin Cawood

Gavin Cawood is the Operations Director for Design Wales, a Welsh Assembly Government-funded service established to encourage and facilitate the use of design in industry, particularly within SMEs. After gaining a degree in industrial design, Gavin became a partner in a product design consultancy with clients as diverse as the Early Learning Centre, Marconi and Xerox. With the opportunity to develop his skills further, he took up an offer to lead the industrial design team at Xerox, where he was responsible for the product design aspects of all Xerox products manufactured in Europe. Shortly before gaining an MBA he started working in Wales to help launch and develop the Design Wales service. Design Wales is now recognised internationally as a leading model for design support for industry.

For the benefit of those who are unfamiliar with your area of activity, can you provide a brief overview of your role as Operations Director at Design Wales?
Design Wales is a design support programme for Welsh industry funded by the Welsh Assembly Government. My role is to oversee all activities, such as a specialist advisory service and seminar programme for industry, a design award for students (Ffres), the production of case studies for use in schools and initiatives to support the design sector itself. To ensure we are delivering best practice we also undertake networking activities on a global basis to understand how design is being supported and promoted around the world. The combination of working on the front line with industry and being very aware of what else is going on around the world ensures we have an appropriate level of authority when asked by our own regional government (and others) to input to their planning.

It is commonly agreed that design can offer many benefits to the organisation; could you take this further and suggest what major benefits design can offer to regional development?
I believe that design has an important part to play in adding value to the development of new products and services that are fit for purpose and that are internationally competitive. Although anyone with experience of design will probably take this for granted there is still quite a job to be done to raise design on the regional economic development agenda. The economic development strategies of most developed regions and nations are based on innovation, technology and possibly entrepreneurship. Within these strategies design usually has a very low profile but more regions and nations are understanding the essential role design has in translating innovative ideas into products and services that are competitive in the marketplace.

What other countries do you admire or draw upon with regard to national design policies?
Very few nations actually have a written design policy. Korea, Singapore, Japan, India and Mexico have them in place but no European nation has a definitive national policy. From our networking activities we have realised that one model for design support or promotion will not fit all nations. The understanding of design and the support it receives is dictated by the local political, economic and education conditions, therefore all the models of support we see are different – even across northern Europe. So for different reasons I admire the initiatives in Korea for their bold approach to investing in design support and promotion on a national level to drive their economic development; in Denmark via the Danish Design Centre for a very professional and forward-looking programme; and more local initiatives such as the Design Center De Winkelhaak in Belgium, responsible for the genuine transformation of at least one part of the city of Antwerp. You can see more case studies of design support and promotion programmes on the website for our European network: www.seedesign.org

From your own experience, what specific needs or assistance do SMEs need as opposed to larger, more established organisations that have a deeper understanding of design?
The culture within SMEs (even quite large ones) reflects the knowledge and experience of the owners and senior management, so shifting this culture to take a design-led approach requires quite a commitment.

What are the common problems that you frequently encounter when an organisation is struggling to implement design within day-to-day activities?
A common challenge that SMEs have to face, even before they might invest in design, is finding the time to step back from their day-to-day operational activities to firstly understand the benefits that design can bring and then translate this into an achievable project. Frequently SMEs start thinking about design when they find themselves in some kind of crisis, or can see themselves falling behind the competition. The challenge for design support initiative like Design Wales is to turn this crisis into an opportunity.

Perhaps you could provide an example of a company that has found success through design initiatives?
Great examples, for different reasons, are:

1 **Bacheldre Mill**
   It produces artisan flour and through a relatively small investment in branding and packaging has greatly expanded its customer base, had a four-fold increase in production and found recognition via several national awards along the way. The development of the brand has also allowed it to expand its product range.
   www.bacheldremill.co.uk

2 **DMM**
   The climbing equipment manufacturer is known internationally for its innovation and quality but its passion is for climbing. More than most products, climbing equipment has to be functional but DMM sees design as vital for developing leading edge products that also have a little bit of magic.
   www.dmmclimbing.com

3 **Melin Tregwynt**
   There has been a woollen mill on the Melin Tregwynt site since the 17th century but by taking a design-led approach, this mill produces contemporary products that find markets around the world. I think this is a great example of a business in a traditional sector finding advantage through an investment in design.
   www.melintregwynt.co.uk

In a recent article you commented that 'for business, design should be the bridge between an idea and the marketplace'; could you expand on this a little further?
I believe that design is a vital step in converting innovative ideas into products and services that are fit for purpose. A great example of this was a client of Design Wales who had developed a medical product to the level of a functioning process but had no idea how to turn that laboratory process into a usable and manufacturable product that could be packaged, branded and distributed – all elements that required a design input.

Do you consider market research and the way this information is then translated into the design brief to be vital to project success?
Market intelligence is a vital part of the design process. It's needed to understand what the competition are doing and to work out how you might compete. Without it you are simply guessing and taking more of a gamble with any new product or service development. As with many things, gathering market intelligence does not have to be rocket science, but many SMEs simply don't take the time to step back and take stock of their target market.

In terms of introducing a new product to the market, do you have any thoughts on how 'success' can be measured? If an SME is investing heavily in a design project, how would it determine its overall success?
Measuring the benefits directly resulting from investment in design can be complicated. The introduction of a new product or service will probably be part of a new promotional campaign and changes to distribution channels. From a business support perspective I would consider an intervention with a company a success if when we walk away they have developed their capacity and culture to develop future products and services – we will have hopefully moved them up the design ladder.

If we fast-forward 10–15 years, what do you think would be the greatest challenges that regions and countries face in light of globalisation?
As was highlighted in the Cox Review, an increasing number of nations will have the ability to produce or deliver products and services that add value through design. In order to compete we will have to continue to push the capacity of our design and creative expertise to stay ahead.

Gavin, to conclude, is there anything else that you would like to raise that you consider of great importance to the design profession in terms of future critical engagement?
I guess building on the answer to the last question, the design sector is also going to have to develop its capacity and specialist expertise in order to offer services that are attractive to international buyers. On a regional and national basis this is no small challenge.

**Vision and Values in
Design Management**

Design
directions

Design
transformations

Design
advocacy

Design
alliances

International design collaboration

This section will now offer two diverse but complementary examples of design management practice, one in Mexico and the other in China. They provide a brief overview of the origins of design management and how the discipline has been shaped and tailored to suit its particular industry need. By comparing the two examples, we will be able to understand the marked differences in the role and application of design management.

Design management in Mexico

Despite the fact that design management has been recognised in Latin America since the 1990s, its development has been awkward and disoriented. A lack of design culture has made the inclusion of design management in business difficult. The region has an imported history and tradition of design that the first professionals brought from Europe, although in recent years, groups of designers from the most developed and experienced nations in Latin America – Argentina, Brazil, Colombia, Chile, Cuba, Ecuador, Mexico and Nicaragua – have begun to strengthen their professions and obtain a representative identity in their work. However, despite all these efforts, design management has come to a standstill due to the misuse and concern over its definitions and perception.

Beatriz Itzel Cruz Megchun
A Mexico City-born industrial designer with experience of working within different industries in the design field in Mexico and Europe. Her current research is focused on the improvement of small technological-based enterprises in Mexico. Her work on design management has been published in different journals in Latin America.

Connecting different meanings | Applying a holistic approach | National design policies | International design collaboration

76|77

Figure 1
Mario Ortiz: visualisation of a children's toy for a Mexican food company which is aiming to increase market share. Initial concept sketches of the toy, exploring issues of form and function.

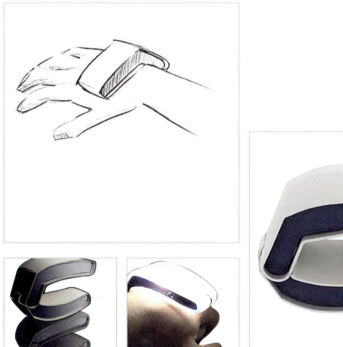

Figure 2
Mario Ortiz: detailed conceptual images exploring the development of a personal light that is worn on the wrist.

**Vision and Values in
Design Management**

Design
directions

Design
transformations

Design
advocacy

Design
alliances

The origins of design management

The concept of design in Mexico was imported from the theory and practice of European schools such as Bauhaus and HFG of the ULM. Since then, university curricula and programmes have been entirely based on these theories. In 1969, the country entered into a period of promotion of design that continued throughout the 70s, with strong support from the government to boost the nation's exports. A new direction in economic politics in the 80s led to a sharp decline in government support. Since then, efforts to promote design have come from designers themselves.

Although short-lived, the government's role in design promotion had an impact on its development within industry. These first approaches started from the idea that industrial design was the most effective tool to boost the performance of small and medium enterprises. Industrial design represented the activity that could continuously improve the performance of companies within the market and industrial designers became the leaders in the development of new products at project level. It can be argued that this was the origin of design management in Mexico and the reason why industrial designers had begun to work like design managers.

Design management – key issues

Decades later and design management has barely moved on. Some people believe that it stagnated because of those designers – practitioners and academics – who brought concepts, methods and ideas from abroad which were not suitable for the industrialisation of the nation. These foreign design influences were rarely applicable to the internal considerations and necessities of the national market. Consequently, design and its management have not had the necessary impact upon the nation's industry framework. The lack of expertise and understanding of design within the activities developed in an enterprise, as well as a lack of the resources (financial, material and knowledge) necessary for an enterprise to survive in the market conditions, have all contributed to the stagnation of design management in Mexico.

Design management education and training

Since 2000, a new generation of designers has been working to boost the development and raise the awareness of design management. This small group of designers – practitioners and academics – has gone abroad to gain knowledge through postgraduate study in countries such as Spain, the UK and the USA and to gain experience by working for worldwide companies. Some designers have concentrated their efforts on the generation of new design businesses and some have dedicated their work to academia.

Those designers in the academic area are facing different problems in the introduction of design management. Most universities in Mexico have not updated their curricula for over ten years. Consequently, there is no institution in the country that offers a degree in design management. There are few universities that even have a module of it. In 2006, the Iberoamerican University (Universidad Iberoamericana) held its first master degree in design strategic design for innovation. Its objective is to train professionals in the design area of strategic innovation of products, services, and communications, with a multidisciplinary focus on the business environment. Students are required to have a high level of analysis, creativity and prospective initiative for the development of innovative, user-centred concepts. Likewise, the Anáhuac University (Universidad Anáhuac) has a Centre of Design Research (Centro de Investigaciones en Diseño, CID) whose aim is to deepen the knowledge of design, specifically to define lines of action with a high social commitment and according to the international tendencies of contemporary design.

Figure 1
Visualisation of a 'compact' furniture system designed for owners who live in small apartments. Designer: Alan Pável Mendez.

Connecting different meanings | Applying a holistic approach | National design policies | International design collaboration

78|79

The knowledge generated for the centre will help provide design consultancy to enterprises and cultural institutions; and provide workshops, courses and seminars in design issues, publications, and didactic material. The centre has two programmes that embrace the following research lines: investigating the process of conceptualisation of design; and design studies, which involves information design, product design and design management.

Design management consultancy

In the case of practitioners, there is no specialised company focused on the pure utilisation of design management, although there are businesses that use design management as part of other functions. Of these companies, however, some are established in other countries and the ones that are in Mexico offer their services to multinational or national large enterprises. Examples of enterprises that are using design in an effective and visionary way, and are recognised nationally and internationally, are in/situm; MADE; and advank.

These companies are well known for design consultancy, showing clients the effective way to deliver value to their companies. Indeed, it is recognised that in the future a small number of companies are going to increase their design management strand, but not specialise completely.

Design management – future challenges

The poor industry conditions in Mexico have attracted the attention of a group of designers, who in 2007 presented to the Ministry of Economy the National Plan of Design for innovation (Plan Nacional de Diseño para la Innovación, PNDI). Its aim is to develop a plan that promotes design, in order to create products with added value and that are innovative and competitive in the market. In order to achieve this goal, design must be considered within the country as a strategic tool. It is down to good design to facilitate differentiation, to reduce costs, to generate an identity and a favourable image, and to care for and preserve the environment. However, one of the main problems that this group must face is the gap between industry, government and education.

As we discussed earlier, design management in Mexico is in its early stages and is therefore underestimated by industry and little used by academics and practitioners. The next step for designers is to increase its awareness and develop its use in different fields.

Figure 2
Compact seating system that incorporates discreet storage space. Designer: Alan Pável Mendez.

Design management in China

China has undergone several fundamental changes since strategies identified in the 1980s articulated ten deep-seated reforms; in particular, opening further to the outside world and becoming an active participant in international exchange and co-operation (Lianqing 1996). Since 1978, China has taken these reforms on board and has become a major force in global markets and, in 2006, Chinese exports were ranked number one in the world (Qian 2007). Although this strength has been built on a strong manufacturing base, improvements in China's infrastructure, workforce, and regulatory environment are also enabling global companies to lower their costs to reap new competitive advantages.

Therefore the need for a service sector, which can support innovation and new product development quickly, has become evident. Under the influence of this development, managing design effectively in China now faces the challenge of contributing to the design knowledge and management pool to enable technological and economic growth.

The origins of design management

Design management first appeared in China in 2001, as a 'design management workshop' through the joint efforts of Central Academy of Arts, China, and University of New South Wales, Australia. Design management has since become a popular subject, provided by independent academic organisations around the country, such as Central Academy of Arts; Tsinghua University; Jiaotong University and Dalian Industry University. In 2004, the Design Management Research Institute was set up in Shandong through a partnership between Shandong University of Art and Design and Staffordshire University, in the UK.

There have been conferences organised by academic institutions such as Tsinghua International Design Management Symposium in Beijing, 2002; D2B – the first International Design Management Symposium in Shanghai, 2006. Furthermore, universities and institutes in China started to offer design management courses both at undergraduate and postgraduate level to meet the country's needs. For example, the Central Academy of Arts ran its first postgraduate certificate course in 2003 and Shandong University of Art and Design has been running a BA in design management since 2002. It has since added an MA to its portfolio (September 2007).

Design management – key issues

Design management in China has been described as: providing a new way of communicating to build up a management system (Huangpu, Designer 3M, China); a strategy to plan the future through design (Design management, SUAD); a mechanism that intervenes, organises, mediates and structures in an increasingly more complex enterprise and economic world. In order to implement design management rapidly, Chinese educational establishments offering design management have looked to successful courses elsewhere in the world for advice on curriculum content and to support staff new to the area. With design management being a mature subject in the West, Chinese universities strengthened their ties with Western partners to promote exchanges. As a result, Chinese design management education methods are largely imported from the West. Related courses considered students' level of understanding of professional practice, business and market awareness and design as a strategic tool where the needs to be satisfied are both internal to the designer and external to the market.

Design management – supporting industry need

However, it is important to consider the differences in industry structures and practices between China and the West and how design management supports local industry needs. In 2007, the design to business ds2bs.com suggested that very few enterprises understand the concept of design management as an imported discipline. Although Chinese corporations have started to realise the value of design innovation, they often face the following challenges in practising it. Would the company be able to obtain the corresponding repayment from design research and investment? Why does the team always lack inspiration? Where is the genuine design innovation power located in the organisation?

Much design activity is concerned with the provision of a professional service, either to a client or to an employer. Industry organisations would feel reassured that the professionals understand their problems and are highly competent and experienced in design practice. According to Huang of China Bridge International, 'design management is the key, to merge design into line within systematised management, and the superintendent only then possibly truly transforms the commercial strategy for Chinese industry to carry out the strength effectively' (Huang 2007). Specifically, three main problems need to be solved in the interior organisations in China: unifying design goals and commercial strategy; promoting a design management concept and strengthening innovation culture.

Jian Ye Deng

Ms Jian Ye Deng is a senior lecturer at Shandong University of Art and Design. She is currently studying for a PhD in Design Management at Staffordshire University, UK.

Her research interests include investigating paradigms of design management education in both the East and West; design management within cultural boundaries; teaching and learning strategies; and the role of higher education in economic growth.

Connecting different
meanings

Applying a holistic
approach

National design
policies

International design
collaboration

80|81

Figure 1
Illustration design by
Ning Li, a former BA
student at SUAD.

Figure 2
Lucky Apple by
Professor Lei Sun,
principal lecturer in
design management
at SUAD.

Figure 3
AD poster design for
Folk Arts Exhibition
by Professor Lei Sun.

Figure 4
Universities in China
now offer design
management courses
to meet the country's
needs.

Figure 5
Poster design Knock
by Qunye Gu, senior
lecturer at SUAD.

Unifying design goals and commercial strategy

Each detail of an Apple product has been meticulously observed, from the packaging and the product itself to the user interface. After the return of founder Steve Jobs, Apple design is again at the centre of the corporate agenda. The industrial design centre has regained enthusiasm and inspiration, leading to commercial market successes such as the iMac, iBook and iPod. However, by observing similar products in the Chinese domestic market, although equally advanced in areas of technology, there is an underlying suggestion that the products are 'copied'. In fact, unfortunately, most Chinese industry design appears to be mired in a vicious circle of introduction, imitation and volume production. Behind this disparity is the apparent absence of clear design strategy. A well-structured design strategy should reflect the enterprise's commercial goal. Design strategy demands continuing investment whereby CEOs consider how to improve their long-term income through design, at the expense of controlling the cost of promoting design.

Many Chinese entrepreneurs prefer to invest in hardware, rather than spending on design research. They are content to pay for the completed design plan but, for the most part, are unwilling to commit to the research itself. The very fact that investment in research is not forthcoming, suggests that products will have less chance of success, once they enter the market, as there is a noticeable lack of competitive ability.

However, many Chinese enterprises have started to realise the influence of design. For example, in 2002, Lenovo China invested one million RMB and established Lenovo Product Design Development Center. In 2006, the company invested more than 10 million RMB in product design, associated with more than 80 professionals in ten specialised design teams around the world (Qian 2007). The Chinese computer company is now in charge of IBM's legendary PC business and has proved itself in the global marketplace. According to Steve Ward, former IBM executive and now Lenovo's CEO: 'Lenovo is well-positioned, with competitive strengths in branding, world-class scale and industry-leading efficiency.' Noticeably, by bringing **R&D** and design strategy into the corporate agenda, Lenovo has a powerful competitive position in the global market.

Promoting a design management concept

Sometimes designers are said to 'properly understand the demands of the business world, but not be sufficiently conscious of the relationship between design and profitability'. Many industry designers in China believe that first and foremost they are artists and, as such, have neglected the fact that industrial design requires a teamwork approach, which in turn demands the coordination of various company departments. This necessitates designers becoming familiar with company branding, marketing and its overall operation.

As such, a designer must be constantly aware of the need to offer services to clients which fulfil not only his or her own needs, but also commercial needs, and to fulfil these better than the competition at cost-effective levels (CNAA 1984). On the other hand, many business leaders lack clear knowledge of the very existence, shape and character of design. By reviewing many Chinese enterprises, it becomes apparent that the companies tend to make their own judgement on design through past experience whilst ignoring the designer or design team's contributions. However, companies' design plans should not be confined to what individual CEOs want, but what the market demands.

'A BCG world survey of 940 senior executives to identify the top 20 innovative companies ranked Apple as number one – the iconic company within the design community. In this creativity economy, design is the new buzz word.'
The Boston Consulting Group

R&D
Research and development, often called R&D, is a phrase that means different things in different applications. In the world of business, research and development is the phase in a product's life that might be considered its 'conception' or initial development. R&D is vital to an organisation's longevity, especially in fast-moving technology-led industries such as telecommunications and pharmaceuticals.

Design management – China Bridge

It has been established that exclusive management board support from the enterprises is essential to encouraging the implementation of design and management. Through successful international case studies and external consultancy projects, enterprises should be in a position to improve the product design process. In addition, it is a conduit to helping organisations understand the value of design through publications and conferences, thereby promoting the whole community to support design. It may further provide a wider and more effective range of staff training programmes (providing work experience, multidisciplinary team development or case studies), to better meet the needs of employees. These courses should cater for managers concerned with design and for people involved in the design process industry in order to keep them up to date with new technologies and practices relevant to their work. China Bridge International (CBI), the first Chinese design management consultancy, is an outstanding practising example of promoting design management concepts within Chinese industry. Its experience of working with some of the best companies in the world – such as iF; IDEO; Siemens and Samsung – means that CBI constantly provides expert advice in the area of design strategy, design research, resource network, course training and workshops. With design management teams offering high levels of expertise from both business and academic areas, CBI is in a strong position to offer support to clients in business growth and is better able to appreciate their individual needs in innovation.

Planning for success

Chinese business entrepreneurs are now starting to realise they need to develop the right innovation mix by integrating product and service, which the basis of competition is shifting away from cost to customer value. At the same time, the Chinese Government and leading Chinese enterprises are working to execute their innovation objectives successfully. For instance, the newly built Wuxi industrial design estate is at present the biggest design industry base in China, holding more than 1,000 design enterprises, and helping to lead China's industrial design into a new phase. In addition, in 2004, Shenzhen, the most developed city in China, proposed the goal of building the 'creativity design capital' and the 'global creativity city' on cultural creativity industry development; the famous Shenzhen creativity industry estate includes Nanhai architectural design industry zone; Nanyuan graphic design industry zone; Tianmian industrial design creativity zone and Jingyi animation design industry zone. Chinese government has implemented a policy to attract more international design enterprises and cultivate more outstanding home design firms.

Design management – future challenges

Both the Chinese Government and Chinese industry are embracing design innovation to enhance their competitiveness and capture future growth. Although Chinese industry has highlighted the many challenges it faces, it must have a clear understanding of the steps needed to become design innovative leaders, and view the changes as just another stage of China's ongoing transformation.

However, the road ahead for Chinese design managers is not a straightforward path and a number of fundamental questions remain unanswered. What are the theoretical and practical concepts that Chinese design managers and design management education need to explore in order to influence the progress of design management in China? Can those concepts lead to new forms that are suited to the emerging environment of international competition in the marketplace? How will those concepts help Chinese design managers make an original contribution that is more than a mere imitation of the West? Further research is needed to fill gaps in our current knowledge and also to document the development of design management in China. However, China has started this journey and continuing discussion will shape Chinese design management in the future.

'Chinese enterprises have started to realise the influence of design.'

Case study
Coordinating growth through design

This case study focuses on Haley Sharpe Design, a well-established design consultancy based in the UK. We discuss how it adopted an IT focus very early on in its growth, taking the audacious step of radically changing its current design processes to accommodate new technologies in a bid to secure new clients. After implementing new ways of working, the company expanded its portfolio of clients and projects, securing work in the Middle East and North America. Through this transformation, and willingness to accept change, technology is now core to every aspect of business operation and thinking. As a consequence, Haley Sharpe Design is accepted as market leader in the heritage and museum design market, continually striving to provide innovative solutions to an ever-expanding portfolio of international clients.

'... by far the vast majority of our current work is located overseas, and we need to develop new ways of working with technology in order to remain competitive and stay in business.'
Alisdair Hinshelwood

The company

Haley Sharpe Design was founded in the early 1980s, employing a dedicated and talented team of designers and support staff with a wide spectrum of skills. With the head office in Leicester, UK, the practice offers a unique design package across a broad range of projects and disciplines from exhibitions and displays through to museum retail environments, literature and visitor attraction design. To meet with clients' needs it has fostered expertise to create a coordinated design approach integrating graphic, three-dimensional and multimedia disciplines. Haley Sharpe Design is one of the top five museum and heritage interior design consultancies in the UK.

The need for change

The need for change was predominantly two-fold: first, Haley Sharpe Design had quickly established itself as a young and dynamic company attracting many clients throughout the UK. With the ability to provide comprehensive client services, from research through to concept development and implementation, the company was operating in diverse areas of activity, from museum and heritage projects to retail interiors. As a consequence of rapid growth, it quickly became apparent that a more strategic focus was needed in order to sustain this growth. Secondly, at the time, the company undertook all stages of the design process using traditional methods of design presentation. Its team of in-house designers would prepare perspective drawings and layouts by hand. These drawings would then be presented to the client and used as the basis for further dialogue and clarification of more detailed client requirements. As a result alterations were often needed to the preliminary concept drawings; again this would require time-consuming effort to complete.

However, in order to improve efficiency, Haley Sharpe Design's Managing Director Alisdair Hinshelwood realised that the company needed to invest in an appropriate IT system. At the time, however, no interior design specific software was available and the company was wary of making the wrong investment decisions. Therefore, the success of this strategy was dependent upon identifying suitable software systems (in particular DTP and CAD facilities) and embedding them within the company's everyday business and design practice procedures, thus creating a fully computer literate company.

So, in essence, managing and coordinating 'change' became of the utmost importance to the company, not only to optimise daily business practice, but also to attract overseas organisations in a bid to secure more work on a global scale.

Figures 1, 2 and 3
**The Museum of Liverpool,
Liverpool, UK.**
Artist's impression © 3XN

**Vision and Values in
Design Management**

Design
directions

**Design
transformations**

Design
advocacy

Design
alliances

Embedding new systems

In the early 1990s, initial contact was made between the company and the School of Interior Design at Birmingham City University (formerly known as University of Central England). Alisdair Hinshelwood explained that the company would like to develop new services to its clients but lacked the necessary in-house skills and knowledge to achieve this goal. After much discussion with the academic staff at the university, a two-Associate KTP programme was developed. The lengthy period of programme definition required substantial refinement in response to a closer and deeper understanding of changing company needs.

The principal aim of the partnership was to explore the development potential for IT in the form of CAD, electronic publishing and computer graphics, building on its existing working practices to increase the efficiency of design staff and to provide a faster and more effective response to customer requirements.

The two-fold aims of the programme were to implement an IT system that was compatible with the designers' needs; and to restructure its existing design process system, fully exploiting the benefits of the new IT system. The first KTP Associate, Chris Pruden, was appointed to undertake a comprehensive audit of current design activity at Haley Sharpe Design in reference to general IT requirements. He systematically analysed the company's existing working practices with a view to sourcing and recommending suitable hardware and software packages for both drawing and project management. On completion of the investigative phase, Chris produced a data flow diagram, which indicated communication channels that each individual project follows as it passes through its different stages of development.

Lynne Smith, an interior design graduate, then joined Chris to continue investigating the company's IT needs. She began to investigate potential CAD packages suitable for the company. They required a visualisation tool that could produce three-dimensional walk-throughs and photo-realistic images, coupled with the need to produce accurate engineering drawings that would enable contractors to manufacture components to the designer's specification.

The principal factor in the company's strategy to implement a full CAD system was the need to satisfy its clients that it was a progressive, technologically driven consultancy. Lynne prioritised the CAD requirements of the company in order that the initial system implementation would satisfy the most important clients. Lynne promoted the use of CAD for producing work that would not normally be produced by hand due to the prohibitive effort involved – such as three-dimensional work and measured perspective views. She was keen to instil the belief that the benefits of CAD provided more than simply an electronic drawing board – and that this ethos had to be embraced if the full integration of new technologies within the company were to be successful.

'Through a willingness to accept change, technology is now core to every aspect of our business operation and thinking.'

'... at the initial stages of the design process, our designers can still use magic markers and pens to produce conceptual drawings if they so wish. Other designers are happy to use technology straight away in order to produce designs, but we take a flexible approach in what works best for each individual designer.'

Connecting different
meanings

Applying a holistic
approach

National design
policies

International design
collaboration

86|87

Distributed design teams

By fully utilising information communication technologies Haley Sharpe Design's 'distributed' design teams can communicate across international boundaries to successfully compete for and manage new design projects. This is largely brought about with the ever-increasing globalisation of design and manufacturing; designers are likely to be co-located and are increasingly having to work across time and space in virtual teams. Haley Sharpe Design is now developing a focus towards distributed design teams, which it regards as an effective and efficient means of bringing a range of knowledge and experience to overseas museum and heritage projects. Also, due to the short duration of some of its design projects, there is a greater need for the company to embrace technology in order to produce a rapid response to design and construction issues that arise on site.

What is interesting is that Haley Sharpe Design has built-in greater flexibility in the way it uses technology during the design and construction process. This has evolved naturally since the new IT system has been implemented, often working incrementally with the technology and new project management system. Rather than slavishly adhering to a rigid inflexible design management process, it has designed its working practices to accommodate the technology as opposed to working within the constraints of technology.

However, when the project reaches the detail design stages all subsequent drawings are then produced on computer right through to project completion. Again, this enables changes to be quickly implemented and communicated electronically to other project partners.

Figures 1, 2 and 3
The Oklahoma History Center,
Oklahoma City, USA.

Internationalising design

Haley Sharpe Design now has offices in both North America and the Middle East to attract and manage commissions from a huge variety of clients. By initiating and implementing sophisticated IT facilities and associated support systems, the company operates on a truly global basis, enjoying growth in business and diversity of design projects. Through the establishment of trans-national information networks, problems, knowledge and contextual information can be quickly shared and passed between offices. This allows greater responsiveness to unanticipated problems or implementation issues. This, in a way, goes beyond traditional company boundaries so that designers based in the UK can be working on a project located in the Middle East and vice versa. Initial design concepts and idea generating activities are all supported and interconnected by IT, allowing greater involvement of people within various aspects of the organisation and, as a consequence, richer design solutions can be offered.

Some of Haley Sharpe Design's typical projects include:
— The Museum in Docklands, London, UK
— The Canadian War Museum, Ottawa, Canada
— The State Museum of History, Oklahoma, USA
— The Sharjah Museum of Islamic Civilisation, Sharjah, UAE
— The National Museum of Antiquities, Leiden, the Netherlands
— The Museum of Liverpool, UK
— Archaeology Museum, Sharjah, UAE.

Compare Haley Sharpe Design from its initial beginnings in the early 1980s as a small office based in the UK, mostly working with regional clients, to now, with a large number of projects overseas.

Summary

We have seen how Haley Sharpe Design has implemented and embraced new ICT technologies to both manage incremental 'change' and establish capacity to seek and secure new overseas clients.

Prior to the full use of IT, the company was predominantly desk-based and struggling to compete in the highly competitive museum and heritage design market. By radically reappraising existing business operation and traditional working practices and management systems, Haley Sharpe Design embarked on restructuring every aspect of organisational activity to plan for strategic growth. At the very core of this ethos was design and, in particular, how design could be maximised to full effect, offering greater efficiencies in operation whilst providing its clients with an enhanced value-added bespoke service. Alongside this, it is commonly known that new technologies are a major component of innovation, which embraces full system integration and networking; agile and customer responsiveness, driving continuous innovative activity. Since reappraising and implementing new design practices, it has managed to double its annual turnover; provide more services to its clients and enter more lucrative overseas markets. Ten years on, over 80% of its current work is located in the Middle East and North America. With new working systems in place coupled with the adoption of a IT focused workforce, Haley Sharpe Design is not only remaining competitive in difficult markets, it is securing major international projects and growing in prestige as an international design practice providing value-added services to its clients.

'Haley Sharpe Design has designed its working practices to accommodate technology as opposed to working within the constraints of technology.'

'In order to undergo strategic change, Haley Sharpe Design undertook a fundamental review of its existing design process systems, analysing how technology could play a major part in everyday practice.'

'By initiating and implementing sophisticated IT facilities and systems, the company operates on a truly global basis, enjoying growth in business and diversity of design projects.'

Figure 1
The Museum of Antiquities, Leiden, the Netherlands.

Figure 2
The Sharjah Museum of Islamic Civilisation, United Arab Emirates.

Figure 3
The Canadian War Museum, Ottawa, Canada.

Vision and Values in Design Management

Design directions

Design transformations

Design advocacy

Design alliances

Revision questions

Afterword

In the early 1990s Haley Sharpe Design recognised the emergence of two key issues that dictated its future in practice: new technologies and internationalisation. In a way they are both inextricably linked, especially in the search for new markets and business growth. At this time, the company understood the value of IT and the need to restructure the way in which it related to its clients in terms of design development work and communication. Haley Sharpe Design took the radical step of changing outdated working practices, taking on more of a technological focus in every aspect of designing, which at the time was an audacious move. With a heightened and formalised framework for responsiveness, technical issues can quickly be resolved and overcome with great efficiency and effectiveness. Planning for design isn't easy, but with intuitive and considered insight, the risks are far outweighed by the benefits.

1 Can new technologies ever replace the creative 'inspiration' of the designer?

2 ICT technologies can radically change the way initial design concepts are developed; in what way are these changes manifest?

3 How can IT capture the voice of the client within design development?

4 IT can speed up the design process, leading to greater efficiencies in performance; where and how are these efficiencies made?

5 ICT technologies have the ability to offer many unique benefits, but what are the drawbacks, especially in respect of cross-cultural communication?

Further recommended reading

Author	Title	Publisher	Date	Comments
Collins, J.C. and Porras, J.I.	*Built to Last: Successful Habits of Visionary Companies*	Random House Business Books	2005	Based on erudite research and cutting-edge thinking, this book illustrates why some organisations are just unbeatable – noteworthy for its use of case-studies.
Deakins, D. and Freel, M.	*Entrepreneurship and Small Firms*	McGraw-Hill Higher Education	Fourth edition 2005	An interesting and handy book exploring dynamics of entrepreneurial firms and their unique characteristics.
Friedman, T.	*The World Is Flat: The Globalized World in the Twenty-first Century*	Penguin Books	Second revised edition 2007	A highly readable account of the shrinking world and its impact on both business practice and social development. Compelling.
Levitt, S.D. and Dubner, S.J.	*Freakonomics: A Rogue Economist Explores the Hidden Side of Everything*	Addison Wesley	2007	The authors offer an upbeat and lateral view of the world and how some things just cannot be explained by mainstream economic thought. Once you start on this page-turner you won't stop – immensely enjoyable.
Porter, M.	*Competitive Advantage*	Free Press	2004	No reading list on management thinking should ignore this author. Groundbreaking and insightful – a true world expert on the subject.

**Vision and Values in
Design Management**

Design
directions

Design
transformations

Design
advocacy

Design
alliances

Chapter summary

Design is imperative to commercial and economic success and the way in which we manage this process is vital to the long-term and continual survival of the organisation. We have seen how design management, through its many faceted roles, has the ability to adapt itself and 'shape' business decision making and operation by influencing key individuals within the organisation. This can occur on a day-to-day basis right through to the establishment of international joint ventures. Design is becoming more globalised and we have discovered the ways in which nation states are adopting and formulating design policies. We have seen how China has embraced design and innovation, in the rebranding of a country with the ultimate ambition of becoming a global leader and developer of cutting-edge technological solutions. The case studies showed us how design management has been adopted within very specific cultural and regional frameworks, driving and fostering change in dynamic and emergent marketplaces.

Review questions

Based on what has been discussed, you should now be able to answer the following five questions.

1 What are the key factors driving the changing definition of design management?

2 What incremental strategies would you propose in terms of taking an organisation up through the design ladder from level 1 to 5?

3 How can design engage with emergent issues such as eco design and corporate social responsibility?

4 Why is it so important that countries develop a strategic national design policy?

5 What do you think are the key differences between China and Mexico in terms of design management?

Connecting different
meanings

Applying a holistic
approach

National design
policies

International design
collaboration

92|93

Further recommended reading

Author	Title	Publisher	Date	Comments
Bruce, M. and Bessant, J.	*Design in Business: strategic innovation through design*	Financial Times / Prentice Hall	2002	A highly contemporary and readable account of strategic design and innovative management processes. Excellent range of contributors makes the book a vital companion for the reader. Very worthwhile to the reader who is interested in exploring the wider context of design and business strategy.
Bruce, M. and Jevnaker, B.	*Management of Design Alliances: sustaining competitive advantage*	John Wiley and Sons	1998	The authors offer a broad and insightful discussion concerning the many benefits and potential pitfalls of strategic design alliances. Ten years on, this book is now more important than ever with the erosion of cultural boundaries offering distinct benefits to companies prepared to enter into design alliances.
Cooper, R. and Press, M.	*The Design Agenda: a guide to successful design management*	John Wiley and Sons	1995	This book is an invaluable guide to exploring all aspects of both design and design management within everyday practice. Highly articulate and easy to understand, it presents a compelling case for adopting a design management orientation in order to seek competitive advantage.
Jerrard, R. and Hands, D. (editors)	*Design Management: fieldwork and applications*	Routledge Taylor Francis	2008	The book aims to demystify the benefits of design investment through exploring case studies drawn from a variety of different contextual backgrounds. Invaluable to the reader if they are considering developing design auditing tools.
Walsh, V. Roy, R. Bruce, M. and Potter, S	*Winning by Design: technology, product design and international competitiveness*	Blackwell Business	1992	Although slightly dated, this book deserves further reading as it provides a strong case for the investment in design. The authors are recognised authorities on design and they bring to bear all their experience and knowledge concerning design and technology.

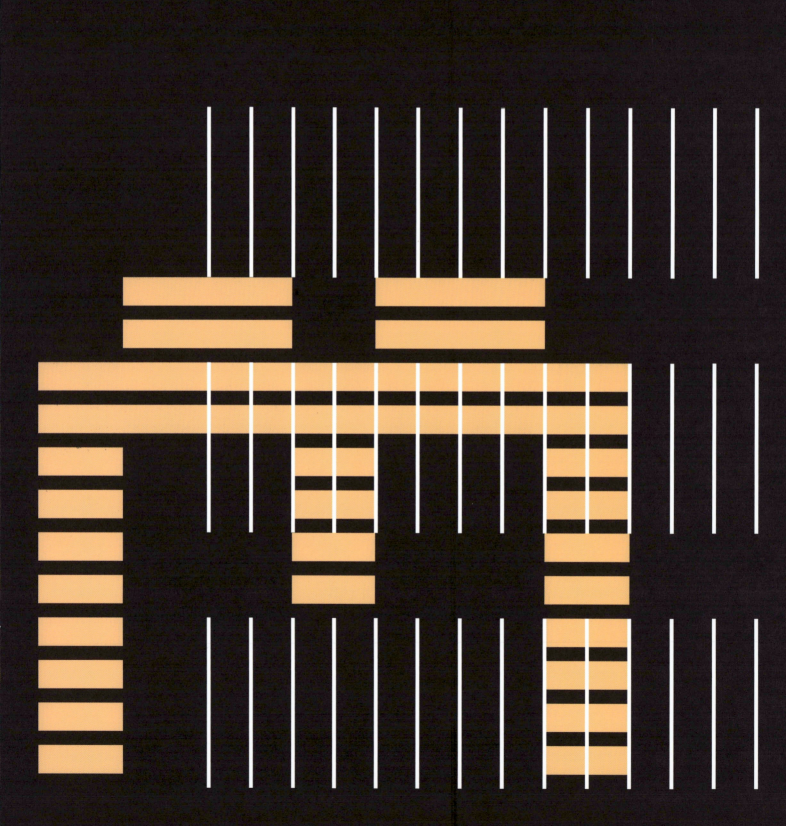

Design
leadership

Driving innovation
through design

Design
strategy

Design
collaboration

94|95

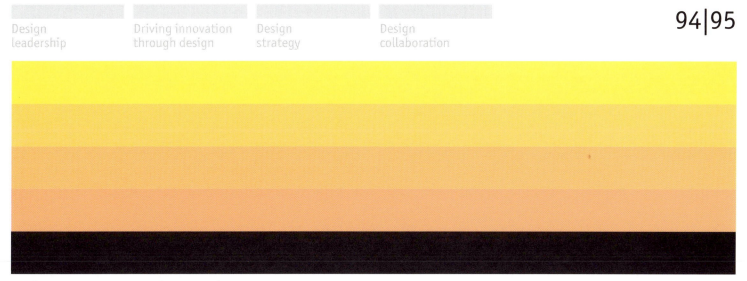

Chapter three
Design advocacy

Design champions are key drivers of change within the organisation. What are design champions and how do they contribute to strategic change and business growth? Leadership by design can drive innovation not only within the organisation but by reaching out to partners within the extended supply chain. With the ability to foster a climate of creativity and innovative activity, new and sustainable strategic futures enable endless possibilities for the organisation.

Design leadership

This section will discuss the rise of design leadership as a separate but intrinsically related discipline to design management. It could be seen as a natural continuation of design enhancement taking prominence within the organisation, with talented leadership in the boardroom being used to fully leverage design to secure corporate aims. The origins of design management are raised, focusing on key texts that provided landmark developments leading to the emergence of design leadership.

Figures 1–3
Raymond Turner was Group Design Director of British Airport Authorities (BAA), responsible for providing design leadership to Heathrow's Terminal 5 project.

Design
leadership

Driving innovation
through design

Design
strategy

Design
collaboration

96|97

Beyond design management

Is design management dead we ask? Is the term outdated and past its expiry date, with no real relevance in meaning or application? After 30 years of growth and discussion, design management is still a much debated and contentious term, meaning different things to different people. Recently, the term design leadership has come to the fore, providing clarity and relevance to organisations, suggesting that design is a corporate asset and has the ability to significantly contribute to organisational effectiveness and strategic vision. On first glance there does not seem to be much difference between these two terms, but on closer investigation they are actually quite separate yet intrinsically related. To begin a closer detailed analysis, it is worthwhile at this point to mention two significant names closely related to the emergence of design leadership: **Alan Topalian** and **Raymond Turner**. It is argued that both design management and design leadership are equally valid and valuable disciplines; however, they are uniquely important in their inherent differences and distinct positions within the organisation.

The late 1970s saw the humble beginnings of design management: the **Corfield Report** (1979) critically discussed the failings of British industry, and at the heart of the report was that industry did not recognise and deploy design effectively enough, let alone manage it strategically. Implicitly, the Corfield Report suggested that industry fully exploit design within the development of new products and, importantly, manage design with a greater emphasis on achieving corporate aims and objectives. At the time, the report's findings and recommendations were ground-breaking and revolutionary, raising the value of design to a higher corporate level. Let's fast-forward to the 1980s, when another seminal text placed design management on the corporate agenda: *Design Talks* (1988), which featured keynote papers taken from the London Business School design management seminars. Even now, 20-odd years after its publication, the contributors discuss and raise issues regarding strategic design management that are equally as relevant today as they were in the 1980s.

As part of the launch of the Design Leadership Forum, Raymond Turner discussed the key differences between design leadership and design management, arguing that the former is more 'proactive' and the latter 'reactive'. So in essence leadership is more concerned with 'vision' than 'implementation', which is the primary domain of management. A position was established to promote dialogue and debate regarding the validity and differences between the two terms. In short, Topalian and Turner argued that the core characteristics of design leadership involve five significant aspects:

1   Clarify where the company wishes to go.
2   Define its desired futures.
3   Demonstrate what those desired futures might be like.
4   Develop design strategies that help the company get there.
5   Turn the desired future into reality.

Taking these five aspects for further discussion offers a very persuasive case for design leadership. So, what does this entail?

'The idea that is not dangerous is not worthy of being called an idea at all.'
Elbert Hubbard

Alan Topalian
Topalian is Principal of Alto Design Management in London. He is author of three British Standards within the BS7000 series on managing innovation and design. 'Probably the most comprehensive and widely researched views on design management are those of Topalian' – so concluded a 1984 international survey of work in the field by the Council for National Academic Awards sponsored by the Department of Trade and Industry and the Design Council in the UK. Alan is considered by many to be a leading authority on design management and his work over the last 30 years has advanced the field considerably.

Raymond Turner
Turner was Group Design Director of BAA, the world's largest privately owned airport company, for nine years. He is retained by BAA to provide design leadership to their Heathrow Terminal 5 project and is a board director of the brand consultancy Marketplace. Before joining BAA, Raymond was a Board Member and Principal Consultant of Wolff Olins, where he was responsible for providing creative leadership and directing design investment for a number of their major clients, including Eurotunnel.

Corfield Report
The Corfield Report on Product Design (NEDO, 1979) stimulated debate into the important role of design in competitiveness that significantly contributed to the development of design management as a strategic corporate resource.

**Vision and Values in
Design Management**

Design
directions

Design
transformations

Design
advocacy

Design
alliances

Signposting the future

Forward-thinking and progressive
organisations are constantly asking
themselves, 'Where could we be in five or
ten years?' New technologies, market
opportunities and overseas demand are
continually presenting areas of activity and
exploitation that could ensure business
survival and continued prosperity. Design
leadership gives a firm identity and voice of
design at senior management or boardroom
level, enabling the organisation to plan and
drive future growth with design as the
combustion engine of innovation and
inspiration.

Cul-de-sacs or superhighways

Which road should one take? Would pursuing
route A be the most advantageous in the
long run, or route B to reap swift rewards?
Having identified long-term strategic aims
for future development, there could be
numerous ways of achieving these goals,
but which one is best? Design leadership is
where the voice of design articulates and
tests the different routes that the
organisation could take. Through this
proactive mindset, desired futures are
tentatively identified, tested, and
appropriate responses initiated. Cul-de-sacs
may seem like an attractive proposition in
the short term, but for the forward-thinking
organisation strategic development is the
only way forward. Design is a route map
identifying the most effective and
sustainable way of getting from A to B.

Exploration and inspiration

Is it better to travel than to arrive? Does the
journey of investigation make the process of
exploration more fruitful and worthwhile?
Design leadership has the charismatic and
imaginary attributes to engage, challenge
and inspire people who would otherwise feel
disenfranchised from the strategic planning
process. With the ability to communicate
on different levels, to often diametrically
opposed functions within the organisation,
design leadership acts like a corporate 'glue'
combining diverse viewpoints and opinions.
Ideas and future scenarios can be tested
through strong visualisation and good
communication skills helps to inform
opinions. In essence, leadership is making
sense of intangible aspirations and
transforming long-held perceptions of
what the future could hold.

Figure 1
Neff is a specialist brand within the Bosch
and Siemens group. The organisation
benefits from a strong sense of design
leadership.

'Designers have a range of specialist skills
which enable them to make a unique and
valuable contribution to technology start-
ups. These skills include creative problem
solving and visualisation techniques as well
as expert practical knowledge of both user
needs and the product development process.'
David Maddison

Design
leadership

Driving innovation
through design

Design
strategy

Design
collaboration

98|99

Alchemy and chemistry

What is the difference between alchemy and chemistry? And why is this difference central to design leadership, you may well ask? Alchemy is the chemistry of science with the added X-factor that takes science into the realm of the supernatural. Are design managers 'chemists' and design leaders 'alchemists'? If you combine intuition, empathy, creativity and inspirational leadership with the ability to understand day-to-day practical business considerations, then this unique force becomes integral to the strategic armoury of the organisation, turning aspirations into reality.

Experience of engagement

Today's consumers are more demanding and discerning than ever. They search for value and meaning in every purchase and engagement with the organisation, not only in the private sector where the transaction of goods take place but also in the public sector, such as healthcare. Let's look at a basic example, such as the purchase of a motor vehicle. The customer would want to experience the motor car in both a meaningful and memorable way. The Aston Martin brand is synonymous with value-added prestige, superiority and elegant sophistication; these attributes of the brand must be manifest in all aspects of customer engagement with the organisation. From the very point of initial contact through to eventual purchase, the experience of engagement must convey these intangibles to the customer.

If successful, a meaningful relationship is cemented and sustained; however, if one aspect of this is unsuccessful then the relationship is lost. Design leadership ensures and embodies strategic intent to drive long-term relationships. If we take the role of leadership further, then inevitably one of its core responsibilities is to instil and support organisational creativity, embracing risk-taking through design. To promote and argue for the value of design at a corporate level, then a support framework must be implemented. For example, design is embedded throughout every aspect of organisational activity within IBM, Kodak, Honda and so forth, but what drives this vision is that risk taking, innovative activity and trial and error are actively encouraged in the search for new answers in business practice and development.

'Too many companies make the big mistake of rushing into design projects without first considering the implications of what they are doing.'
Design Council

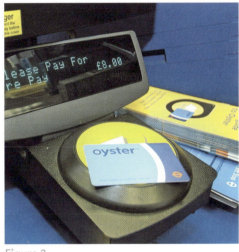

Figure 2
The Oyster card service has been designed to reduce inconvenience for commuters on the London Underground tube system.

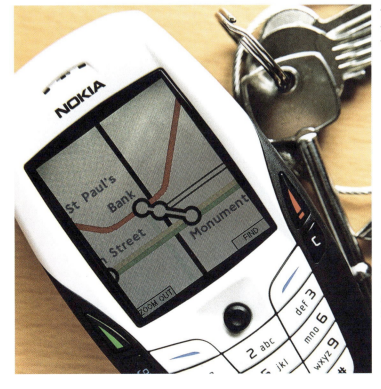

Figure 3
Nokia is continually striving to provide services to its customers that reflect and support their hectic lifestyles.

**Vision and Values in
Design Management**

Design
directions

Design
transformations

Design
advocacy

Design
alliances

Fostering a culture of creativity

A risk-taking approach is easy to promote, but to actually implement such a climate of creativity is incredibly hard. Many organisations are willing to try but do not fully understand what it entails. With pressures to increase productivity and performance within the workplace, failure is still commonly regarded as a negative thing. To overcome this and to support creativity, some enlightened organisations allow employees to experiment, or be allowed to work on individual personal projects in work time. It is hoped that by supporting personal projects, those ideas and concepts that are explored and nurtured may eventually be taken into full production at a later stage.

The freedom to develop ideas without the fear of failure and reprisal enables innovation, which benefits the individual, team and organisation as a whole. The risk of failure is an incredibly potent force that inhibits creativity, stifling experimentation and play, which are the key components of innovation. To provide a supportive atmosphere for creativity involves new modes of working, increased flexibility and adjusting the common industry orthodoxy that failure is at all costs to be avoided.

Rethinking the organisation

Creativity has the power to change perception and the way in which we view ourselves. Creativity is a skill; it takes practice, perseverance and a lot of hard work. In short, it is the ability to apply existing skills and knowledge in new and innovative ways to new contexts. With technological developments emerging on a daily basis, knowledge and creativity are becoming the new skillsets that are demanded by organisations. Structural change is transforming the working environment, where national economies are placing greater emphasis on the personal skills of the employee; at the core of this, organisations are seeking employees who can apply knowledge in ever more creative ways. Design leadership is focused on two aspects of creativity: first, product creativity – in terms of enabling designers to foresee new problems and overcome them; and secondly, perhaps more importantly, managerial creativity. This involves rethinking how we organise, plan, develop and commercialise ideas supported by new dynamic managerial structures. To rethink existing business models of routine practice and develop a more creative one requires belief in the value of creativity from the top – and design leadership is best suited to achieving this cultural transformation.

'Nearly half of businesses where design is integral have seen turnover, profit and competitiveness increase. Growing businesses are far more likely to be getting these benefits than companies with static or shrinking turnover.'
Design in Britain

Summary

The recent emergence of design leadership as an evolutionary advancement of design management raises many questions. Is it design management with new clothes or a logical developmental step in its ongoing maturity? On closer investigation, the debate is much more complex, trying to understand and separate the nuances and differences between the two. First, the debate is timely, because as we have seen and witnessed, design is a powerful boardroom weapon in the search for differentiation and ongoing business success. Through this discussion, and as a natural consequence, the design agenda is raised and positioned at the core of organisational activity.

Who is the best person to lead and manage is a more complex issue; more shades of grey than black or white. It could be argued that design management is inherently a proactive force similar to design leadership, but it applies its value and persuasive effects in very much a 'silent' or subtle manner. Rather than have two definitions competing for attention and utmost importance within the organisation, why not have one holistic term that embraces the values of both perspectives: strategic design management? Since the late 1970s design management has grown in importance and, by and large, Topalian and Turner have been central to its development and implementation within organisations.

However, with design management being embraced, adopted and adapted in relatively new economies such as India, south-east Asia and in particular China, the next five to ten years offer unique opportunities for clarity and ongoing debate between the two viewpoints. For now, this worthwhile and valuable debate continues.

Figure 1
Festo is a worldwide leading supplier of pneumatic and electrical automation technology with an illustrious history of developing innovative products.

**Vision and Values in
Design Management**

Design
directions

Design
transformations

Design
advocacy

Design
alliances

Interview
Alan Wall

Alan Wall is the director of Buxton Wall
Product Development Ltd. A designer with
over 30 years' experience, he has worked as
a design consultant both in the UK and in
the USA. Wall graduated in mechanical
engineering and progressed to a postgraduate design course and so into
consultancy. The Buxton Wall McPeake
Consultancy, established in 1979, offered a
comprehensive 2D and 3D design support
service. Buxton Wall Product Development
Ltd was established in 2002, primarily to
concentrate on royalty-based projects.
However, design consultancy and new
product development remains an important
aspect of the workload.

**For those unfamiliar with the work that
you do, could you provide a brief overview
of your role and responsibilities?**
When I first meet a potential client I try to
understand as much as possible about what
they hope to achieve, timescales, budgets,
the competition and so on. My first job then
is to produce a proposal document that sets
out a brief (as I understand it), a design
programme sub-divided into stages with
associated costs and timescales, and my
terms and conditions. This is an important
document for both parties to agree to before
work commences. I am then responsible for
ensuring that the work is done on time, and
within budget, and liaison with my client
and other suppliers. This is the classic
structured approach, which most designers
conform to. However I am sometimes
commissioned to throw the rule book out the
window and get a result by whatever means!

**Can you give us an example of a typical
client and project on which you would
normally work?**
There is no typical client: they vary from the
big international companies down to one-
man companies and inventors. The support
required also varies from simple front-end
concept generation through to providing a
comprehensive design programme, which
would probably include liaison with other
suppliers (e.g. toolmakers, moulders,
keypad manufacturers and so on). Some
designers specialise in specific market
segments but we do not, and so I have been
lucky enough to be involved in design
projects that include toys, transportation,
pet products, medical/scientific equipment
and consumer plastics. Projects range from
dog toys to mass-spectrometers, which
perhaps gives some clues as to why I have
found this to be both an entertaining and a
satisfying career!

Design
leadership

Driving innovation
through design

Design
strategy

Design
collaboration

102|103

From your own experience, do many of your clients fully understand the value of design?

Not surprisingly, this does vary. The blue chips are generally au fait but SMEs vary. Small companies are often wary at first but usually become enthusiastic once they see what we can do and realise we are on their side! Sadly design support is often viewed as a 'grudge purchase' in the UK and sometimes a company's attitude is coloured by a less than satisfactory previous experience. I do feel that we have to work extra hard to prove our worth. I can't claim 100% success but I think in general we have done pretty well for our clients down the years.

Since you have been practising in industry, what are the key developments you have had to overcome in terms of staying in business?

I started out in design consultancy in the early 1980s, just at the tail-end of the period where most product design work was done by hand at the drawing board with Letraset for graphic designers. This changed rapidly, first with Macs for our graphic designers and then 3D CAD for us product designers. The cost of hardware and software was very high at the time so this was a big change for designers. From this point on it was a major cost for design companies and it was absolutely necessary to stay in business. Our first workstation with 3D CAD software cost around £35,000 (a current cost equivalent would be twice that). Fortunately today costs have dropped significantly in real terms although serious software is still quite expensive.

Has the rise of new and sophisticated technologies changed the role of designing?

In very broad terms, the role of designing remains the same: by first generating a concept, which answers the brief, and then working with the client to bring the solution to the marketplace. The detail of the design process itself has changed: now it is 3D CAD at an early stage, rapid prototyping, data transfer to suppliers (e.g. toolmakers) and of course, extensive use of the internet for research and email for close liaison with client and suppliers. All kinds of software are employed to generate realistic images of the emerging product, to design the labels and keypad, the packaging and so on. Time to market is a key issue.

Does this new technology remove the need for creativity? Can technology ever replace creativity?

Designers have to invest a lot of time learning to use the relevant software, which is a shame because after all it is only a design tool. A big danger here is to become so immersed in computers and software that basic design skills and creativity are pushed into the background. It doesn't help that a superficially polished computer image can look good at first sight. Personally I still like to see a designer with good drawing skills who can explore ideas quickly on paper and communicate them via illustration (simple sketches or, less often now, the finished marker visual). At this point in time, this is still the quickest way to get through the initial concept stage of a project.

What would you consider to be the most important stage of the design process?

It is undoubtedly the front-end concept stage. Any solution selected for ongoing development will incur costs downstream that will last for the life of the product. So first there may be toolmaking and other implementation costs, then the production unit cost, distribution, maintenance, 'in the field' success against the competition and many other relating issues. So get it right and the product 'flies', is profitable and shakes the opposition. Get it wrong and the product will not do well in the market, be less profitable and may even fail. And let's not forget good aesthetics, which may be top of the list for a consumer product but also counts high for a mass-spectrometer.

How much emphasis do you place on personal relationships, or let's say 'chemistry' with the client, leading to overall project success?

It is a key ingredient in any business relationship and it is hard to go that 'extra mile' with a difficult or unsympathetic client. The best scenario is where mutual respect and trust develops and then you get a genuine team effort. This also paves the way for a longer-term relationship, which all design companies hope for. The downside is if the principal contact within the client company moves on, then the relationship can suffer. Their replacement might well have their own preferences for a design house and this is known as the 'new broom' scenario. These days, takeovers, mergers and closures can make a relationship redundant overnight.

How do you measure the success of a product that you have designed? Do you try to ascertain feedback from a client, in terms of product sales or user feedback?

Success from the client's perspective is inevitably linked to the bottom line. A product that becomes a UK market leader and sells in excess of two million units is a convincing story. The model of a new design ready in time for a launch at the main international exhibition (saving 12 months) is good news. If a new design outsells projections by 400% then everyone is delighted. But good design is sadly only part of the mix. Sometimes a really good design solution may be praised by all and sundry but fails for other reasons, such as an adverse economic climate or aggressive counter-marketing by the current market leader.

Is there anything you like to add that we haven't covered, but you consider important to raise?

We are all naturally concerned about where manufacturing in the UK is heading – after all, product designers provide a support service. Volume products have long since gone to the Far East but high-value, low-volume products have tended to stay here. Designers hoped that the design work itself would stay here even if manufacture moved overseas and this has been true to a certain extent. But quality manufacture and design is increasingly available in China, which at first sight is bad news for us here in the UK. However, right now (as of October 2008) there are dramatic upheavals taking place in the world economy. As a consequence it may well be less attractive in the near future for manufacture (and design) to move overseas, which would be good for all of us involved in design and new product development.

**Vision and Values in
Design Management**

Design
directions

Design
transformations

Design
advocacy

Design
alliances

Driving innovation through design

Innovation is a complex process of taking vision through to reality by combining knowledge from different sources and transferring technology from one domain to another. We take a close look at how innovation is the engine of change and business success, driving growth and future prosperity through collaborative partnerships from diverse sources. At the core of this dynamic and fast-moving activity is design, advocating progress and market differentiation through visionary behaviour combined with subtle design leadership.

Opportunities
Innovation triggers can come from a
combination of different sources.

Figure 1

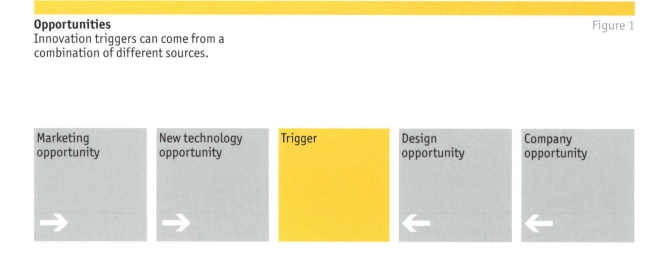

Marketing
opportunity

New technology
opportunity

Trigger

Design
opportunity

Company
opportunity

Design
leadership

**Driving innovation
through design**

Design
strategy

Design
collaboration

104|105

What is innovation?

The **PDMA** defines innovation as 'a new idea, method, or device. The act of creating a new product or process.' The act includes invention as well as the work required to bring an idea or concept into final form. It is important to make a clear differentiation between innovation and invention and according to the **CIPA**, an invention is 'simply something new, something that has not been thought of before and which is not obvious.' Invention is therefore the creation of something entirely new to the world, which has not involved the development of an existing product, process or system. The lightbulb, the digital watch, the Biro, the microwave oven and the telephone are all examples of inventions. Innovation essentially refers to change and this can be applied to the products/services offered by an organisation and the ways in which these are created and delivered. A new design of car and a new car insurance package are examples of product innovation. A change in the manufacturing methods and equipment used to make the car and the new office procedures and sequencing used to develop the insurance package are examples of process innovation.

Innovation and business

Baxter defines innovation as, 'a vital ingredient for business success'. Companies must continually introduce new products and modify existing ones in order to prevent their more innovative competitors gaining market share. There is a strong correlation between market performance and new products, which clarifies the importance of innovation: 'Whilst competitive advantage can come from size, or possession of assets, the pattern is increasingly coming to favour those organisations which can mobilise knowledge and technological skills and experience to create new products, processes and services.' (Baxter, 1996.)

Innovation through activities

Innovation is not 'a single action but a whole process' made up of a series of events and activities and involving a number of people and disciplines. The process varies from company to company but despite these variations there is an underlying pattern of important stages. The innovation process on a basic level can be viewed as three phases: the trigger, the opportunity and the need. Innovations may also be categorised by the type of trigger, by what originally initiated the process. Triggers for innovation can come from a combination of sources and disciplines.

The ideas that initiate the innovation process may originate from a wide variety of sources. An invention is just one type of trigger and usually involves new technology, which can come from the consumer behaviour, market activity or from a change in design. Triggers often relate to three particular disciplines: technology, marketing and design. 'Technology push' refers to ideas that are created and/or developed in internal R&D departments or technological ideas that have been adopted from other industries. 'Market pull' defines a trigger that was conceived in response to the end-user's needs and/or demands. Also included in this category of trigger are those which were prompted to counter competitor activity. 'Design-led' innovation triggers refer to the ideas that change and improve the function aesthetics and performance factors of the product/process as perceived by the consumer. This includes design improvements in manufacturing processes, which may increase efficiency.

Is there an opportunity?

Once the idea is identified, resources should be allocated, skills diverted and support given to seize the opportunity available. Deployment of organisational knowledge and capability ensures the idea is protected and nurtured for its potential success. The experience of innovation provides opportunities to expand and develop skills and know-how.

Is there a need?

It is argued that in order for the idea to be commercially successful there must be a need. Often inventions fail because there is no perceived or actual need for it. Need can come internally in a strategic sense as well as externally from the consumer, and both are important elements of success.

'Design is an investment not a cost. It is a continuous thought-provoking process that affects every part of business.'
Stephen Byers

PDMA
The Product Development and Management Association is a global advocate for product development and innovation. Its website provides an excellent resource featuring case studies and an extensive glossary.

CIPA
The Chartered Institute of Patent Attorneys is the professional and examining body for patent attorneys (also known as patent agents) in the UK. The Institute was founded in 1882. It represents virtually all the 1,730 registered patent attorneys in the UK.

**Vision and Values in
Design Management**

Design
directions

Design
transformations

Design
advocacy

Design
alliances

Market opportunity

Figure 1

The market provides many rich opportunities
for expansion and commercial growth.

New technology opportunity

Figure 2

Technology can trigger innovation from
within and beyond company boundaries.

Move up market

Technical
developments

Improved product
specification

Market
opportunity

Expand exports

New technology
opportunity

Product spin-offs

Change in market
demand

Gap in the market

Adaptations from
other industries

Continuing to innovate

It is suggested that innovation success is
a multidimensional concept, interlinking
factors relating to the strategy objectives
with internal and external benefits. A
one-off success requires little more than
good timing and a bit of luck. However, to
repeat innovation success demands careful
coordination and mobilisation of skills and
know-how in the long term.

Measuring innovation success is a complex
problem, as the criteria change with each
company and with each case. Companies
must establish their own performance
measures. Quantitative data, for example,
might include the number of hours devoted
to new ideas or the number of new ventures
in a year, whereas qualitative data could
rate company morale and motivation and
examine the ratio of skills and knowledge
that have been gained from various projects.
Much can be learnt from the success criteria
developed for product performance. Souder
et al (1998) suggest a number of critical
factors for success (see Table 1).

Critical success factors

Table 1

1 A unique, superior product	A differentiated product delivers added value to the consumer, unique benefits and provides a competitive advantage.
2 A strong market orientation encouraging a customer-focused new product process	Good consumer knowledge and feedback enhances the desire for such products and improves marketing activities.
3 The right organisational structure, design and climate	A **cross-functional team** that integrates different discipline perspectives.
4 Sharp and early product definition	Definition of the product concept, consumer benefits and core market helps formulate an accurate positioning strategy.
5 More emphasis on consistency, completeness and quality of execution	Research, testing and evaluation to improve quality and performance at every stage.

Design
leadership

**Driving innovation
through design**

Design
strategy

Design
collaboration

106|107

Company opportunity   Figure 3
Company stimuli to trigger innovation.

Design opportunity   Figure 4
Design-led innovation triggers refer to ideas
that can change and improve product and
service attributes in the eyes of the
customer.

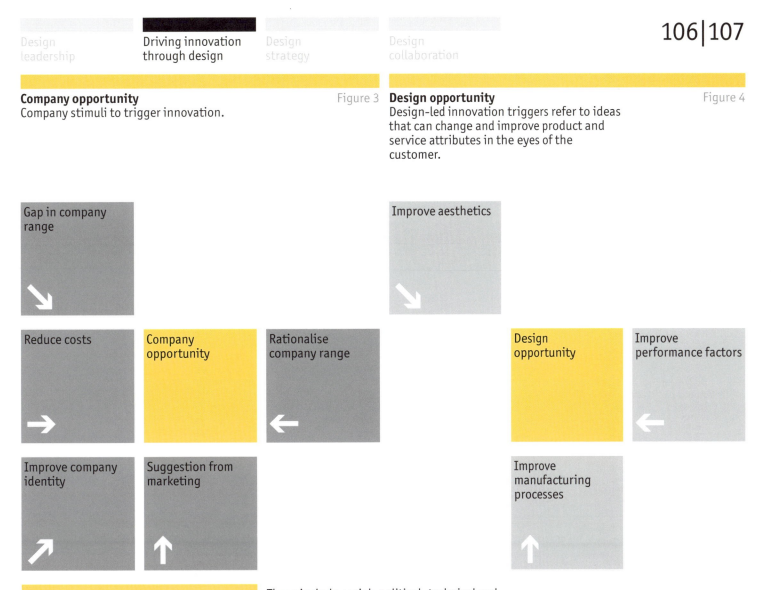

Risks and rewards

Product innovation does not always lead to
company success and the failure rate of new
products is a frequently quoted business
statistic. 'For every 10 ideas for new
products, 3 will be developed, 1.3 will be
launched and only 1 will make any profit'
(Page, 1991). Statistics vary due to the
different definitions constituting a new
product and what constitutes product
success. However, the figures above
highlight the immense risk involved in
product innovation. The cost incurred during
the development of new products can run
into millions and a good example of huge
loss involves the Edsel Ford or the 'E' car,
which was a spectacular failure, despite
Ford's $400,000 investment in 1952.
Certain aspects of the risk involved in
innovation are unpredictable.

These include social, political, technical and
market factors. Therefore the innovation
process must be managed effectively and
carefully in order to decrease the risk of
mistakes and to ensure that if failure occurs
lessons are learned to avoid the same
experiences in the future.

Adair Turner, **CBI** Director General, identified
that 'the lack of ideas is worrying. It is quite
a turnaround, since the UK is supposed to be
good at ideas but weaker at exploiting them.
Unless companies can come up with new
ideas they won't have any innovations to
exploit in the future.' More encouraging
research indicates that companies are
becoming more responsive and reacting to
customer pressures. One survey identified
that over four-fifths of manufacturers have
introduced new innovations in the last three
years and to counter the lack of ideas,
companies are developing links with other
firms and forging ties with research
institutes.

Cross-functional team
A team consisting of representatives from
the various key functions involved in
product development, such as marketing,
engineering, manufacturing/operations,
finance, purchasing, customer support and
quality control.

CBI
The CBI's mission is to help create and
sustain the conditions in which businesses
in the UK can compete and prosper for the
benefit of all. The organisation provides
access to governance, policy making
information and a vast resource of related
business and legal support.

**Vision and Values in
Design Management**

Design
directions

Design
transformations

Design
advocacy

Design
alliances

Supply chain-driven innovation

Having identified the key considerations at the initial stages of new product development, our focus should now move on to the valuable and often neglected partners in the process of developing innovative and novel products – suppliers. **The Supply Chain Council** offers a clear and succinct definition of the supply chain: 'The supply chain – a term now commonly used internationally – encompasses every effort involved in producing and delivering a final product or service, from the supplier's supplier to the customer's customer. Supply chain management includes managing supply and demand, sourcing raw materials and parts, manufacturing and assembly, warehousing and inventory tracking, order entry and order management, distribution across all channels and delivery to the customer.'

In short, suppliers are experts in their own lines of business activity; to develop a reasonably advanced product (in terms of technology and highly engineered parts) many suppliers would be involved. Their involvement could range from simply supplying component parts to engaging in a closer involvement with the organisation providing expertise and knowledge. If we add all the suppliers together involved in developing one new product, the numbers are impressive. For example, there are a huge amount of suppliers involved when developing a new Boeing aircraft (see the illustration on page 111) or a state-of-the-art motor vehicle range for Toyota. Within this vast network of suppliers lies a great wealth of knowledge that could be exploited within new product development.

At one time, the supply chain system was quite a basic process: company A needed parts, they identified a suitable supplier, after contact and negotiation parts were supplied on a regular basis, and there was minimal involvement beyond that. However, this model is incredibly outdated and almost redundant, with customers now having considerable say in what they want; this is commonly termed 'demand-driven innovation'.

Demand-driven innovation is a highly responsive and flexible type of innovation that not only satisfies customers' needs but exceeds them. In order to do this, a system needs to be in place where the organisation can obtain quality feedback, most often through the marketing department or after-sales. This information is taken forward into the development of subsequent products that incorporate these demands and desires. If successful, the product is viewed as desirable and valuable in the eyes of the consumer, thus leading to continual sales and customer loyalty. There are many different and often complex variables that need to be considered and accommodated in order to remain flexible and respond to constantly changing and shifting customer demands. The first variable is the relationship between the design function and marketing, whereby rich qualitative and quantitative data can be obtained, analysed and translated into design requirements. The second factor is forging closer, more collaborative relationships between all the differing suppliers, whereby the design team can consult and seek specialist knowledge when developing initial concept ideas for either new or modified product families.

Suppliers
Suppliers can provide a great wealth of knowledge and expertise within the design development process.

Figure 1

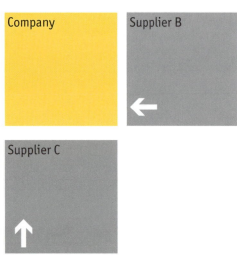

Supplier A

Company

Supplier B

Supplier C

Supply Chain Council
This international organisation offers its members support and guidance in all areas of supply chain management.
www.supply-chain.org

Design
leadership

Driving innovation
through design

Design
strategy

Design
collaboration

108|109

With this power shift from the manufacturer to end customer, the role of continuous and rapid innovation becomes paramount. In the period before computer technology and sophisticated software programs, companies retained the balance of power whereupon they slowly developed products and offered them to the market. Now, we are witnessing a seismic shift from the organisation to the consumer. Companies that fail to understand or respond to this shifting power are the ones that see falling sales and low market uptake of their product offerings.

Companies are having to continually innovate, not only in terms of design enhancement, but by seeking innovation in the way they engage with their customers, understanding their needs and requirements and transferring this sophisticated data into firm design specifications and requirements. One notable example of this is 'mass customisation' where mass market products are tailored and accommodated to appeal to and suit individual needs. A fine example of mass customisation is Levi jeans, where the customer can choose online specific requirements of their garments that fit their physical characteristics and purchasing preferences.

'A lot of trial and error goes into making things look effortless.'
Bill Moggridge

Supply chain knowledge
The design team can utilise knowledge from the supply chain and use it within the NPD process to offer new and innovative products to the marketplace.

Figure 2

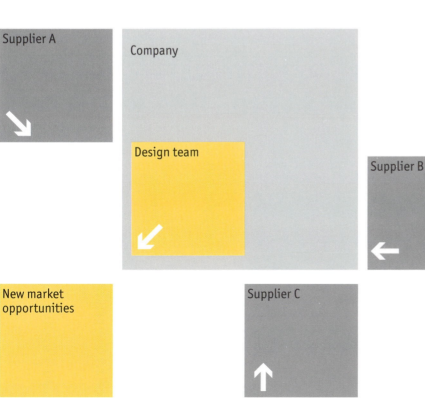

Supplier A

Company

Design team

Supplier B

New market opportunities

Supplier C

Summary

Innovation is the lifeblood of organisations; continually updating or providing new and innovative products is a prerequisite to business longevity. However, to achieve this requires foresight and flexible planning, being able to respond to and accommodate market demand within very tight timescales. Customers are more discerning and particular in their own purchasing decisions; competition is demanding, with customers dictating change and rapid differentiation within the marketplace. As a result, organisations are forging closer working relationships with their suppliers, working together to share intimate market knowledge and highly specialist manufacturing expertise to create new market opportunities through design and new product development. Case studies featured within this book illuminate how the designer as advocate for change can act as a catalyst for innovation through collaborative partnerships within the supply chain.

Design funnel
The designer connects suppliers, customers and marketers through collaborative activity.

Figure 1

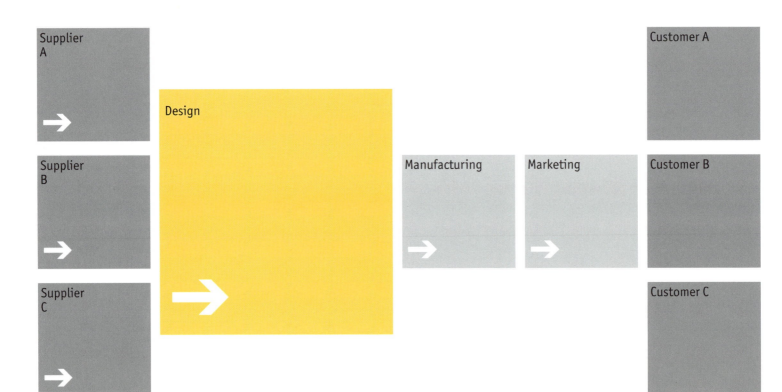

Design
leadership

Driving innovation
through design

Design
strategy

Design
collaboration

110|111

THE COMPANIES

U.S.	CANADA	AUSTRLIA	JAPAN	KOREA	EUROPE
Boeing	Boeing	Boeing	Kawasaki	KAL-ASD	Messier-Dowty
Spirit	Messier-Dowty		Mitsubishi		Rolls-Royce
Vought			Fuji		Latecoere
GE					Alenia
Goodrick					Saab

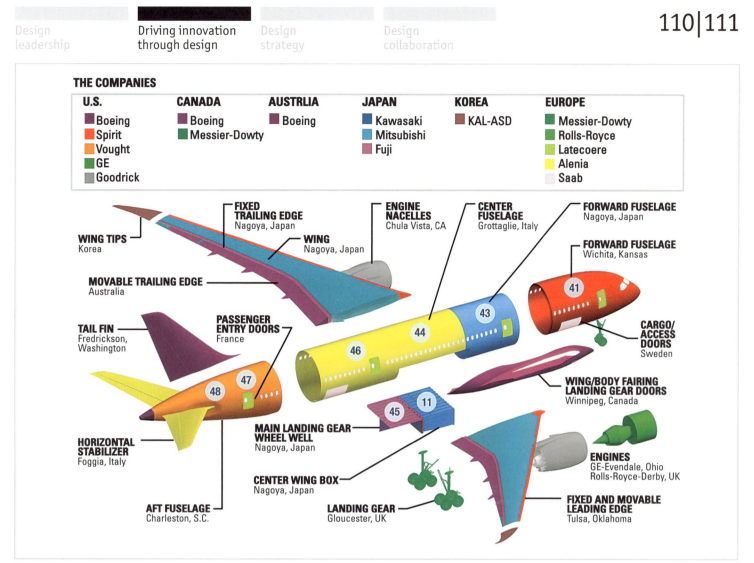

Figure 2
There are a vast number of international suppliers involved when developing a new Boeing aircraft. Boeing has a sophisticated understanding of design and the way it is coordinated throughout every aspect of organisational activity.
Copyright © Boeing.

'It is very easy to be different, but very difficult to be better.'
Jonathan Ive

Case study
Product success through design leadership

This case study investigates the pivotal role of the designer in driving supply chain innovation. It begins with establishing the need for the radical redesign of an existing product, offering a step-by-step discussion of the key stages of product development. The original design brief was very flexible and open, allowing a greater degree of interpretation by the design team. The role of careful research and investigation at the initial stages provided invaluable insight into the existing product in use. Through a careful and close working partnership with supply chain partners, the designer managed to utilise specialist knowledge and embed this expertise into the design detailing phase of product development. Finally it concludes with a discussion on the merits of multi-agency involvement throughout the duration of the project.

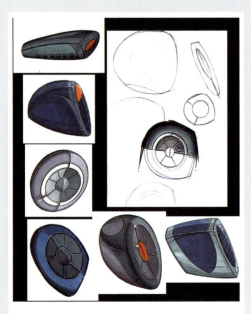

Figure 1
Initial conceptual sketches of the console exploring shape and form.

The company

Promethean Limited is a UK-based company specialising in the supply of systems that harness ICT for group teaching and learning in schools and training establishments. Promethean was founded in 1996 and its technology has established a global profile, with the company quickly becoming one of Europe's leading developers and manufacturers of InterACTIVE systems. Promethean was awarded Millennium Product status by the Design Council in 1999 and its systems are now widely accepted as being at the leading edge of technology, with 6000-plus installations in the UK alone.

The designers

Buxton Wall Product Development Ltd was established in 2002 by Bob Buxton and Alan Wall. The intention was to run the agency in parallel with the Buxton Wall design consultancy, but to focus on royalty-based projects only. Today this is still the primary activity of the UK-based company, but in addition it now offers a comprehensive design consultancy service. It has been involved in the design of many successful products for different markets. The designers are familiar with most manufacturing techniques and work with their clients to help them get to market by the quickest and most cost-effective route.

Figure 2
The first generation of the hand-held Activote console.

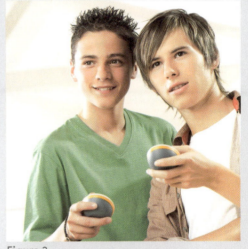

Figure 3
Pupils with the Activote system.

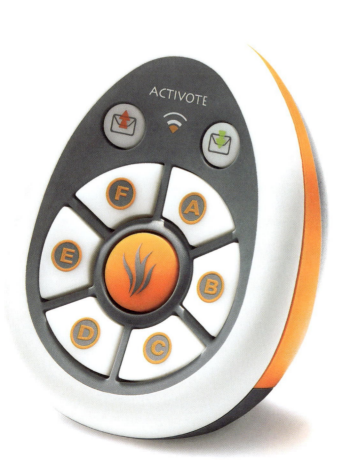

The Activboard concept

In essence, the Activboard concept is new technology made into a user-friendly system that aims to replace traditional display systems within the classroom, boardroom and lecture theatre. It is a whole group teaching and learning resource. But, most importantly, it is not a tool designed to be used solely in an ICT room – it is cross-curricular. Although the Activboard has a matt white finish for glare-free protection, it is still possible for the user to utilise it at its most simple level – as a dry wipe marker board.

The primary purpose of the board is as a projection surface to be connected to a personal computer or a video cassette player. This is when the Activboard can be used to replace the dry wipe marker board, blackboard, OHP, flipchart and television. The projector sits in front of the Activboard and shines the computer or video image on to its surface. In a mobile situation the projector may be on a table or trolley, but projectors can also be ceiling mounted.

When connected to a PC the screen image, normally displayed on a monitor, is projected on to the Activboard, essentially transforming it into a 75-inch monitor. However, because it is electronic, the user may use a battery-free pen on the screen in the same way one would use a mouse with a PC.

Using the software provided, the user may also annotate in electronic ink over any PC application, web page or image. These annotations are digital and can therefore be printed off, exported as web pages or saved to a disk. In addition to freehand annotations the Activboard comes with over 100 pre-drawn annotations, which include maps, science equipment, grids and boxes. Therefore, a teacher may control the PC whilst remaining at the front, sharing the resources with the group.

For complete group interactivity an Activslate is provided with the screen. This allows control from anywhere within the room so the teacher may move around and still be able to control the PC. Equally, it enables students to contribute without having to leave their seats.

The Activboard can also play host to radio transmissions. The company has developed a 'classroom response system', which is similar in intent and function to 'ask the audience'. In addition, devices may be registered to pupils and individual performances may be assessed and calculated.

'Even though the ideas are quite rough, it is essential to get on board all of the suppliers that we have identified to work on this project and gauge their opinion. Their expert opinion is often very valuable to the end product.'

Design
leadership

Driving innovation
through design

Design
strategy

Design
collaboration

114|115

Product development

The design brief

The redesign of the existing product was primarily to do with the way it was utilised by the end-user. Initial customer responses suggested that there was a distinct lack of tactile and visual feedback to the end-user. The system as a whole works extremely effectively; however, user interface problems demanded a significant reappraisal of the design of the handheld voting device. After initial research by the designer, Michael Thomas, a number of issues arose concerning the original product design.

Michael Thomas points out that: 'the overall form was one of the big problems with the original hand device. The problem was that it was very much like a TV remote control and one of the big failings was that the children, when voting, used it like a remote control, actually pointing it in the air. They won't think or visually recognise what they are doing in terms of the voting process.'

User research

Having followed the brief to identify the initial problems, and having established the needs of the client, the designers went on to research the user side. They visited a school in Sheffield, UK, that had been trialling the project. Not only did they talk with the students to find out their issues but they also worked with the teachers and the management of the school to find out what they wanted from the system. This provided the design team with an intimate knowledge of how the product was used, its current failings and how to refine and enhance its existing design.

Design concept development

In tandem with field research within the schools, the design team investigated the current market and also relative products to this particular handset to try and focus that into the idea generation process. They then began to produce initial ideas, which were presented at an internal idea review. This stage involves reviewing ideas to ensure that they satisfy all the conditions laid out in the brief and the proposal and make sure that the designers were going forward in the right direction. Through close involvement with key stakeholders at the initial stages, the design team developed many conceptual proposals to be taken forward at the internal idea review. Decisions were made based on sound and varied expert opinion from a variety of industry professionals present at the review. The decision-making process also had to take into account the company's strategic future plans.

Figure 1
Highly rendered representation of the console prior to full production.

Figure 2
The final product.

**Vision and Values in
Design Management**

Design
directions

Design
transformations

Design
advocacy

Design
alliances

Design detailing

At the design detailing stage, an embryonic idea for the final product is taken forward, refined and developed into a workable solution. Selected suppliers play a closer involvement in materials selection and production tooling, refining issues concerning its manufacturability. The designers were working in unison with all of the product suppliers, constantly communicating back and forth making sure that their design decisions were faithful to the design brief. The designer says: 'Initially we had to heavily rely on rapid prototyping, utilising CAD data to verify our design decisions and make safety checks before the commitment straight down into tooling. We used that to communicate our decisions, again using the rapid prototyping to communicate right across the supply chain network; then we move closer to the tooling process where rapid prototyping will fall off, but other suppliers will come in such as the packaging and graphic suppliers, logistics, technical data and things like that.'

Implementation

In all other stages of the design programme, the design function had been central to the whole project, but at the implementation stage, the designer took a step back with the client moving into a more pivotal position. This is largely due to investment factors where the client has to make strategic decisions regarding financing the product, now liaising more directly with the suppliers. However, the designer still retained an important role working with both the client and suppliers to make sure that design intent is still achieved.

At the pre-production stage, the design function is primarily concerned with ensuring that design intent is fully achieved. Although they have been ensuring it throughout all stages of the process, they are on hand to respond to any issues that are raised prior to full production. Meanwhile, the client is now liaising with the suppliers to secure the most cost-effective way to develop the product.

Summary

When the product enters the production stage, the designer's role becomes less pivotal; they may simply offer advice about warranty issues and refinements to later models. The end product is the embodiment of all design decisions taken throughout all stages of the NPD programme.

This case study has illustrated a variety of key issues central to the product design and development process. At the very beginning of the project, the designer conducted extensive research within the school classroom to see how the children use and interact with the product. As a result of this first-hand information and knowledge, design concepts could be generated to enable dialogue between the design consultants and Promethean.

'On this particular product, the key design decisions can be identified quite easily and all of those design decisions have come through the collaboration; through the whole design process with the user, the client, the marketing department and the suppliers.'

Design
leadership

Driving innovation
through design

Design
strategy

Design
collaboration

116|117

Figure 1
The end product is the embodiment of the
design decisions taken throughout all stages
of the NPD programme.

**Vision and Values in
Design Management**

Design
directions

Design
transformations

Design
advocacy

Design
alliances

Revision questions

Afterword

As a product design process develops, more people and companies become involved to offer specialist advice and knowledge on functional and technical considerations. This is how innovation can occur; the technical term for this is 'innovation through the supply chain', whereby key suppliers and stakeholders contribute expertise within certain points of the design programme. However, for this to successfully happen and be effectively managed, it relies upon the skill and persuasive abilities of the designer to carefully coordinate and manage this complex process. It could be argued that design involves many skills and abilities far beyond creativity and innovation.
As this case study illustrates, invaluable communication skills, intuition, knowledge and empathy for the end-user were all vital ingredients to the success of the radical redesign of the interactive voting device.

1 Why is it important that the design brief is carefully crafted to enable the designer flexibility of interpretation and creative opportunity?

2 What are the unique benefits of ethnographic research when collecting primary data?

3 Why is it important to include a wide variety of stakeholders in the design development process?

4 Why is it vital that all manufacturing issues are considered and resolved prior to production?

5 What other uses of the Activote system would you recommend to the organisation in terms of developing new market opportunities?

Design
leadership

Driving innovation
through design

Design
strategy

Design
collaboration

118|119

Further recommended reading

Author	Title	Publisher	Date	Comments
Baker, M. and Hart, S.	*Product Strategy and Management*	Financial Times / Prentice Hall	2007	This highly contemporary student textbook offers an intelligent account of the management of product design and development and corporate strategy.
Baxter, M.R.	*Product Design: Practical Methods for the Systematic Development of New Products (Design Toolkits)*	CRC Press	1996	Long-standing and popular student textbook on product design. Highly informative and accessible.
Bessant, J. and Tidd, J.	*Innovation and Entrepreneurship*	John Wiley and Sons	2007	Introductory text discussing innovation and entrepreneurship; excellent use of case studies makes the book both informative and accessible.
Tidd, J. Bessant, J. and Pavitt, K.	*Managing Innovation: Integrating Technological, Market and Organizational Change*	John Wiley and Sons	2005	This textbook offers a broad perspective on the role and nature of innovation at a strategic organisational level – invaluable.
Ulrich, K.T. and Eppinger, S.D.	*Product Design and Development*	McGraw-Hill Higher Education	Fourth edition 2007	Classic handbook succinctly discussing all aspects and issues of successful product development. The fourth edition is testament to its popularity and wide appeal to all design students.

Design strategy

Designers and design managers are best suited to identifying new market opportunities in highly complex and diverse business contexts. This section describes why and how design should be included within the strategy formulation process and the benefits it has to offer in the quest for strategic growth.

Holistic design   Figure 1
Design is a holistic activity unifying all areas of business operation.

Perception of design   Figure 2
Design is important in the way the company is perceived by 'external' stakeholders.

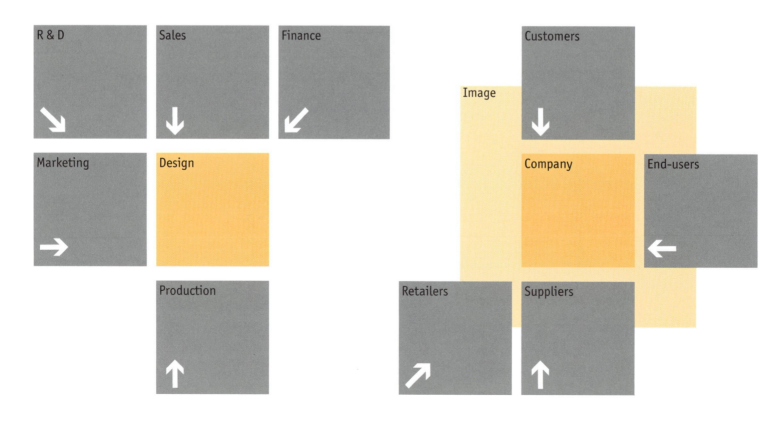

Design
leadership

Driving innovation
through design

Design
strategy

Design
collaboration

120|121

Silent strategists

Common industry practice in strategy development and formulation is undertaken by senior management, with scant input from other business functions and, more often than not, without the designer's involvement. In reality, a small group of senior people devise corporate strategy that has a huge impact on everyone else within the organisation. Decisions are based on logical thought, rational and objective analysis of raw data obtained from a variety of sources that normally include sales figures, market information and projected sales. However, it could be argued that designers are equally well suited to contribute to strategy development, offering their unique skills and lateral perspectives from an intuitive sense. Design has always been closely associated with marketing, especially when developing new products and services. When we add design management to this process, design becomes even more strategic as the designer unifies all the disparate business functions together, taking a holistic view of 'the big picture'.

With this in mind, it would be reasonable to suggest that there is a strong argument for the inclusion of design within strategic development. Earlier in this chapter, we saw how Alan Topalian and Raymond Turner present a strong case for design leadership and its valuable contribution to corporate strategy. **Peter Gorb** raised the issue of 'silent' design in the 1980s, arguing that there are many designers within the organisation, but without the title and status, contributing to the design decision process without even knowing it – hence the term 'silent design'. Can we take that same philosophy further, suggesting that designers contribute to corporate strategy without even knowing it, as 'silent' strategists? Design is intrinsically and intimately involved in developing new products, creating new identities and value systems through every designed element of the organisation, which in turn affects how the organisation is perceived by stakeholders both within and outside the company.

Consequently, this impacts upon business performance, market visibility and long-term sustainability – all strategic considerations. It is well known that the benefits of intelligent and considered design are significant and, in turn, if design is not carefully and sensitively applied the effects are equally significant. With these dynamics inherent in every strategic decision that is formed, should not design be represented within the boardroom? It may be argued that the effects and consequences of design are considered and accommodated within the boardroom but the design champion's physical presence less so.

Communication of values
Design communicates the values of the company to all 'internal' stakeholders.

Figure 3

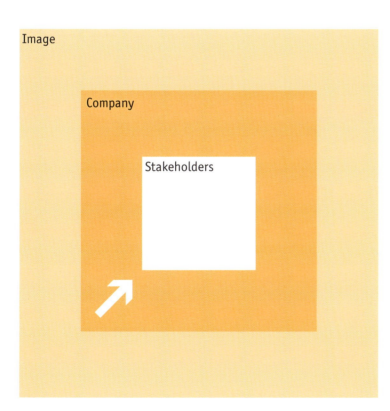

Image

Company

Stakeholders

Peter Gorb
Gorb was Senior Fellow in design management at the London Business School, where he pioneered the teaching of design to managers. He has published widely in the field of design.

**Vision and Values in
Design Management**

Design
directions

Design
transformations

Design
advocacy

Design
alliances

Boardroom
Strategic design considerations need strong
leadership within the boardroom.

Figure 1

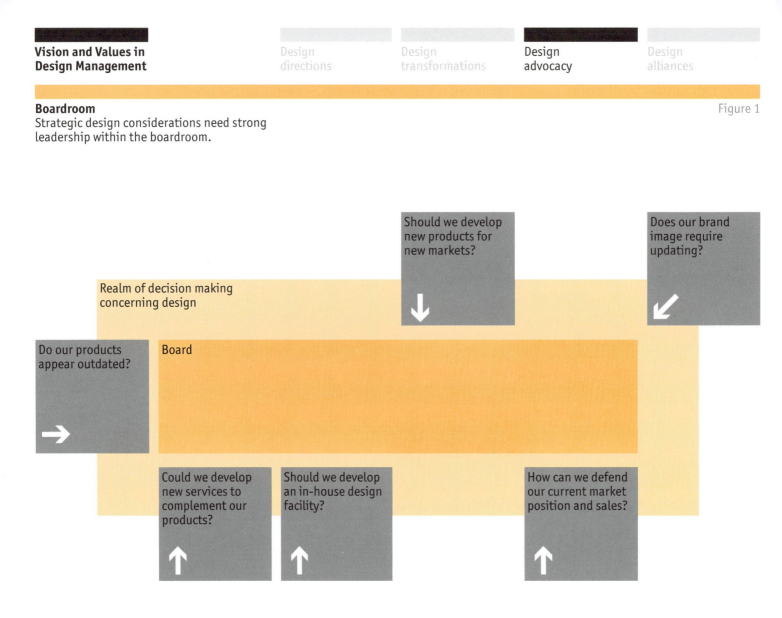

'The responsibility for strategy making must be
broadly distributed. Top management must
relinquish its monopoly on strategy creation.
In this sense you can't have innovation in
business models without innovation in
political models.'
Design Council

Design
leadership

Driving innovation
through design

Design
strategy

Design
collaboration

122|123

The Prince and the Pauper: designers as strategists?

What is it about design as opposed to other business functions that could offer great value and uniqueness to boardroom policy making? Apart from manifesting strategic intent, which is the implementation of vision, design also 'envisions' new futures and business scenarios that cannot be overlooked. So what are these unique characteristics that are valuable to strategy development? First, crossing boundaries of 'possibility' or generating unknown futures; if we refer back to the characteristics and skillsets of what constitutes a designer, the terms innovative, creative, ambitious and risk-taking all come to the fore. Combine all these attributes when either developing a new product or service, or modifying an existing product range; endless opportunities of market exploitation are raised and tested. Through blue-sky thinking and uninhibited concept development, new markets could be identified for potential entry.

As a simple example, if company A solely produced lightweight waterproof jackets and wished to develop new market opportunities, they could, through design, develop ranges that appealed to ramblers and hikers (increase waterproofing through the use of new materials); or to cyclists (more pockets on the back to carry extra items such as waterbottles) and so on. So with design involvement at the initial stages of consideration, new concepts, modified ideas and market research can considerably contribute to the strategic development of a product range, leading to new customers and business growth. Developing concepts and new ideas is one small part of the designer's armoury, the other key ingredient is communicating and visualising them.

One major formative aspect of design education and the practice of design is to conceptualise and visualise abstract ideas to broad audiences. This can take many different forms, most common being 2D visuals and animation and 3D models and prototypes. The famous Victorian 'heroic' engineer Isambard Brunel often sculpted cheese to communicate the complex form of his civil engineering projects to lay audiences in an attempt to engage them in discussion and consultation.

With the use of new technologies and software, interior designers and architects can take a user on a virtual tour through the internal spaces of a structure, visualising every space and designed detail in a way that was unimaginable a generation ago. Product and industrial designers can present to clients panoramic 360° views of their ideas in virtual space, which provides a rich and fuller context to the 3D artefact in development. Suggestions, comments and modifications can easily be sought and implemented, often with the client present, which presents a cost-effective and time-efficient means of concept development.

'Designers bring energy to strategy. They find ways forward. Their currency is possibility and their scope is vast. We need their creativity – perhaps more than ever.'
Design Council

Levels of innovation
From level 1 to blue-sky thinking.

Figure 2

Blue-sky thinking					Innovation
Level 4				Innovation	
Level 3			Innovation		
Level 2		Innovation			
Level 1	Innovation				

**Vision and Values in
Design Management**

Design
directions

Design
transformations

Design
advocacy

Design
alliances

Planes, trains and automobiles: which way forward?

Having established a broad context as to why and how designers can contribute to strategy development, it is now worthwhile focusing on potential aspects of strategy formulation. In essence, a strategy is the most effective way of achieving a clearly defined goal. In that though, there could be many avenues or routes to choose from, but which one would yield the best results with minimum outlay and reduced risk? To provide a simple illustration of this conundrum, let us say we wished to travel from the UK to Beijing in China: what would the best strategy be? First, is cost a factor? If so, would obtaining a variety of low-cost train tickets be worthwhile? Yes, the price would be greatly reduced, but the timescale of travel would be lengthy travelling across Europe and beyond – therefore cost is appropriate but the journey time is excessive.

However, if the issue was not cost but speed, then air travel would be the best option. If cost and time were irrelevant but the 'experience' of travel was paramount, then perhaps a luxury cruise would be better suited. As we can see, a straightforward trip between A and B could involve three strategic choices, therefore clearly identifying key aims and objectives is an important part of the decision-making process.

Common routes to strategy formulation could involve a variety of design interventions. The first one could entail positioning a certain level of value to an existing product or carefully positioning a new product or service to a specific market segment. A company may wish to develop a range of products that are distinctly 'up-market' thus attaching a premium price tag, or develop a low-cost range appealing to a broader, less defined customer audience, to achieve higher sales volumes instead. Another fruitful way of developing a robust strategy is to audit internally competencies and knowledge retained within the organisation.

The Design Atlas offered by the Design Council is an excellent tool that signposts key points of consideration and areas of focus, enabling an organisation to understand itself in terms of expertise but also to offer avenues for future development. If the organisation decides to develop an ambitious product/service range but does not have the ability internally to execute this strategy, how would they overcome this? Buy in expertise? Subcontract or develop capacity from within? All these are major aspects to consider when choosing the most effective strategy for implementation.

Which way forward?
Strategy is the most effective way of achieving a clearly defined goal.

Figure 1

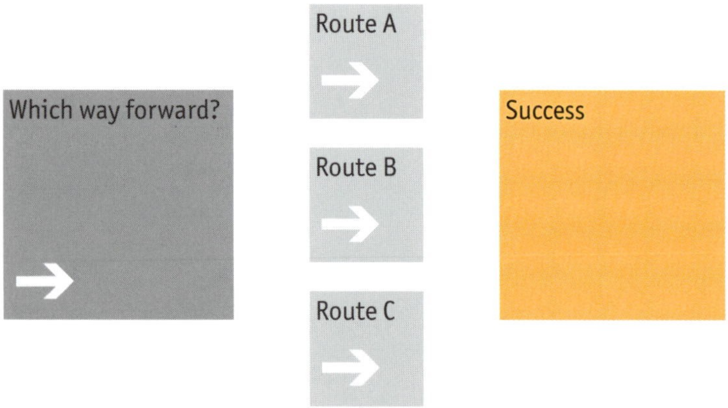

Routes to design enhancement

Figure 2

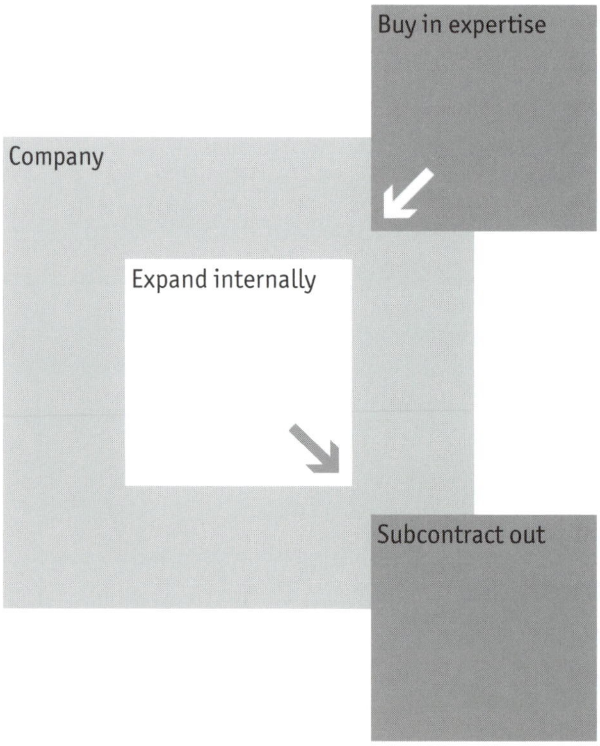

Which way forward?

Route A

Route B

Route C

Success

Company

Buy in expertise

Expand internally

Subcontract out

Design
leadership

Driving innovation
through design

Design
strategy

Design
collaboration

124|125

The Magnificent Seven:
designers to the rescue

Having presented a strong case for the inclusion of design within the strategy development process, below are seven key reasons why the designer should be invited into the boardroom:

1 **Empirical:** 'seeing is believing' and designers worship this doctrine more than any other discipline. In order to understand a design problem, designers make sense of its broader context through first-hand research and observation. Through this process, unique perspectives are discovered through the prism of investigation, which offers strategy a broader sense of purpose.

2 **Empathic:** adopting a user-centred approach to concept development. Designers develop an understanding of the problem and subsequent solutions through the end-users and customers, regarding them as a vital source of inspiration and intuition. Through this empathic approach, 'uncaptured' customer information helps to stimulate innovation and to 'delight' customers in the final designed outcomes.

3 **Political:** ensuring both 'intent' and 'integrity' through the passage of design development and that the original design brief is adhered to. Every decision made through this process is embodied within the final outcome, and in order to achieve this, the designer will deploy their persuasive skills to facilitate and manage relationships with all the represented stakeholders. Through the politics of design, strategic intent is ensured.

4 **Perfectionist:** designers by their very nature are perfectionists and highly critical of the desired solutions that they pursue. Ideas and concepts are developed, tested and refined; if the brief articulates that product A should appeal to market audience A, they will strive for perfection in order to achieve it.

5 **Free-thinking:** in order to generate novel ideas and conceptual proposals, blue-sky thinking and other lateral 'thinking' tools are fully utilised. Through divergent and convergent thinking processes, innovative products and services could be identified whilst also helping improve business performance.

6 **Flexible:** strategy is a fluid dynamic that is constantly shifting and changing; embracing change and being flexible is part and parcel of design. Responsiveness to the fast-moving business environment and the ability to rise to the challenge is seen as a richly rewarding aspect of being a designer.

7 **Communicators:** strong verbal and visual communication skills engage stakeholders in the design process, and enable complex and abstract ideas to be communicated to wide audiences, some of whom are unfamiliar with design. Communication enables dialogue and the sharing of ideas, with the designer driving this participatory activity.

The Magnificent Seven
Seven key attributes of design within the strategy formulation process.

Figure 3

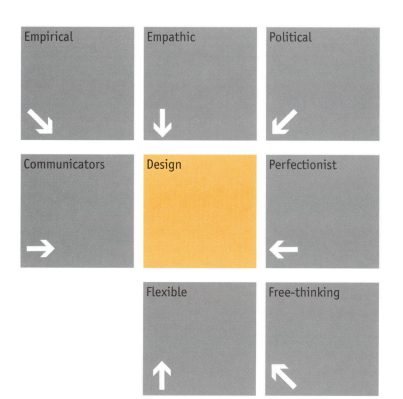

Design Atlas
An audit tool used to help an organisation assess its capability for handling design activity. Design Atlas was informed by research into the drivers of success associated with design project activity. The tool has been tested by design counsellors working within advisory services such as the UK Business Link network. It has formed a core element within many Design Council-supported projects.

Case study
Innovation through collaboration

This case study offers a unique insight into the multi-faceted role of design and, in particular, the skills of the designer to overcome many design and technical considerations when bringing a new and innovative product to the market. Sensitive communication was core to the success of this project, as was an ability to speak to many different experts and supply chain partners, sharing and embracing many different and often contradictory viewpoints. The combination of knowledge and expertise from beyond the design company was taken forward and embedded within discrete stages of the design development programme. In retrospect, the very success of the Exertris fitness cycles could be attributed to two distinct aspects: first, the original but simple concept devised by the inventors; and secondly, the skill and professionalism of PDD to take the idea through to the marketplace.

'How might exercise be made more interesting?'

Design
leadership

Driving innovation
through design

Design
strategy

Design
collaboration

126|127

The company

Exertris, founded in 2001, is a start-up company primarily funded by venture capital. The directors, both engineering graduates from Brunel University, are passionate about keeping fit and they decided to combine their leisure interests with a radical business concept. Exertris's interactive workout cycle was launched in October 2001. The company is currently based in London.

The design consultancy

PDD is one of the leading design consultancies based in the UK. They have more than 25 years' experience in striking the balance between future opportunity and practical reality in world markets. Their experience spans consumer products, high-technology equipment, medical, data communications and packaging sectors. They employ over 65 specialists who have skills in research, product design, engineering and multi-media/interaction design.

'It's an amazing piece of innovation – you've really got to use it to believe it. Our teamwork with PDD has been very rewarding; we are delighted to have them as a partner in our future.'

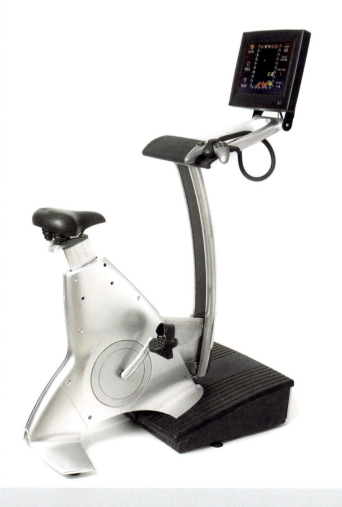

Figures 1 and 2
The Exertris fitness machine.

The economic context

Research by Mintel highlights that nearly six in ten adults have taken part in at least one sporting activity on a regular basis in the past year. Regular sports participants are more than likely to be male than female and there is a strong correlation with age – more than eight in ten 15–24 year olds take part, with a steady decrease with each successive age group. The socio-economic group is an important factor, with nearly three-quarters of ABs (professional workers) but only a third of Es (unskilled workers) taking part regularly. The reasons for taking part are for relaxation and the social aspect of sport: 26% and 24% respectively; while only 15% say they take part in order to lose weight. Keep-fit, aerobics and stretch were the most popular fitness activities among those questioned. Some 12% had visited the gym and/or did weight training on a regular basis and 7% were jogging at least once a month.

The product

Exertris developed a 'fitness experience' concept to radically break away from the monotony often associated with the user interaction with exercise equipment. Reading newspapers or watching TV monitors only provided a transitory distraction. Exertris wanted to develop a machine that creates a total mind and body experience by linking advanced, interactive software directly with the physical effort applied on the exercise bike.

Exertris suggests that its concept: '...is unique; the system motivates, it challenges, it stimulates.' The design has the same footprint as a standard exercise bike. Its ergonomic, modular design incorporates a self-diagnostic testing approach making the system easy and affordable to maintain. The system supports a number of advanced features:
— one touch gas-assisted frame adjustment
— advanced gearbox and electro-mechanical braking system
— interactive software and games: Gems; Solitaire; Orbit and Space Trippers.

'The first of its kind, it combines a beautiful, ultra-modern cycle with revolutionary interactive technology that combats "work-out-weariness" and makes the time fly by.'

Figures 1 and 2
Conceptual proposals for the design, outlining key details and product in use.

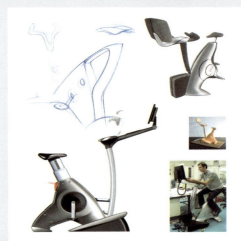

Design
leadership

Driving innovation
through design

Design
strategy

Design
collaboration

128|129

The design development process

The directors of the company had done extensive market research into fitness products and had visited 'virtually every fitness and leisure company in the south-east of England'. The initial brief was in essence, how to develop a game or interaction that was physically linked to the exercise that the user was doing. The directors approached PDD with this initial design problem, requiring expertise in both the development and implementation of the cycle machine and the games software.

Concept development

Firstly, PDD turned the idea into a 'proof of principle' that could actually work. Once both parties agreed that the idea could be taken further into the commercial sphere, Exertris then began the task of raising money for the venture. Through the process of iteration and mutual sharing of ideas and understanding the full potential of the idea, PDD and Exertris developed a close working partnership.

Very quickly, PDD managed to create an innovative mechanism fundamental to the concept. David Humphries at PDD is quick to point out that 'we managed to patent the special connection between the way that the software "kicks back" and the gearing mechanism in the cycle.' At any one time, the project team was diverse in its composition in terms of the range of expertise working on the concept. The engineers had a strong input on the cycle, designing and testing a minimum of four ideas. Based on the initial design concepts, and the new patent on the gearing mechanism, Exertris were able to secure more funding through venture capital to take the design further towards commercialisation. Through the development of the cycle, Exertris forged close links with the software consultants working on the project. Their input proved crucial when working with the other experts, linking the differing disciplines together.

Prototype testing

PDD built the initial prototype of the cycle in-house and then tested them at local gyms. The designer says, 'we are going to be working with the first gym that will officially house a bank of 15 of these machines; just about every major gym in the country has got one of these being tested.' He goes on to say, 'through testing these bikes in the gyms, we found it was not an issue getting people on these cycles – but actually getting them off them... you have got to remember it's a complete experience, because of that inter-connection, which has never happened before.'

Figure 3
Exploded view of the Exertris machine.

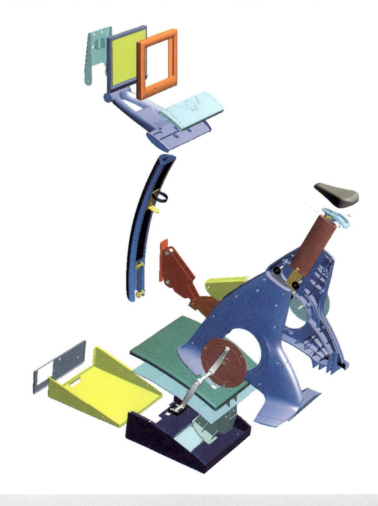

Crossing boundaries

A key part of the success of this project was the design project leader networking across different organisational boundaries and disciplines. The project leader was not an engineer, although the project was an engineering-led programme. But he had great networking skills that allowed him to call in experts when the project needed critical knowledge input and he integrated the functions into one focused team.

David Humphries, the director of strategy at PDD, comments that: '...what I find very interesting with these types of projects is that where you have a lot of technical input some designers don't really identify with that; equally, people on the other side don't necessarily identify with industrial design. But, there are some people who feel really comfortable going across all that because they see it more holistically.'

PDD transferred the knowledge and expertise of their links with industry into the project, relying on their network of external suppliers of components, materials and sometimes processes.

Figure 1
Early research and testing of the prototype.

Design
leadership

Driving innovation
through design

Design
strategy

Design
collaboration

130|131

Design contribution

The success of this project could be attributed primarily to the cohesive nature of the designer's involvement throughout all stages of the programme. His role and skill was to glue together all the differing functions associated with the cycle machine, bonding them into a focused cross-discipline team. By communicating to the different groups, both explicitly and implicitly, he managed to enable them to share knowledge and technical skills, greatly contributing to its overall successful completion. David Humphries comments on the role of the project manager:

'...We go through the commercial side before a project manager is appointed. When a job is appointed then so is a manager, who could be one of a number of people. That is partly down to who is available but also who would be "right" for the job. It's a combination of many things, but ultimately it's to do with skills and what type of skills would the job require. You cannot have a CAD specialist if the job is 70% design engineering or vice versa.

'[The project manager] incidentally is not an engineer, he's an experienced industrial designer, but with good networking skills he can go to whoever he wants and has the personality to call in experts when he's out of his depth.'

It could be argued that these types of (design) enablers are very comfortable crossing boundaries, talking to anybody at any level, bringing people in and persevering until they get the right answers from the relevant experts. David Humphries further adds:

'...That's helped here at PDD because that's a part of the company culture, how we're structured. It's all about integrating different skill bases to encourage that; but at the end of the day it's about individuals and some are better at it than others... the project manager takes the complicated supply chain inputs in his stride, even though he's not an expert in a lot of the issues involved. More importantly, the people on the other side feel very comfortable working with him – it's a great strength.'

Summary

Ideas are relatively cheap and easy to produce; transforming those ideas into commercial reality is fraught with risk and overall failure. The two young entrepreneurs realised this at a very early stage, deciding to minimise the risk and engage a well-known design consultancy to enable them to turn their ideas into reality. The engineering technology was unique and well thought out, but it required significant strategic design enhancement to 'package' its appeal. By entering into a strategic design alliance, risk of failure was greatly reduced, mostly due to the extensive commercial experience of PDD and their expertise in taking pure ideas through to fruition. However, the process wasn't without major obstacles, especially when taking cutting edge technology and applying it to a fitness cycle. To overcome these barriers, the project team enlisted the support and knowledge of specialists in the field to resolve production problems. Alongside these manufacturing difficulties, long-term planning and vision was established, to provide extra added benefits to the users. New games were initiated and embedded within the machines' technology, providing a distinct unique selling point. This reflected the brand values of the company, namely that of making exercising an enjoyable and rewarding activity. Exertris has now firmly established itself as a leading provider of fitness equipment, with innovation at the core of its success.

'The games range from a space invaders style, good versus evil game, to the traditional Solitaire card game in order to offer something for everyone.'

**Vision and Values in
Design Management**

Design
directions

Design
transformations

Design
advocacy

Design
alliances

Revision questions

Afterword

This case study has clearly demonstrated that the involvement of the design team, in particular the lead designer, drove innovation through collaborative activity. By clearly identifying what skills and specialist knowledge were required to keep the development ongoing, contact and partnerships were forged to overcome seemingly insurmountable problems. However, rather than seeing developmental issues as barriers, they regarded these design and technical considerations as opportunities to explore from unique and diverse perspectives. Design was used as an 'enabling' tool whereby the process of activity and output established a common ground for all the disparate disciplines to meet and freely share ideas and expertise. It goes to show the multi-skilled nature of a design team that could transcend many different boundaries to share one common language: that of sensitive and considered communication.

1 In order to test the integrity and validity of an initial design idea, what tools and techniques would you use?

2 The design development process is fraught with risk, how would you go about reducing the risk of overall project failure?

3 Finding a designer is relatively easy, selecting the 'right' designer is difficult; what would you look for to inform your decision of appointing the right designer?

4 Sharing vision and the unique benefits of your idea are important to establishing a firm foundation for design development work with the design team, how would you go about this?

5 How do you measure the success of a project? Apart from unit sales, what other metrics would you use?

Further recommended reading

Author	Title	Publisher	Date	Comments
Baxter, M.	*Product Design: practical methods for systematic development of new products*	Chapman Hall	1996	Highly recommended text, offering an extensive discussion of new product development, complete with tools and techniques for creative thinking.
Bruce, M. and Cooper, R.	*Creative Product Design: A practical guide to requirement capture management*	John Wiley and Sons	1996	Based on their extensive research, the book illustrates the importance of up-front planning and the value of user-centred thinking.
Cooper, R.G.	*Winning at New Products: accelerating the process from idea to launch*	Perseus Books	Third edition 2001	Robert Cooper is a world expert on the subject of NPD and this book provides an excellent insight into his extensive experience focusing on the design process.
McGrath, M.E.	*Next Generation Product Development: How Increase Productivity, Cut Costs, and Reduce Cycle Times*	McGraw-Hill Professional	2004	Meticulous and highly considered discussion on the strategic value and application of new product development – invaluable to students and practitioners alike.
Smith, P.G. and Reinertsen, D.G.	*Developing Products in Half the Time: New Rules, New Tools*	John Wiley and Sons	Second edition 1997	Again, very much in the same vein as R.G. Cooper, the authors offer a series of sophisticated tools and techniques in order to increase efficiencies within the NPD process.

**Vision and Values in
Design Management**

Design
directions

Design
transformations

Design
advocacy

Design
alliances

Design collaboration

This section is provided by Dr Cristiaan de Groot, discussing his extensive involvement with the Hothouse, which is an innovative 'creative think-tank' based within UNITEC University, New Zealand. Hothouse offers perspectives on setting up a collaborative innovation community. Dr de Groot talks about the initial concept of Hothouse, providing examples of new-to-the-world products arising from its collaborative activities. Later on in the book he provides further discussion about Hothouse and its strategic aims for collaborative activity.

Collaborative innovation   Figure 1

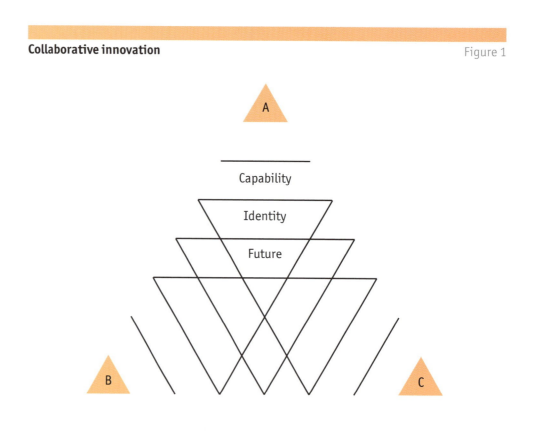

Design
leadership

Driving innovation
through design

Design
strategy

Design
collaboration

134|135

An introduction to the Hothouse

The Hothouse is a design-led open innovation lab in New Zealand that supports the collaborative development of new products and services between young designers and multiple businesses. The Hothouse uses advanced forms of open innovation to bring these multiple parties together to achieve real breakthrough and significant progress, using the capabilities and difference of many contributors.

The main idea behind the inception of the Hothouse is that novel ideas and innovations can be generated between organisations and that these organisations can be motivated to work collaboratively by introducing a designer to act as a third party project developer. The context within which this principle is being applied is the New Zealand economy, which is dominated by SMEs. These have growth potential that can be unleashed if their intangible resources (experience, knowledge, IP) are leveraged without drawing upon the very issues that hold growth back (time, vision). Therefore, the introduction of a young designer, mentored and supported by a trusted university-type organisation, helps to coordinate collaborative relationships, and further, to set up a community of collaborative innovation where multiples of these relationships can be conducted.

Collaboration

In the past, collaboration in business has been largely limited to process engineering and alignment in vertical supply chains. Horizontal collaboration, i.e. across different firms, and even from different industry categories, has been limited to either cross-licensing situations in IT and pharmaceuticals, or to process benchmarking where firms share knowledge of best practice. A radicalised version of open innovation (as described by Miles, Miles and Snow in *Collaborative Entrepreneurship*), gets diverse firms operating in wholly different markets cooperating on innovations, and often generating new companies as a result.

Open innovation

Open innovation is a concept being used globally to describe communities of individuals or firms that collaborate to bring about innovations. Other concepts such as COINs (collaborative innovation networks) are similarly oriented. The principle behind these contemporary models of creative cooperation is that new meaning is created through difference. Indeed, it can be said that all meaning is the product of difference.

The constructive or designerly dimension of creating new meaning through difference is the power of combination, or combinatorial thought. Historically, this principle has been powerfully described, for example, by Poincaré: 'ideas rose in crowds; I felt them collide until pairs interlocked, so to speak, making a stable combination.' Einstein also wrote that: '... combinatorial play seems to be the essential feature in productive thought.'

That novel ideas can be generated by combinatorial thinking is in itself not new. What current examples of open innovation point towards is that multiple organisations or individuals can generate these combinations faster and more predictably when facilitated by tools and structures that support the collision of their meaningful difference. The internet has been pivotal in supporting these collaborative conversations, enabling combinatorial thinking to occur across time and space, allowing the right people to be thinking about the right challenges or opportunities. Typically organisations upload the challenges they face, or the IP that they are willing to share, and stimulate others to play with it under their own direction. Some of the online platforms are open-source, some are the spin-offs of large multinationals. Examples include www.crowdspirit.com; www.innocentive.com and www.fellowforce.com.

'The Hothouse employs a secure website where the members access the projects they are involved in to keep up to date and offer feedback and ideas. The community is further strengthened through regular workshops and presentation sessions.'
Dr Cristiaan de Groot

**Vision and Values in
Design Management**

Design
directions

Design
transformations

Design
advocacy

Design
alliances

The operational model

The Hothouse community of organisations and individuals has been created largely by invitation. The organisational members have been identified through two qualities, namely their design-led credentials and their level of difference from each other (i.e. they occupy different markets).

Collaborative projects are best initiated when there is enough knowledge available to identify potential overlap in one or more ways. Such information exchange is usually brought about through existing professional or personal relationships where over time conversations move from specific or prosaic questions and answers to more wide ranging comparisons of strategy and business model design. However, the normal organic process of people and organisations getting to know one another is likely to be too slow for the purposes of an innovation community. In the Hothouse we have developed a layered model for extracting the requisite information for establishing common ground between disparate potential collaborators.

This information can be collected either through an interview conducted by young design talent (students/graduates) or within a workshop session where several community members share their information in real-time. The data sets of two or more organisations are then brought together into one diagram, and the potential for a project developing from that particular union is then identified using relatively simple systemic modelling tools and conceptual landscape exercises.

The operational model of the Hothouse has evolved over the last 18 months, beginning with a 'cohesion' model of creative collaboration, and recently moving towards a 'brokerage' model. The cohesion model is one where the community is encouraged to be in continuous contact with each other, with the aim that good ideas will be generated amongst many poor or recycled ideas. We have found that this kind of operation requires a great deal of energy to sustain and is characterised by a high level of 'redundant' conversations and ideas. That is to say, conversations or ideas that lead nowhere and therefore have a negative impact on the excitement and commitment that members have towards the community. The Hothouse has since moved on to a 'brokerage' model whereby the young designer acts not only as a project developer, but also as a conduit or connection between the firms, effectively brokering the relationship. This has the effect of reducing the level of redundant or irrelevant information being exchanged and thereby keeping all the involved parties engaged on a positive and productive platform.

Setting up: process

Research conducted by Miles, Miles and Snow indicates that the development of a community based on creativity and enterprise will require:
— A common interest
— A sense of belonging
— An explicit economic purpose
— A sponsor
— A shared language
— Ground rules for participation
— Mechanisms to manage intellectual property rights
— Physical support of the sponsor
— Cooperation as a key success factor

They also found that setting up collaborative and creative communities is possible, and that idea filtering is a necessary step. There are various scorable components in four distinct categories:
— Idea attributes
— Risk factors
— Potential demand
— Resources (existing...)

This idea assessment, or more accurately an idea-screening or filtering tool, has its roots in management consultancy where hired guns come into organisations and help redefine the innovation pipeline for large commercial organisations. This tool is therefore presenting the designer with a business-orientation or perspective in the context of deciding which ideas should be taken forward. This perspectival shift is probably quite a good thing for designers since they are notoriously bad at making decisions, especially when it comes to their own work. 'You have to be able to kill your own babies' as they say in the advertising industry – and so it is with design.

Design
leadership

Driving innovation
through design

Design
strategy

Design
collaboration

136|137

Setting up: communication

More than the brand, the name or the identity, it's the communication of 'how' you intend to conduct your work that matters most.

Generating and evolving illustrations or visual maps of the collaborative innovation process has a variety of roles and functions within the development of any experimental project that has a wide group of connections all needing to buy into the way it's shaping up. Without visuals your communication material looks like an annual tax return, and has little chance of garnering the type of quality feedback that the emergent project so dearly needs. Most significantly the ongoing process explanations are the designer's version of moving towards the infamous 'Hollywood-pitch'. Designers think in pictures, so describing new ways of working will undoubtedly begin looking pretty complicated (see our initial efforts as an example, complete with 'off-angle' perspective – figure 1).

Over the course of time, and much feedback, the process visual become less important as a source of designerly status, and more focused on their primary role in business, i.e. communicating the process to critically important others. Unfortunately, when it comes to describing the well-spring of their unique contribution (creativity and innovation), designers tend to get all mysterious, complicated, or both. This usually results in multi-layered graphics that have no functional benefit when trying to persuade the CEO of a large organisation that they should partner up with you and some crack-pot scheme in the pursuit of the 'as-yet-undefined' next-big-thing. Innovation is slippery, creativity is worse, and collaboration is a melting-pot of potential misunderstandings. So celebrate when you finally uncouple the design-ego from the communication of the core model, the project can now expect credible traction.

Setting up: building connections

While the premise of any community of creation must offer potential members strategic benefits that align with the strategic ambition and vision of an organisation, the effective cooperation and collaboration of any and all organisations is reached via the interest and energies of individuals.

The Hothouse concept

Figure 1

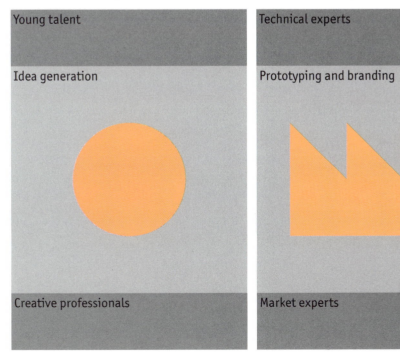

Hothouse workshops

Young talent

Idea generation

Creative professionals

Hothouse development lab

Technical experts

Prototyping and branding

Market experts

Hothouse exit

Entrepreneurs

Commercialisation

Investors

Source: Dr Cristiaan de Groot.

**Vision and Values in
Design Management**

Design
directions

Design
transformations

Design
advocacy

Design
alliances

Projects

Not all projects retain the interest of the organisations that initiated them, or contributed to the original development of prototypes. Many reasons exist for early or premature departure from a collaborative project, including the typical ones such as personnel change, significant change in the economic climate or the share price of the organisation in question. More interesting, and possibly unexpected, are other reasons for organisations to exit of their own accord that are to do with limits and boundaries rather than the forces of change. If there is a significant emphasis on the practical involvement of a collaborating partner, the creative and adaptive limitations of organisations can often be exposed through the early stages of prototyping a product or service, and thereby trigger an awareness that this particular kind of endeavour is not for them. It is possible that greater preparation for the rigours of development and prototyping (through extended communication) could forge a greater strength of ambition; however, you cannot plan for all eventualities.

Regular and effective communication is the most pivotal dimension in retaining partners in any collaborative project. And the reverse is also true, as ineffective and irregular communication will unsettle and disquiet professional expectations and undermine the trust that is later required when progress in the project becomes difficult. Expectation setting, project management, early scoping of the project parameters and mutual establishment of success criteria are all important factors to successful partnering.

Certain projects that eventuate as orphans, with no other partnering organisations than the initial designer/facilitator/broker, are more than likely the most radical and potentially successful of all. Without contributors, potential manufacturers, and most importantly distributors, such potential will amount to nothing. Such circumstances leave two options open for extracting further value from the project. One is to pursue the project further through searching for new project partners. Depending on how far the development has been carried out, these partners need not be replacements (which are hard to find) and instead can fulfil the requirements of the next stage of commercialisation such as distributors, investors and so on.

The other option is to use an orphaned project as a communication or publicity vehicle by which to garner continued interest in your community and attract new organisational partners or creative talent. This option is not necessarily the last resort since community growth is important and most projects will hold enough future promise to prevent their premature exposure to the media.

The prototype shown here (figure 1) is one such orphaned project that has been used for communicational purposes once it had been established that no significant intellectual property or further investment could be efficiently attracted. This is a decomposing garden ornament that engages users in a narrative experience. Specifically, it is a garden gnome made of biodegradable plastic that contains a 'seed-bomb' inside. As the outer casing erodes, a skeletal form is revealed, allowing rainwater inside which activates the seed-bomb. This seed-bomb is composed of soil, various flower or vegetable seeds and fertiliser. As the gnome disappears plants grow in its place, animating the lifecycle of death, decomposition and rebirth. The design intention is that it becomes an educational gift of sorts whereby old and young can build educational relationships out of doors, promoting questions and story telling of how the natural world works.

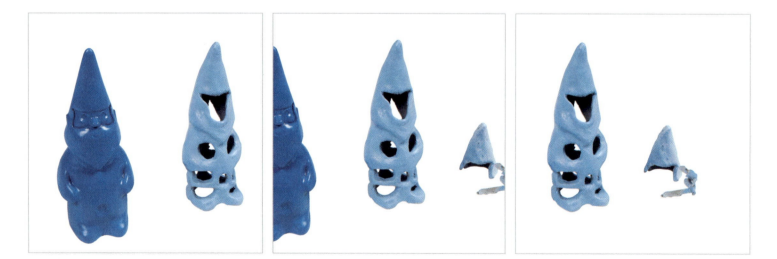

Figure 1
The biodegradable gnome erodes over time, releasing seeds contained within.

Design
leadership

Driving innovation
through design

Design
strategy

Design
collaboration

138|139

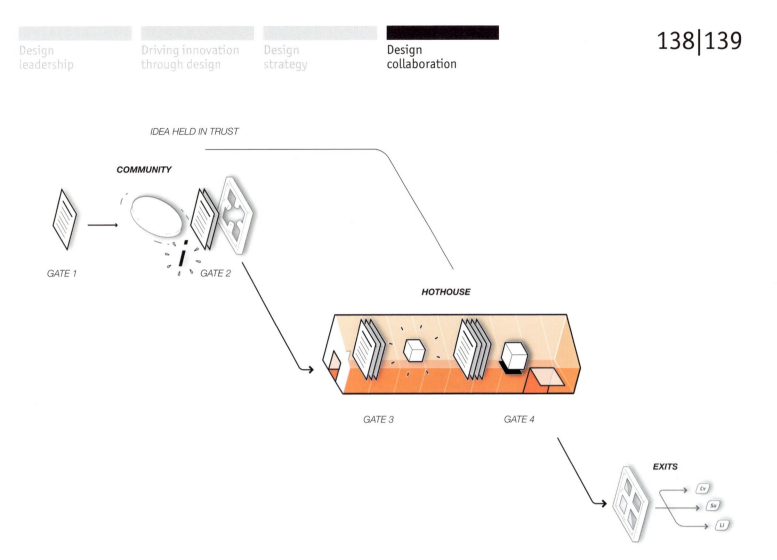

IDEA HELD IN TRUST

COMMUNITY

GATE 1

GATE 2

HOTHOUSE

GATE 3

GATE 4

EXITS

Figure 2
The intellectual property and product
process map that underpins the Hothouse
concept.

'New technology and mass migration are
helping to make the world a smaller place,
but we still persist in thinking of ourselves as
more different from each other than ever.'
James Harkin

**Vision and Values in
Design Management**

Design
directions

Design
transformations

Design
advocacy

Design
alliances

Interview
Peter Quinlan

Peter Quinlan is the head of the product development department at Cityspace (see the case study on pages 158–165). He is responsible for research and development of all hardware products, processes and procedures. Key aspects of his role include sourcing, assessing and appointing suppliers, agreeing commercial terms and quality processes, as well as project managing key Cityspace contracts.

How important is design to Cityspace? Not just product design, but other more subtle aspects of design such as signage, use of colour, and the emotional aspects of design in the terminals that you create?
Extremely important; we are recognised for our quality and presentation. Our close attention to all aspects of design impacts on all areas in the company, from products to marketing.

I first became aware of Cityspace when you were instrumental in developing the iPlus information terminals system about seven years ago, and in particular its crime reduction attributes. Has designing against crime (DAC) always been at the heart of your design approach?
Not consciously. I think my approach has always been very DAC but mainly because it leads to improved uptime, user experience and operational savings – it's also, of course, very 'green'.

How did or does Cityspace capture all past experience of its products in use? You say that past experience of products in use is vital in informing your approach to enhancing current designs and so on. In what ways do you capture all this vast past experience?
Traditionally we have maintained all our products and have built a comprehensive performance-related database over many years. Most of our products have touch screens and all are connected to some form of communications provision. As such we have the ability to build maintenance reports and gather feedback from the product and get well organised, instant information. Additionally, we have developed a feedback and field-testing process for working with our external staff and ensuring product performance meets expectations. We draw on all this experience both to shape our approach and test regimes. It is often not the test that's hard to do; it's working out what tests you need to do – this is where knowledge and experience really kick in.

Design
leadership

Driving innovation
through design

Design
strategy

Design
collaboration

140|141

How much importance do you place on the design brief when initiating or developing new products? Is crime and the issue of crime reduction 'explicit' within the brief and throughout the briefing process?

The briefing process – assessing, agreeing and clearly documenting the exact requirements – is the single most important part of the product development process. It is also, often, the hardest to do. A good brief provides a specification to work to and a tool for measuring the deliverables against. It aims to take the subjective out of the requirement and ensure people clearly understand what we are making and most importantly what they are getting. Crime reduction is an ongoing aim and always part of the brief, but explicit requirements are product dependent.

The success of the Smart Point units is based upon the central aspect of 'modularisation'. Can you tell us a bit more about how this simple, but very successful, concept came about?

As a child I played with Lego a lot! When I was growing up, Lego was a set of regular shapes (square, rectangle or block) with a common fixing method. From these blocks you could make anything. The Smart Point is a set of blocks with a common fixing method. Modularity brings a huge amount of other advantages – it's hard to pinpoint the most important, but I'd say 'easy and cost-effective adaptability' plus 'reduction in manufacturing costs'. When producing low volumes, the cost of setting up tooling and plant is generally far greater than the actual item produced. The aim is to amortise these set-up costs over the greatest quantities possible. By taking a modular approach we increase the quantity of individual components, can create usable stock and, further, achieve a spin-off cost saving in assembly – it's much easier, quicker and more certain to assemble many of the same component. I could write a book just on all the advantages of modularity but probably a tour around Ikea would be convincing enough!

What emphasis do you place on exploring and utilising new materials and manufacturing technologies in the development of new products?

We are always looking for, and where appropriate utilising, new materials and methods, but there is also a lot to be said for the tried and tested. My approach is to perfect a solution to a problem and then apply that same solution everywhere I can. For example, over the years, we have tried quite a few different approaches to hingeing doors; we think we perfected it on the Multipoint and so just used the same for the Smart Point. I don't want to keep re-inventing the wheel.

Could you provide any good examples of how you either used new materials or embraced new manufacturing techniques?

I can give you plenty but I'll focus on a recent change we made because it is a very common problem and I like the approach we took to the solution. We have never liked backlighting with fluorescent tubes; they don't consume a great deal of electricity but need changing (expensive on the street) after about 12 months and provide visible 'stripes' in the backlit image. My colleague Gavin Cassidy spent a lot of time researching solutions and we selected edge lighting with LED strips and a very recent (and very special) innovation in plastic that is coated with a light dispersing print. LEDs use very little power, generate very little heat and last 10 years, the edge lighting and coated plastic method gives a fabulous, even backlight with no stripes. The initial cost is higher than fluorescent but is recovered the first time we do not need to visit the site and change the tubes. My ideal kind of solution: green, innovative, cutting edge, cheaper over the life of the product, more reliable, better quality and does not impact on the environment within the Smart Point (we are always fighting heat).

Regarding Smart Point, where next? The terminals that we have discussed in the case study, are they just the beginning of a long development programme taking Cityspace into new business directions through the utilisation of strategic design?

Absolutely, we have already produced and installed new variants of the Smart Point to cater to specific requirements – next time you are at Stansted Airport have a look at the three of them in Arrivals.

For Stansted, we needed to provide dual interactive screens/printers – our modular approach allowed us to simply bulge the signature keyhole of the central section to create extra space. I love the look of the finished product and was delighted by how easy it was to achieve – we did not need to re-design the whole kiosk, just one area. Again because of the modularity we were able to get on with production on the rest of the components whilst only at design stage for the area we were changing – we delivered and installed under budget and two months early. We have done other versions for the rail industry and recently developed a four-sided version with 65-inch broadcast screens on top. Sounds unlikely but the aesthetic works and again the design challenge is pretty simple. We are now using the basic Smart Point aesthetic approach – modules, split lines, rounded corners, stainless steel surrounds to focal points (the signature keyhole) across the board. Get the core product right and all else becomes very manageable.

Thank you for sharing your thoughts on the way in which both you and Cityspace value and use design. Is there anything that you would like to add that we haven't covered?

I'm passionate about design and detail and could talk for hours but to try and summarise: I love cleverness over brute force and I love to get things right. I advise all those connected to design to seek opinions, listen to advice, don't be scared to ask the same question over and over (you need to understand; they already do), to take care selecting an expert on a subject, then trust the expert and give them their head. Be innovative, out-think your problem rather than over-engineer a solution (people tend to use lots of material, nature uses shape and form), always focus on the whole life cost and if you remember detail is everything, quality will follow.

**Vision and Values in
Design Management**

Design
directions

Design
transformations

Design
advocacy

Design
alliances

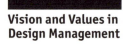

Chapter summary

The recent emergence of design leadership
as an evolutionary advancement of design
management raises many questions. Is it
design management with new clothes or a
logical developmental step in its ongoing
maturity? Moving on to the role of design in
innovation, and how it can be used to draw
upon expertise within the supply chain,
provides further weight to the argument
that design is a resource that should be
represented at boardroom level in the
strategic planning process. Relationships are
crucial in the product development process,
not only those with other companies in the
supply chain; but also those with suppliers
and customers in the development of new
products that are right for the market. The
two case studies illustrated how design
champions were central to the overall
development of initial ideas right through
to commercialisation, and how they used
their powers of communication to drive
vision and inspiration through design.

Revision questions

Based on what has been discussed, you
should now be able to answer the following
five questions.

1   Alan Topalian and Raymond Turner argue
    that design leadership is distinct from
    design management; where do you see
    the key differences and similarities?

2   Can you identify any good examples of
    design leaders? If so, what makes them
    different from design managers?

3   What is the difference between
    'innovation' and 'invention'?

4   Why are supply chain partners valuable in
    developing new and innovative products
    and services?

5   What other characteristics of design do
    you consider to be important in the
    strategy formulation process?

Design
leadership

Driving innovation
through design

Design
strategy

Design
collaboration

142|143

Further recommended reading

Author	Title	Publisher	Date	Comments
Aaker, D.A. and Joachimsthaler, E.	*Brand Leadership*	Free Press	2002	The authors are two leading experts in the subject and this book never fails to impress with its detailed discussion and analysis of brand leadership.
De Bono, E.	*Lateral Thinking: A Textbook of Creativity*	Penguin Books	New edition 1990	Edward De Bono is the godfather of lateral thinking and creativity; this is a true classic that remains unsurpassed.
Hollins, B. and Hollins, G.	*Over the Horizon: planning products today for success tomorrow*	John Wiley and Sons,	1999	An excellent introductory textbook to the subject, complemented by an array of case studies: illuminating and engaging.
Kelley, T.	*The Art of Innovation: Success through Innovation the IDEO Way*	Profile Business	New edition 2002	Tom Kelley provides a breathless and energetic discussion of all things IDEO and the highly creative ways in which it produces innovative products for its clients.
Trott, P.	*Innovation Management and New Product Development*	Financial Times/Prentice Hall	Fourth edition 2008	A solid account of NPD and ways in which to manage the process of innovation. Written by a leading figure in the field, this is a valuable resource book.

**Vision and Values in
Design Management**

Design
directions

Design
transformations

Design
advocacy

Design
alliances

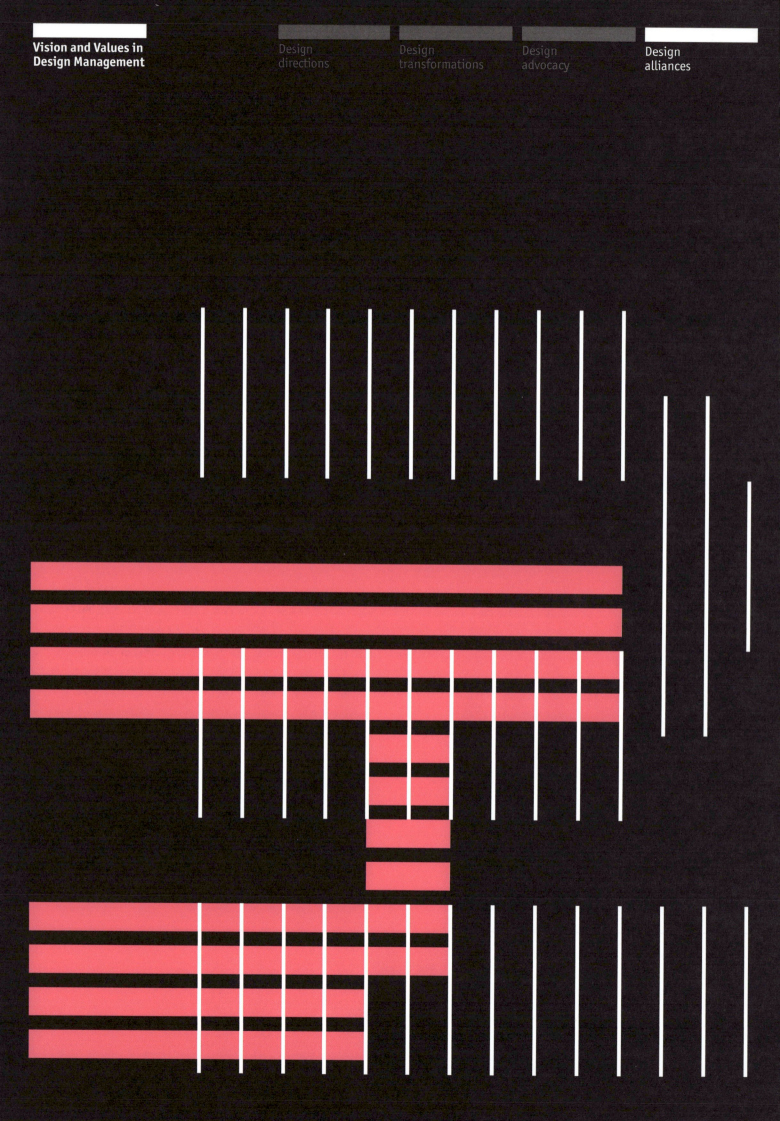

Chapter four
Design alliances

Design alliances focuses on emergent issues impacting upon an organisation. It looks at how design is forced to change its identity and role within the organisation to combat market complacency and the ever-changing demands of consumers and end-users. With the rise of compassionate consumerism and societal transformation new challenges face the designer on a daily basis, requiring swift responsiveness and future foresight in both thinking and practice.

Emergent issues in design

This section will discuss the new landscape of ideas, market forces and social transformations that are driving change in the way we view, perceive, use and understand design. Assaulted by continual change and complex socio-technical forces, organisations are having to adapt and adopt new ideas and experimental methodologies to compete and flourish on a global playing field. One sizable driver for change is the constantly shifting political landscape, with new economies developing and others being dramatically reconfigured.

Figure 1
Eurofighter is a notable product of virtual design team involvement.

Emergent issues
in design

CSR and design

Innovation in
services

Where next?

146|147

One only has to look towards south-east Asia and the Indian sub-continent, which contains a significant proportion of the world's manufacturing and outsourcing of technology orientated activities. With new market opportunities opening up on a daily basis, demographers and marketers are continually compartmentalising and slicing markets into ever smaller sizes based on individual lifestyles and personal aspirations. This in turn forces the designer to understand and produce designed solutions that excite customers and end-users through a variety of different points of engagement. Technology is advancing at such a high velocity that new products today will more than likely appear outdated and obsolete tomorrow – telecommunications is a notable example. Societal change is also becoming harder to predict, never mind quantify, with demographic groups atomising to almost microscopic proportions. Social scientists and marketers are identifying and categorising social sub groups and their inherent value systems, as they demand a greater degree of personalisation in the products and services that they buy and more importantly 'experience'.

The nine challenges covered on the following pages are only some of the key challenges that have either arrived or are in the process of establishing a critical velocity, requiring urgent attention by the organisation.

Some are focused on technological or market-led change, others on significant geo-political developments such as globalisation; however, the majority are a combination of all these factors as it is often impossible to separate such forces into neatly defined compartments.

Demographic change

One of the significant changes within the demographic landscape is increased life expectancy, especially within the European Union (EU). This in turn leads to many changes in the products and services offered by organisations today. First, we are living longer, more productive and independent lives with a greater emphasis on enjoyment and leisure activities. As the population steadily ages, products and services are demanded that overcome both physical and mental limitations – such as housing, for example, where access and mobility considerations are foremost in the design development process. In terms of services, we are witnessing a proliferation of organisations offering social, leisure activities and carefully packaged tourist 'experiences' for the over-50s. In the UK, Saga Holidays is a leading market organisation offering a variety of travel products for the discerning older client. **Saga** is such a strong and well respected brand that it has recently launched a social networking website dedicated to the over-50s, which offers a strong alternative to established industry rivals such as Facebook, Myspace and so forth.

Time economy

Time is a precious commodity; people no longer have the time to shop around. Consumers want retailers to make choices for them. According to a survey published in 2006 by consumer analysts at the **Henley Centre**, the British value time more than they do money. Some 41% of respondents mentioned time as their most valuable resource, while only 18% believed that money was most important. Consumers demand that retailers make decisions for them: they want premium products and services; low-fat food; healthy diets; tailored mobile phone plans that reflect and support increasingly time-intensive lifestyles. Due to the poverty of free time to plan, facilitate and enjoy our eclectic lifestyles, more and more consumers are prepared to trade off income in order to buy back more time. More importantly, the implicit assumption is that time is treated as a valuable and scarce resource in today's economy. In recent years the Henley Centre has also identified a drift towards 'leisure canapés', in which time-poor people dip their toes in different leisure activities in order to squeeze as much as possible out of their free time.

Saga
The Saga Group is a comprehensive organisation offering a full range of products and services to the over-50s community. For further details on Saga go to www.saga.co.uk.

Henley Centre
The Henley Centre was founded in 1974 by academics associated with the Henley Management College in Oxfordshire, UK. Three of its original core principles have remained consistent: the importance of understanding consumer behaviour; a rigorous approach to analysing data and a focus on the future.

**Vision and Values in
Design Management**

Design
directions

Design
transformations

Design
advocacy

Design
alliances

Virtual organisations

With the advent of the information age in full flow, the evolution of organisational structures has taken a significant leap into the virtual world. Within the next decade, virtual organisations will be as commonplace as physical ones – almost standard in business practice. Virtual organisations succeed based on the premise that they share and apply specialist knowledge to complement their cyberspace partners. Four key characteristics underpin their success: first, each partner's expertise and core competencies complements the other organisations within the network; secondly, responsiveness is essential to business practice, with time becoming the critical factor; thirdly, trust is paramount as the organisations are separated geographically but the working relationship is bonded by information networks. Without trust, organisations will be unable to quickly pull together the necessary resources to take full advantage of an emerging market opportunity. Finally, fully exploiting communication technologies to cement and flourish the relationships determines overall success within business operation.

If these four factors are understood and taken advantage of, the virtual organisation becomes a potent force in its ability to provide value-added, highly innovative products and services to emerging markets, overcoming boundaries of distance and time.

Market fragmentation

Traditional tools to divide the marketplace into neat, symmetrical segments are becoming obsolete. Crude categories such as age; gender; occupation and education are as outdated as vinyl records and terrestrial TV. Markets are now being atomised into a kaleidoscopic array of micro 'collective-identities' based on aspirations, personal fulfilment and personal value systems. **Peter York** was an early pioneer of segmenting the market into simple lifestyle characteristics, such as the Sloane Rangers and Yuppies, but now the demographic landscape has advanced considerably further, requiring sub-definitions within market segments. Gone are the Yuppies and in their place are Yeppies, the 'Young Experimenting Perfection Seekers' who are less single-mindedly materialistic, but also more ambitious in terms of personal fulfilment.

This is just one of numerous categories emerging, with each niche requiring specific product and service benefits that complement their expectations and purchasing motivations.

Mass customisation

The 'one-size-fits-all' model is officially dead. The era of high-volume manufacturing supplying the marketplace with anodyne, generic products (and, more importantly, the product services) has been rejected by the market. Differentiation is now the mantra of industry and commerce, where technologists and designers create unique and superior products aimed at micro-niche demographic audiences. Mass customisation means that the consumer can get exactly what they want, at a price they are willing to pay. With this new paradigm forcing change on existing manufacturing models, organisations are having to reconfigure every aspect of operational practice to develop 'products for one' whilst still producing and distributing high volumes within realistic budgetary constraints.

> 'There are ideas as labels to help us describe and understand our changing world and the people in it; ideas as innovations to help us to change things; ideas to help turn businesses around and make money; most of all, there are ideas to make us, our organisations more exciting.'
> **James Harkin**

Peter York
A social commentator and management consultant and broadcaster on social styles and trends. Peter York was co-founder of the influential management consultancy SRU with Lord Stevenson.

Non-renewable energy sources
Sources of power that cannot be replaced once they are used, because the energy source has taken millions of years to form (i.e. coal and oil).

Emergent issues
in design

CSR and design

Innovation in
services

Where next?

148|149

Sustainable lifestyles

Socrates was attributed with the comment 'I am always amazed to see just how many things there are that I don't need,' which is more relevant today than ever. As energy consumption increases, along with the reliance on **non-renewable energy sources**, consumers are increasingly worried about the environmental impact of their lives. Both legislative and consumer pressure is forcing industry to review current standard practice and offer strong and viable alternatives to the way in which products and services are manufactured, distributed and recycled after expiry. But beyond this, localised and national action groups are campaigning for a return to sustainable and ecologically friendly ways of consumption, that embrace supporting the local community whilst engaging and honouring their responsibilities to a wider audience. Attitudes and expectations of consumers are moving more quickly than the speed at which businesses and other organisations have been able to adapt.

Corporate social responsibility

Customers and end-users are becoming increasingly concerned with the social, economic and environmental impact of business practice. So much so, organisations are having to adopt responsible leadership in every aspect of daily operation and provide a greater degree of transparency in accountability. Numerous surveys show that members of the public prefer companies which are 'seen' to be positively contributing to the environment and society as a whole. A good reputation is one of the most valuable intangible assets a company can have, and maintaining it is a key motivation for companies to engage in responsible business. Design is a strategic tool in the way the organisation adopts 'compassionate' practice and the way the organisation communicates its commitment to CSR to all its stakeholders.

Figure 1
Today's young consumers are more focused on personal fulfilment than material gain.

Figure 2
Nokia understands the core values of its customers and the importance of recycling.

**Vision and Values in
Design Management**

Design
directions

Design
transformations

Design
advocacy

Design
alliances

Crime and anti-terrorism

The most recent and sophisticated analysis of crime in England puts the total annual cost at a staggering £60 billion (**British Crime Survey**). Although recorded crime has decreased slightly, more than half of the population in England and Wales considers crime as the number one problem facing the country. The UK Design Council, supported by the government, has produced policy initiatives for industry, commerce and the design profession to develop a deeper understanding of the issue, aiming to change industry practice in the way new products and services are conceived and taken to the marketplace. Following on from CSR, crime reduction practice is a signal to consumers that businesses have a responsibility to reducing crime and that they are committed to combating it through the development of crime 'resilient' offerings. The case study on pages 158–165 provides a more detailed overview of this emergent issue.

Technological convergence

Innovation, new markets and technology are often found in the collision point between new and existing technologies. Likewise, companies in certain industries can draw inspiration from the way other industries use technology. In essence, this means that innovation can be encouraged if companies become better at identifying new technological development opportunities outside their own area of activity or industry, in light of technological convergence. The internet is perhaps the most widespread example of technological convergence. Virtually all entertainment technologies – from radio, television and video to books and games – can be viewed and played online, often with greater functionality than they have in their primary technology.

Summary

Factors driving change can come from a variety of different sources, more often than not from arenas of activity completely alien and beyond the reach of design. However, rather than viewing 'change' as a negative issue, so often change can afford and provide new impetus for opportunities leading to new and radical innovations in the marketplace. Designers flourish on change as it continually provides a rich seam of inspiration to be taken forward and embedded within the creation process.

Figures 1 and 2
The Karrysafe bag incorporates robust anti-snatch features that reduce the risk of theft from the person. This was developed in collaboration with Central St Martins School of Design, London.

British Crime Survey (BCS)
This comprehensive survey is an important source of information on levels of crime, public attitudes to crime and other criminal justice issues within England and Wales (Scotland and Northern Ireland carry out their own surveys). The results play an important role in informing government policy.

**Emergent issues
in design**   CSR and design   Innovation in
services   Where next?

150|151

Figure 3
A new and innovative bike stand that
reduces the risk of theft incorporating
'design-against-crime' thinking. This was
developed in collaboration with Central St
Martins School of Design, London.

'You cannot approach large problems
surrounding sustainability with an
accountancy mindset. You need to approach
it with a divergent mindset . . . and then you
need to narrow down creative solutions.'
Dr Caroline Davey and Andrew Wootton

**Vision and Values in
Design Management**

Design
directions

Design
transformations

Design
advocacy

Design
alliances

Interview
**Dr Caroline Davey and
Andrew Wootton**

Dr Caroline Davey and Andrew Wootton are co-directors of the Design against Crime Solution Centre at the University of Salford. They have undertaken extensive research into reducing criminal activity through design-led interventions. They are also well-recognised authorities on Corporate Social Responsibility, working with a number of organisations to embrace socially responsible practice.

For those unfamiliar with the work that you do at the DAC Solution Centre, could you provide a brief overview of your role and responsibilities?
We are both co-directors of the Design against Crime Solution Centre at the University of Salford. This ground-breaking initiative researches, designs and delivers a comprehensive range of services tailored to the needs of design, development and planning professionals. The Centre supports the adoption of effective design-led crime prevention by police forces across the UK, and promotes an innovative, human-centred approach. Since its inception, the Solution Centre has sought to transform the nature of design-led crime prevention.

Corporate Social Responsibility (CSR) still does not have a clear definition. How do you define it?
CSR doesn't have a clear definition, but it's one of the main things that we have looked at. We first looked at a definition offered by the World Business Council for Sustainable Development (WBCSD) and they define it as: 'Corporate social responsibility is the continuing commitment by business to behave ethically and contribute to economic development while improving the quality of life of the workforce and their families as well as the local community and society at large.' However, it's quite wordy and not really a definition at all; so that's the problem with it, it's very vague to say the least! The problem that businesses have with it concern certain levels of influence; obviously with CSR they can control what goes on within the business and their partners. It's all about delineating boundaries; the level of influence decreases as it moves further beyond organisational activities. To add clarity on these issues, a good example is our work with socially registered landlords, i.e. a housing association. They have a combination of both direct and indirect influence through their activities, and we have helped them increase their commitment to CSR. They are supported by public funding, so adopting a strong CSR commitment is very important to them. What we found is that CSR is heavily linked to sustainability. Corporate responsibility (sustainable development) can be divided into three distinct aspects – corporate social responsibility, corporate environmental responsibility and corporate financial responsibility.

Emergent issues
in design

CSR and design

Innovation in
services

Where next?

152|153

So is CSR under the umbrella of something else or are these three tenets under the umbrella of CSR?
We are more concerned with doing something practical with it, so we divided it into two strands. The first strand is organisational management activities – structures, management style, reporting and so on; the second is CSR itself – reporting and ethical practice. External activities go alongside this: production, services and systems to support it; so one side is socially responsible design and the other socially responsible governance. One is internal, the other external.

Consumers are still quite cynical about believing the commitment of businesses to CSR. Why do you think this is the case?
When you look at some of the companies that claim to be socially responsible, you tend to find that they use design for marketing. So it looks like corporate social responsibility with window dressing; which is more to do with communication than actually doing. The large, multinational petroleum organisations claiming to be fully CSR committed I find very interesting!

Do you think this common, almost negative perception of CSR has hampered its development?
Yes absolutely, I think it could be attributed to how society is organised. It's difficult to argue for anything other than profit in pure business terms. The main problem is that companies are not aware of the benefits that CSR can offer them, mostly viewed as just an expense. However, they could build a strong sense of customer loyalty through CSR practice; take for instance the Co-operative Bank and the way in which it invests customers' money, ethical banking. It doesn't help that the many positive benefits of CSR practice are not communicated well to businesses.

How do you think businesses can overcome these widely held views?
I think the only way businesses are going to overcome these widely held views is through 'enlightened leadership'. You need to have business leaders who buy into their role in wider society rather than just shareholders generating profit.

CSR talks about stakeholders as opposed to shareholders and you need to have leaders who are actually going to communicate well that CSR isn't just good for the bottom line to be seen to be doing but actually has value for wider society. And again, green issues, the environment, global warming and energy efficiency are becoming a matter of consumer choice, in that if you don't adopt CSR then people will switch away and move to rivals with a more ethical standpoint.

What is the 'Triple Bottom Line' and to be fully CSR committed does the organisation have to embrace these three key tenets?
The triple bottom line is people, planet and profit; and obviously that links to the three pillars of sustainability. I don't think it helps that you have CSR and sustainability all competing for attention, with one saying we are more important than the other. Often, sustainability is confused with 'environmentalism' which doesn't include the three pillars. Profit needs to be reconsidered as not just economic benefits to the company, but profit meaning economic benefit to wider society; it's about added-value to society.

How and where does design fit into CSR practice?
Unfortunately, design is used mostly for marketing, communication and reporting. We view and use design as a force to create opportunity, offering benefits to wider society, the planet, and even economically. We try to harness the creative power of design to approach it in a different way. You cannot approach large problems surrounding sustainability with an accountancy mindset. You need to approach it with a divergent mindset (which is how design operates) and then you need to narrow down creative solutions. This whole area needs creative thinking, and thinking that designers can offer. Designers have a big role to play.

You have worked with many organisations regarding CSR, can you give me a good example of your involvement?
A good example is our involvement with the police, especially in terms of CSR and in particular the whole regeneration process – the design and development of new buildings. We have done loads of work with Greater Manchester Police (GMP), helping them with the design development process – engaging with the planners, architects and developers to create more responsible projects.

The planning and design process is quite complex from a number of points of view. What tended to happen in the past is that the police would be sent plans of new developments at the very end prior to final planning approval, by which stage all the design had been done. The problem was that the police could then come up with a potential crime issue (such as car theft), which needed to be addressed. Putting the brakes on at that late stage caused all sorts of problems and costs to the developers. So what we did for GMP was to design a new process to help them engage much earlier, at the concept stage; offering advice much more on a consultancy basis. In terms similar to that of a design consultant, enabling the developers to make real changes that would reduce crime. It ends up being a smoother process, because it isn't all stopped at the end, and better crime prevention comes through closer integration with the designer. This process has been implemented within Greater Manchester by the police and we are looking to roll it out throughout other forces in the UK.

What are the future challenges for CSR?
I think we are living in a very cynical society for a number of reasons. We cannot afford to do nothing; and as a result of cynicism we just do nothing. One of the main things is the change in the media; the media more than ever are quite sensationalist about issues to do with crime, well basically social responsibility issues. It encourages us to believe that problems are too big for us to do anything about. In the case of crime, it makes people unduly afraid; if you actually look at the crime figures you are quite unlikely to be a victim of crime, less than you would believe by watching the news. There is basically a problem that people don't get full access to the facts. Some of these issues are incredibly complex with no simple solutions attached to them. That's the problem, people want simple solutions and normally the idea is to blame someone; who can we blame for this? There are people refusing to take responsibility, partly because they are not necessarily made aware of all the facts.

**Vision and Values in
Design Management**

Design
directions

Design
transformations

Design
advocacy

Design
alliances

CSR and design

The importance of corporate social
responsibility in daily business practice cannot
be ignored. With the rise of 'compassionate'
consumerism customers and end-users are
demanding a greater degree of responsible
practice from the organisation, and more
importantly, greater transparency in the
operation and reporting of CSR practice. This
section will provide an overview of CSR and
why it is so important to embrace, not only
in the eyes of the consumer, but how CSR
practice can provide new ways of thinking
and behaviour whilst establishing closer
working partnerships with suppliers within
the extended supply chain.

'Today, corporate social responsibility goes far
beyond the old philanthropy of the past –
donating money to good causes at the end of
the financial year – and is instead an all-year-
round responsibility that companies accept
for the environment around them and for the
best working practices.'
Design Council

Emergent issues
in design

CSR and design

Innovation in
services

Where next?

154|155

CSR: a brief overview

In today's globalised marketplace, there is growing acceptance that the corporate sector must face up to its responsibilities to the wider world. As well as minimising their impacts on the environment, more and more companies are getting involved in areas such as human rights, fair trade, local economic development and non-discriminatory employment practices. CSR continues to be a highly topical and debated subject, raising philosophical issues for the organisation about its role and responsibilities and its relationship with its stakeholders. Although debate continues to rage about CSR there is still a long way to go to pin down what it means and its true value. Anecdotal evidence suggests that it is just concerned with glossy annual business reports and superficial public relations, with organisations seeing it as a distraction or a threat. Alternatively, some see the issue as no more than sound business practice. Others regard it as a source of business opportunity and improved competitiveness.

CSR is indeed highly relevant to all companies, large and small, to those operating regionally, nationally as well as internationally in global markets. In other words, it may be argued that CSR is as much as anything a way of thinking about and doing business. And that way of thinking needs to be mainstreamed across all business operations and into company strategy; design is an integral part of this thinking. However, it is not just a task for the public relations department but needs to permeate across every aspect of the company, in business development, marketing, finance and design and so on. For CSR to reach its true potential, full and strategic implementation throughout every facet of business performance is vital.

The ways that particular companies embrace the challenges of CSR must in essence reflect their individual circumstances. The approach, challenges and opportunities would be very different between a small software company operating exclusively within the UK and a multinational petroleum company such as BP or Shell. The distinction between daily practice and communication of CSR has also been the focus of much discussion. To what extent should reporting and a public profile be taken to indicate a responsible business?

The distinction however is not that clear cut: for a consumer facing business, communication is central to its CSR practice. Customers need clear information if they are to exercise choice. Socially responsible investment (SRI) products, which continue to grow although still a small share of the current market, reflect this type of demand.

CSR has continued to develop well beyond its philanthropic and community roots with a growing focus on the business case. While there is strong evidence of the actual and potential benefits to individual organisations its direct link to competitiveness is difficult to quantify; nonetheless, companies themselves have shown direct positive impacts on their business. An increasing focus on the global reach of organisations and therefore the international dimension to CSR has sparked considerable debate about the value and limits of CSR in dealing with many complex and sensitive issues associated with globalisation. But responsible business practice or sustainability is commonly acknowledged by all sides as vital to ensuring globalisation works for the poorest and as a means of bringing benefits to developing countries.

Figure 1
There is growing acceptance that the corporate sector must face up to its social responsibilities. Reducing our impact on the environment, by investing in sustainable energy, for example, is at the forefront of CSR practice.

CSR and competitiveness

CSR encourages organisations to look at a wider range of stakeholder interests, which can widen understanding of the potential risks and opportunities for the business while offering wider social or environmental gains. Closer links with consumers may lead to greater awareness of their needs, which could result in the organisation becoming more competitive in terms of product quality. In some cases, CSR could also lead to greater efficiency (in cost savings from the take-up of best practice waste minimisation techniques), and as a consequence this could lead to the firm becoming more competitive in terms of prices. But there is no 'one-size-fits-all'. Differences in their scale, nature and spheres of activity will influence how different companies contribute to social and environment goals and the competitiveness challenges that they face. Some individual companies such as BT and the Co-operative Bank already quantify the impact of CSR activities on their competitiveness.

CSR challenges within design

Inclusivity

To fully embrace CSR practice, open dialogue, encouragement and transparency are all prerequisites. Through mutual understanding and consensus, the differing and valuable contributions of all stakeholders can contribute to successful and meaningful design development activities. This can be done by engaging not just with customers and end-users, but further beyond with suppliers, manufacturers and retailers, encouraging them to get involved in a number of ways. By fostering a commitment to CSR the organisation can transform attitudes and skills, embedding a new responsible focus throughout every aspect of business practice. The design development process is an inclusive activity, with dialogue and empathy as key tenets. CSR practice and responsibilities neatly blend in with the values of inclusive holistic design, stimulating better decision-making and a broader understanding of the problem at hand.

Democratising the design process through inclusivity can lead to the development of more meaningful designed outcomes that demonstrate a true commitment to responsible corporate behaviour.

Motivation

CSR attitudes and thinking can reinvigorate tired and jaded market audiences through the impetus of a new and purposeful way of thinking. A key strength of CSR is providing a more holistic viewpoint of current business practice and output, stimulating responses and their impacts far beyond the financial. Through this shared understanding between business functions, new ideas and energy can permeate through the organisation leading to new market opportunities for either current or new products and services. By fostering a commitment to empowering all stakeholders in business activities, a closer connection and understanding is established between the organisation and their constituencies, leading to a fluid exchange of ideas and possibilities for future partnerships. 'Responsible renewal' comes through not just engaging with customers, but also with wider society, creating pragmatic, market orientated designed solutions with benefits to a wider audience than first anticipated.

Figure 1
Pressure groups such as Greenpeace continually monitor the ethical practice of organisations and governments around the world.

'Employees are one of the key stakeholders for any business and evidence is growing of the importance employees attach to companies demonstrating their CSR record through progressive employment practice as well as through their behaviour as good corporate citizens.'

Emergent issues
in design

CSR and design

Innovation in
services

Where next?

156|157

Values

Building in design 'values' at an early stage is arguably the best way to embed CSR thinking that makes the most impact within design practice. Ideas and concepts generated within the front end of the design process cost relatively little compared to costs incurred further down the process, especially when ideas need to be taken into full-scale production. Research by the Design Council argues that 15% of time and energy devoted to the concept stages of design development lock in the subsequent 85% of costs, therefore correctly identifying the problem, generating subsequent solutions and taking these through to production depends on the rigour and focus applied at the initial front end of project activities. If we take this into account when applying CSR thinking, identifying the long-term impact and consequences of every design decision taken regarding the sourcing and use of materials, energy-efficient production methods, and environmental performance of the final product, building in values at the earliest stage is a true commitment to responsible thinking practice.

Strategic design management 'thinking' is best placed to embrace and drive the organisation's commitment to both CSR and Design against Crime development, capturing and encouraging awareness through open and constructive dialogue at the earliest possible stages of consideration.

Commitment

An organisation that embraces inclusivity, motivation and values and communicates these in an intelligent and meaningful way illustrates its true commitment to CSR practice. It was discussed before that some companies pay lip-service to achieving CSR goals in very much a limited and superficial manner, focusing on 'reporting it' as opposed to 'doing it'. Research has pointed to a public appetite for companies to communicate more about their CSR performance. But a lack of publicity cannot be taken to indicate a disregard for CSR.

The attention and potential for criticism that a raised profile can bring may make reporting a lower priority than substantive action. So there are choices to be made. Nevertheless, the drive for greater transparency as a means to improve accountability and trust has continued, as seen in the further development of voluntary reporting guidelines.

'The UK Government has played a key role in enabling, encouraging and recognising action – from engaging businesses in regenerating our communities, promoting voluntary benchmarking to rewarding success through awards and kitemarks. Above all the DTI has linked corporate social responsibility with competitiveness.'

Case study
Design thinking: designing against crime

This case study focuses on the design of the Cityspace 'Smart Point' information terminal. It discusses how the design brief provided a focal point for discussions, both within Cityspace and with the design consultancies GTD and Tobermory. Based on extensive experience and through discussion and testing, the design brief was developed from an original 'brief' – an initial statement of aims – to a fully detailed 'scope' document outlining a large variety of potential design considerations that would enable the product to withstand criminal abuse in a public environment. Following further internal design and mechanical engineering consultations, instructions were issued in the form of a detailed PID (Project Initiation Document) and appendices.

VOIP
Voice over Internet Protocol is the technology for providing voice communications over networks such as broadband internet.

Figure 1
Smart Point combines multiple functions into a single structure, helping to minimise street clutter and put essential services where they are most needed.

Emergent issues
in design

CSR and design

Innovation in
services

Where next?

158|159

The company

Cityspace and Adshel are both part of the Clear Channel Group. Cityspace benefits greatly from Adshel's experience in design, deployment and maintenance of street furniture, from bus shelters to bill boards.

Cityspace and Adshel have been installing street furniture for many decades and consider themselves to be the leading world brand in the market, operating over 3,000 street furniture agreements with municipalities in 20 countries. Cityspace offers an electronic service that provides free, up-to-date, passive and interactive information on travel, towns and cities in a visual and attractive format.

Touch-screen technology and attractive graphics are used to combine transport and editorial information with video, music, **VOIP** and maps. In operation since 1997, Cityspace services have proven successful in cities across the UK and abroad. As each city has different needs and issues to address, each Cityspace network is implemented in close consultation with the municipal authority to provide a solution tailored to the local area.

It was essential to incorporate crime-reduction thinking into all aspects of new product development. Cityspace consulted extensively with both Adshel and Adshel's clients to draw on considerable experience in the development of a crime focused strategy. Peter Quinlan, Head of Design Development at Cityspace, takes us through the initial design stages outlining key considerations that needed to be taken into account when developing Cityspace products.

'Our key drivers are: to have our kiosk usable the maximum period of time; to control the cost; to control impact of crime and to ensure our designs allow us to return our products, at very low cost and with little disruption to the public, to a 'just out of the box' appearance at any time during their expected 30-year service life. Crime presents a major challenge in our doing that.'

**Vision and Values in
Design Management**

Design
directions

Design
transformations

Design
advocacy

Design
alliances

The Smart Point range

The Smart Point range is a fully customisable modular terminal, providing interactive travel terminals and real-time information for the travelling public at points of departure and interchange. The range presents a bold, modern image and a cost-effective means of delivering services at any point of need. The terminal's state-of-the-art design offers complete flexibility, allowing an organisation to choose the services and technology required to meet its corporate objectives. The product can either be deployed on its own or as part of a wider network of screens and terminals available from Cityspace Transport.

The initial design brief: the new Cityspace Smart Point range

The essence of the brief was to redesign the existing iPlus information terminal, utilising the specialist knowledge of leading street furniture design consultancies and Peter Quinlan's experience in closely managing the design, purchase, manufacture and installation of all Cityspace products.

The challenge was to capture in one design a decade of experience in delivering unattended, on-the-street interactive and broadcast information services. It was essential to minimise the cost of maintenance and the impact of crime. Also, equally important was the need to provide full and cost-effective adaptability throughout the entire life of the unit. There were many issues concerning this generation of product that needed to be addressed.

Key considerations within the design brief

The main considerations within the design brief were based on extensive experience from earlier projects, as many issues arose from feedback and knowledge of existing products in use. By including and soliciting the views from a diverse range of stakeholders, the following aspects were raised and included within the design brief:

Modularisation

Component parts were designed so they could be replaced quickly and cost-effectively. By designing parts of the unit within a modular format, making repairs is relatively inexpensive. Consequently, with panels and screens easily replaced, the product is able to withstand everyday wear and tear; it looks pristine after five, 10 or even 15 years of constant use.

Key

Document title	Process stage
Description of document	Description of stage

Project boundary
Decision is made on whether to stop or proceed

Cityspace product development process
Cityspace has developed a comprehensive framework that outlines all the key stages of product development, from idea to inception. This is built on PRINCE2 (PRojects IN Controlled Environments), a process-based method for effective project management.

Corporate

Pre-project

Idea	Mandate	Explore idea	Marketing
	Contains the subject matter of the project, allowing everything to start: project background; objectives; constraints; scope; interfaces; outline business case; roles and responsibilities; project tolerances; potential customers and users.	Research possible approaches to key aspects of the project.	Marketing document possibly including renderings of the potential idea(s). This stage also includes an outline scope, plan and budget.

Emergent issues
in design

CSR and design

Innovation in
services

Where next?

160|161

Help Point and CCTV

In case a user ever feels at threat, a Help Point facility combined with CCTV ensures a greater sense of safety through the product. Utilising VOIP, with or without a webcam, the public have 24/7 access to a travel call centre or emergency services.

Positioning

This issue was largely communicated through the tacit knowledge of Peter Quinlan. Information units were positioned under the surveillance of CCTV cameras so that if the units were vandalised, or someone was attacked, the likelihood of arrest would be increased. Safety of the user is always a concern and a strong consideration in the selection of locations; for example, great care is taken not to block line of sight for road traffic.

Lighting

The information units emit low levels of lighting to provide a sense of security and safety after dark. This insight came particularly from a project manager who, from a female perspective, ensured the issue of lighting was addressed within the modified unit.

Figure 1
Peter Quinlan brought considerable experience to the design, development and implementation of Smart Point.

'Over the years we had developed an excellent and highly specialised team. We were determined to deliver a new standard in street furniture.'
Peter Quinlan

[continues overleaf]

Project

Feedback	**Business case**	**Authorisation**	**ITP/brief**	**Planning**	**PID/plan**
Marketing collateral presented internally and externally for feedback and development of idea.	Document providing an overview of the project, why it is needed, approaches considered, benefits expected, key risks, costs, timelines, investment appraisal and overall evaluation.	Decision by management based on business case to proceed, repeat previous steps or stop project.	Includes summary of business case, aims and objectives, deliverables, timelines, roles and resources, legal and financial and management sign-off.	Instructions in ITP developed to establish detailed scope, plan and budget.	Detailed document including team structure and roles, project objectives and deliverables, budget, acceptance criteria, summary of business case and a detailed project plan. This may differ from original ITP.

Summary

The Smart Point range is the embodiment of the considerable experience of the design development team and the collective knowledge of earlier versions of information terminals. Also, and most importantly, the range fulfils the strategic aims and ambitions of the design brief.

First, it is a cost-effective and financially robust piece of design that offers its clients value for money. Thanks to its modular configuration, all parts, panels and screens can easily be replaced efficiently, thus ensuring the longevity and durability of the product system. A service engineer can easily and quickly replace damaged parts on location and without fuss or disruption to pedestrians. The robustness of its design ensures value for money; its value can be measured through ease of maintenance and cost-effective servicing in the long term.

Secondly, as Peter Quinlan argues, it is an incredible piece of design in terms of the value of engineering quality versus effectiveness. Working within tight parameters brought about considerable innovations. Every aspect of Smart Point was designed within a tight budget; manufacturing considerations and overall quality were paramount to its success.

Thirdly, 'future proofing' was a key consideration, as Smart Point is based upon the premise of offering technology to its end-users within a fast, safe and easily accessible manner. It is difficult to predict technological developments within the period of a year, let alone a five-year horizon, but the design team have had to anticipate technological change within the basic architecture of its overall form. With the advent of new products and services, faster processing, increased memory and miniaturisation, flexibility was vital within the final designed piece to embrace and utilise these developments as and where required.

Overall, Smart Point is the embodiment of Cityspace's strategic aims for street furniture. It provides a robust and cost-effective means of offering comprehensive information to the end-user in an easily accessible manner at the touch of a screen. For commercial reasons, a desire to offer a high level of service and because of its highly public presence, the issue of crime and criminal abuse was a key design consideration. This issue had to be addressed not just at a superficial level, but at a fundamental level throughout, from initial concept, through to manufacturing, implementation, operation and servicing.

So where does design management have a role to play within this complex process? The design team and design leader, Peter Quinlan, have managed to take all previous experience and knowledge forward to the development and implementation of Smart Point. Tight budgets, corporate aims and user requirements have all been considered and accommodated within the ensuing design solution, which balances the conflicting demands of value for money, design flexibility and enhanced user experience for both today and tomorrow.

Peter Quinlan concludes by saying, 'We are extremely proud of the Smart Point; it has reduced our costs by over half and delivers a new benchmark in street furniture. The Smart Point range is loved by clients, local authorities and our maintenance team; further, by the use of classical architectural reference points, it aesthetically complements any environment and, of course, looks beautiful.'

[continued]

Development	Prototype drawings	Prototype	Product pack	Close	PIR
Detailed research and design development required to deliver product and needs of project.	Includes everything required to make prototype, such as (1) top level drawings and sub assemblies; (2) eDrawing models; (3) detailed parts drawings; (4) DXFs; (5) BOM; (6) data sheets.	Build prototype, test and modify design.	Includes an updated drawings pack post-modifications, marketing literature and any other supporting documents.	Project is completed and feedback provided.	Analysis of project, cost, timelines, structure and deliverables. Aim to highlight what was done well and what could be improved in the future.

Emergent issues in design   CSR and design   Innovation in services   Where next?

162|163

'As a fun alternative, one of the Smart Point options is the "through hole module", a large, eye-level opening that allows the user to look through the kiosk. I love this idea; it is unusual, generates interest and yet cost nothing; monetarily or environmentally.'

Figure 1
Even at night, the illuminated Smart Point provides a safe haven for its users through clear lighting and strong visibility.

Figure 3
Smart Point with the optional 'through hole' configuration. It affords a greater sense of connection between the user, the Smart Point and its immediate environment. The high degree of visibility ensures that the user feels safe.

Figure 2
Reducing the need for disruptive on-street work, Smart Point benefits from easy-fit, replaceable swap-panels with an anti-graffiti coating.

Vision and Values in Design Management

Design directions

Design transformations

Design advocacy

Design alliances

Revision questions

Afterword

The Smart Point range is a notable example of designing against crime in action. The UK Design Council has long been promoting the contribution and the role of design in combating crime and anti-social behaviour. By and large, this has been brought about by government initiatives to enlist the support of a wide variety of agencies and professions with unique skills and knowledge in the reduction of criminal activity. Through the involvement of the Design Council and the Home Office, design has been recognised as a valuable resource to play a key part in this policy initiative. This case study exemplifies the unique aspect of crime reduction activity through design: to protect the product from misuse and vandalism and to protect the user. With many more examples of designing against crime coming to public attention, the role and worth of design has been considerably raised, making it one of the key considerations in crime reduction within society today.

1 Is it fair to suggest that the designer can meaningfully contribute to crime reduction?

2 At what point within the design process do you think the issue of crime should be raised?

3 Should design-against-crime thinking be expensive in terms of additional attention and effort?

4 Why should businesses engage with designing against crime; what benefits do they gain from this?

5 How can you measure the success of design-against-crime thinking? Can it be measured at all?

Emergent issues
in design

CSR and design

Innovation in
services

Where next?

164|165

Further recommended reading

Author	Title	Publisher	Date	Comments
Cooper, R. Davey, C.L. and Press, M.	*Design against Crime: Methods and Issues that Link Product Innovation to Social Policy*	International Journal of New Product Development and Innovation Management	December/January 2002	Excellent and detailed account of the inter-relationship of adopting design against crime practice and its wider impact on society.
Davey, C.L.	*Conducting Case Studies: Design against Crime*	Design Policy Partnership, University of Salford	2001	A step-by-step introduction to auditing and researching design against crime case studies.
Design Council	*Think Thief*	Design Council	2003	An accessible and user-friendly introduction to understanding all things design against crime and utilising appropriate tools and techniques.
Design Council	*Cracking Crime through Design*	Design Council	2001	Brilliant series of case studies illustrating how organisations have successfully adopted and implemented design against crime practice.
Design Policy Partnership	*Off the Shelf: Design and Retail Crime*	Design Council	2001	Thought-provoking account of the true cost of crime in the retail sector and a variety of ways of preventing crime.

**Vision and Values in
Design Management**

Design
directions

Design
transformations

Design
advocacy

Design
alliances

Innovation in services

This section introduces the emergent issue of service innovation and how 'bundling' services around a product is a key source of sustainable competitive advantage. It begins by offering a basic overview of what constitutes service innovation, outlining the benefits and drawbacks connected to adopting a service innovation strategy. If adopted successfully, service innovation offers many unique benefits to the organisation not only in terms of income generation but also as a vehicle to establish longer mutually rewarding benefits to all partners involved in the relationship.

we find millions

Xerox Global Services professionals can transform your firm's
document processes to create revenue while driving up productivity.
Result? Improved top and bottom lines.
There's a new way to look at things.

Figure 1
Xerox places the customer at the core of its
business strategy.

'Only 32% of UK companies have introduced a new product or service in the last three years. Where design is integral, 67% have done so.'
Design Council

Emergent issues
in design

CSR and design

Innovation in
services

Where next?

166|167

Services: a brief discussion

Innovation is one of the five key growth areas of productivity, alongside skills, investment, enterprise and competition. Increasingly, firms do not see themselves to be 'services' or 'manufacturing' but more akin to providing 'total' solutions for their customers that involve a combination of both products and services. Services in essence 'wrap-around' or embrace both manufacturing and environmental offerings. Much has been said about how innovation drives economies and the success of individual firms, but strangely enough services have received little attention in terms of how firms innovate in order to differentiate and succeed in competitive market environments. Innovation as we know is the 'successful exploitation of new ideas'. We could apply this definition to all firms in the economy and it is equally relevant to services innovation.

While innovations in products may be more easily recognised and understood, there are fewer examples in services innovations. What we are witnessing is a growing trend amongst manufacturers to offer or 'bundle' services related with what they produce. This isn't a new idea, admittedly, but what is happening is that manufacturers are offering an increasingly sophisticated range of services related to their products. A brief example of how far this development has increased could be illustrated using the company Xerox. Thirty years ago, Xerox started providing both long and short-term leasing and service agreements to its customers, moving beyond the manufacture of photocopying machines to providing a service to maintain their effective use within the workplace. Here we can see the shift from selling a photocopier towards selling a combination of services, thus leading to a greater sense of customer satisfaction. This has led to greater changes in Xerox's innovation strategy. It is worth noting that innovation is now seldom undertaken in isolation by a single manufacturer such as Xerox, but more through networks of manufacturing and service firms working together as strategic partners.

And conversely, we are witnessing service companies who are moving into partnership with manufacturing companies offering services such as ICT and research and development expertise. Having established that service provision is a vital area for strategic growth, let us focus in more detail on the role of services and how design can both promote and sustain innovative activity within this area.

Figure 2
Siemens provides industry solutions covering everything from planning and construction to operation and maintenance over a plant's entire life-cycle.
Siemens Press Picture.

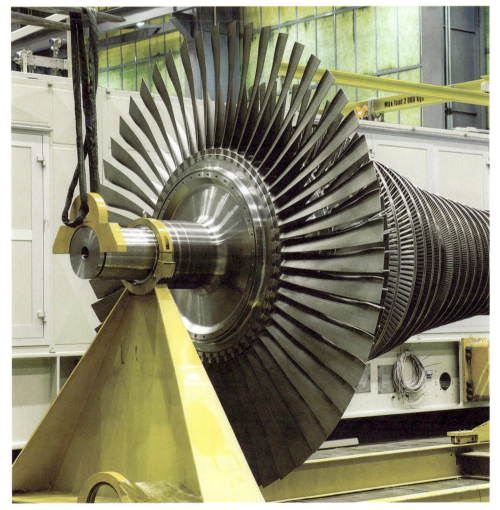

**Vision and Values in
Design Management**

Design
directions

Design
transformations

Design
advocacy

Design
alliances

Beyond the product?

The transition from providing products to offering a service that surrounds the product takes us into the realm of 'service encapsulation', where a whole host of services could be offered to complement the core product. The following five aspects could be connected to the product (either in entirety or individually):

1 **Continual monitoring**
This could be the continual monitoring of an IT system provided by Siemens ensuring it performs to its fullest specification. This type of service is often associated with ICT where the risk and consequences of system failure could be both operationally and financially disastrous for the client company. Continual monitoring provides a sense of 'peace of mind' and heightened protection.

2 **Purchase finance and leasing**
Commonly associated with motor vehicles. Lexus, BMW and other leading motor manufacturers offer packaged deals involving low-cost tailored finance plans and premium leasing agreements to accompany their motor vehicles. This tailored service is a key source of differentiation between the leading motor vehicle manufacturers, continually providing extra benefits and incentives to maintain customer loyalty and retention.

3 **Operation and support activities**
This could be associated with specialist machinery or production equipment where expertise is required to continually ensure safe and continuous operation. Due to its sophisticated complexion, readily available expert advice and support is central to the customer-client relationship.

4 **Retrofitting and updating**
A typical industry example would be the aviation sector where new technologies and systems are constantly being developed and introduced in practice. With safety and security being paramount, constant updating of parts and machinery is vital to the safe operation of the aircraft.

5 **Maintenance and repair**
This service is commonplace throughout a variety of different and diverse industry sectors. It could range from a 12-month annual service attached to a pedal cycle or a 24,000-mile service for a motor vehicle – through to the free first-time dry clean of a tailored suit or garment.

This aspect of blurring the boundaries between product and ancillary associated services leads us into the domain of the 'design experience' so often connected to leading brands as a source of competitive advantage. Or, if we take this issue further, another simple example could be connected to a meal for two at a leading restaurant. The meal is the product, a simple three-course menu, but the added value could be designed-in to include first-class table service and concierge assistance. Taken in entirety, the 'experience' of the meal encapsulates both product (food) and service (delivery plus) that reflects the aspiration and inherent brand values (vision) of the restaurant company. Taken further, if the company has created a flexible online table booking system (partner one) and subsidised taxi service home from the restaurant (partner two), this, it could be argued, is a key innovation strategy working in conjunction with collaborative partners.

Figure 1
Amazon is a good example of a company that offers 'beyond the product'.

Emergent issues
in design

CSR and design

Innovation in
services

Where next?

168|169

Risks and rewards of service innovation

Having outlined the business advantages of service innovation, it is worthwhile to ask 'if this is so easy why aren't more firms adopting this strategy?' First, there is a plethora of new technologies available for the organisation to use within business operation; however, how these are integrated and absorbed within the firm is problematic. Research by **Robson and Ortmans** found that factors associated with the cost and risk of innovation, as well as regulations, tended to be the most widely identified barriers to innovation of high importance. They also suggested that 'a lack of information on technology' was the least important barrier to innovation. Below are the ten main barriers highlighted to innovation; however, none of these are markedly more important than the others:

1   Customers don't or can't pay
2   Regulations create barriers
3   Costs and risks too high
4   Lacking key staff
5   Too busy to innovate
6   Customers are unresponsive
7   Innovation isn't necessary
8   Innovations easily copied
9   Organisation not equipped to innovate
10 Lacking appropriate technologies

To focus on these ten points in further detail, they can be subdivided into three distinct groups. The first group concerns the demand side from the customer's perspectives. That is to say, the customer either does not want, or can't afford, to pay for innovations. This suggests that they do not perceive a need to pay extra for something that they do not want. 'Why should I pay more for something that doesn't really benefit me?' This is a fair point; why would a company invest tens of thousands of pounds for something that doesn't offer anything extra in the eyes of the customer? The second main issue concerns the internal strengths of the company. Basically it's a resourcing issue, not just in terms of financial resources but also human ones as well. This could entail not having the key staff in place with the necessary skills and knowledge to implement such technologies, or the way the organisation is structured makes innovation a difficult task. Thirdly and finally, these could be generally categorised as 'other factors' that are immensely difficult to overcome never mind implement. These could concern the replication of your innovation by a rival or regulatory barriers making implementation too costly or risky to take on board.

Of course there will always be drawbacks to innovation (remember innovation implies risk and uncertainty). However, by undertaking thorough research prior to embarking on such a strategy, these issues could by and large be surmounted, providing access to the rewards of a successful adoption of service innovation.

'Manufacturers make most use of design throughout new product and service development.'
Design Council

Robson and Ortmans
Stephanie Robson and Laurent Ortmans from the Department of Trade and Industry published their research as 'First findings from the UK Innovation Survey', 2005.

**Vision and Values in
Design Management**

Design
directions

Design
transformations

Design
advocacy

Design
alliances

Service innovation: managing complexity

Although it is not easy to adopt a flexible
and robust service innovation strategy, if
considered intelligently and applied
sensitively, the rewards could be
considerable. However, this process needs
to be managed and organised at a strategic
level in order to be effective in terms of
both allocation of internal resources and
suitability for the firm's core customers.
Competitive advantage undoubtedly can
come from innovation of services, however
we need to remember that these initial
advantages slowly erode as rival companies
imitate or, for want of a better word, copy.
Therefore it is important that the firm
continually innovates, thus ensuring
constant advantage and forcing rivals to
play a game of 'catch-up' in order to stay
in business. The point is clear, innovation
matters and if organisations don't change
their product/service offerings then their
survival and growth is in question.

The management challenges to service
innovation are significant. Three
considerations surrounding this challenge
are worthy of brief discussion, these
include: servicisation; customisation;
and outsourcing.

1 **Servicisation**
As discussed before, there is an
increasing trend towards 'wrapping'
services around a product (this is
particularly more pronounced within the
manufacturing industry). For example,
with water purification systems, the firm
is less likely to compete on the basis of
product excellence alone, more likely
competing on the basis of adding value
through support services such as
maintenance, servicing and so forth. This
has two inherent and strategic benefits –
first, it increases the range of revenue
generation whilst also building a long-
term relationship with customers; and
secondly, this relationship could help
elicit important feedback, which could be
taken further in terms of innovative
activity in the future.

2 **Customisation**
A second major development within
manufacturing has been that of
increasing customisation. There has
always been a constant market for
personalised custom-made goods – and
taking this further, 'custom configured
services' (such as personal shoppers,
personal travel agents or personal fitness
instructors). Until recently, however,
there was a general acceptance that this
personalised service carried a premium
price tag and that mass markets could
only be served with relatively standard
product and service offerings.

3 **Outsourcing**
Lastly, the final major driver of
innovation is the growing trend towards
outsourcing of business activities. This
strategy has been growing for quite some
time now, with 'back-office' activities
being outsourced to reduce costs.
Activities usually include IT services,
payroll management and call-centre staff.
This growth has been significant and
increasingly global in reach, usually
driven by the advantage of low labour
costs especially in people intensive
services like call centres. One of the main
benefits of outsourcing business activities
is that the complexities of managing
these activities on behalf of a client
means that the outsourcer has to develop
considerable innovation skills which
could represent a powerful source of
service innovation.

'Public sector modernisation needs to be built
on a new approach to design which gives
users a creative voice in how services are
presented to them.'
Charles Leadbeater

Emergent issues
in design

CSR and design

Innovation in
services

Where next?

170|171

Summary

In this section we have discussed the nature
of services, arguing that service innovation
is a key source of competitive advantage and
differentiation. What we are seeing now is
the enlightened manufacturers 'wrapping'
services around their product offerings. This
is not only to increase revenue but also to
forge longer, more mutually rewarding
partnerships with their customers in order
to obtain vital information in their quest for
continual innovative activity. The product is
one primary aspect of business activity, but
with careful thinking and strategic direction,
the product could provide impetus for
development and growth, leading to closer
working relationships with a host of
different partners. However, innovative
activity is not without risk, with a multitude
of considerations that need to be taken
into account. Careful upfront planning can
overcome the majority of these pitfalls,
however, research is vital to overall success
and avoidance of failure. There are many
routes to service innovation once the need,
demand and vision has been decided.
Coupled with a clear understanding of
customer needs, this strategy could yield
significant benefits for long-term
sustainable growth.

Figure 1
British Telecom (BT) has two Indian call
centres, in Bangalore and Delhi, employing
over 2,200 staff.

Vision and Values in Design Management

Design
directions

Design
transformations

Design
advocacy

Design
alliances

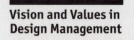

Interview
Dr Cristiaan de Groot

Dr Cristiaan de Groot runs the commercially focused collaborative design outfit Hothouse at Auckland's Unitec in New Zealand. Dr de Groot moved to New Zealand in 2004 but local companies weren't interested in his ideas, so he took a job at Unitec, where he has been moulding young minds as a senior design lecturer ever since. The Hothouse he set up in 2006 is funded by the Tertiary Education Commission, but aims to use the eventual revenue from its products and services to pay its way. Following on from the section in Chapter three (see pages 134–139), Dr de Groot explains in further detail some of the thinking behind the Hothouse project.

How does the Hothouse work?
We approach companies who have a reputation for innovation for being design-led and ask if they want to be involved. The students mine the companies for information – their physical and intellectual capabilities, their values, where they are going, what trends will impact them in the future. The company representatives come back here for a three-day ideas fest with the students and we end up with several hundred ideas. We filter them down; good ideas need either market potential and/or significant interest in shaping future markets, so they can still be somewhat conceptual, or more exploratory, but we look for big markets, $100m opportunities that will attract investors. Then the students develop them. The idea is that students and the companies get part of the intellectual property, and can be involved in the start-up business if there is one. We've only got prototypes at this stage, but Dean Prebble (Director of Unitec's New Zealand Centre for Innovation and Entrepreneurship) is the conduit between investors and entrepreneurs who might be interested in investing.

Why do businesses need Hothouse?
Here's a philosophical statement for you: meaning is generated through difference and if everything is the same then there is no meaning. So you think OK, you could bring mobile phone companies together with food organisations and banks and you'd get a lot more volatility and difference. As I have learned about New Zealand and the economy and the picture of industry, I saw there was a fit between some of the concepts I'd been thinking about. People were calling for SMEs to grow and innovate, but typically those companies don't have the resources, the perspective or the time. I thought maybe the best way to do that was to provide a third party to get a bunch of companies together and think up and develop great ideas.

Emergent issues
in design

CSR and design

Innovation in
services

Where next?

172|173

How are you different from any other collaborative design venture?

Globally we are quite unique. There are only about half a dozen instances of this around the world. Most places operate along linear lines – you've got something and we'll help you develop it. Hothouse is more about network based and experimental innovation. Not just thinking outside the box but thinking outside your category, your market, your current capability. My typical example is, what do you get if you put Navman and Kathmandu together? A Navmandu. But GPS enabled rucksacks and tents are a no-brainer. If you combine Navman's capability around wireless devices and location awareness and Kathmandu's knowledge about fabrics and construction methods for outdoor clothing, and marketing to people with active lifestyles…that's where the Hothouse students would play.

What do businesses get from being involved in a Hothouse project?

They'll get introduced to companies that in their wildest dreams they never thought of collaborating with, find opportunities for new directions rather than just line extensions for their current range. And potentially they'll be a part of new start up ventures with very little risk to themselves. They don't have to put any money in, but even if they're just part of the development process they'll have a stake in the IP.

How do the students benefit?

When students smell the potential in ideas and see that serious players are interested, they want to be there for the business start-up. Pretty much all the students have become consultants for other projects that Unitec is asked to do, and some have spun-off other projects with investors and companies outside of Hothouse. Their perspective shifts. Hothouse stimulates what were artsy humanities-based design students to actively seek business opportunities.

Are there any ideas with commercial potential?

We've got a laptop bag constructed using sports technology so it's good for protecting your laptop but it's not a hard briefcase. And it's got inbuilt technology to amplify your wireless signal. We've also got a set of eco bath toys. Normally a child takes the shark and it eats everything, but with these the shark eats the seal and the seal eats the fish and the fish hides in the seaweed. This idea is an example of where this project comes into its own. We got in touch with a local toy distributor/entrepreneur who told us that the bath market is shrinking because apartments are being built throughout the world without baths. So we ended up re-working the idea, making them less bath dependent, expanding the market potential. And there's the biodegradable gnome. We saw the gnome as a great vehicle for education around ecosystems, seasons, stuff like that. The gnome 'holds' seeds inside it and as it starts to biodegrade the seeds germinate inside its base. As the gnome slowly goes skeletal and disappears, up comes something new and living.

What are some of the challenges in developing the ideas?

Sourcing materials is really hard. Generally in New Zealand you can only readily find the materials that have already been requested by other people, otherwise it's a 12-week wait. Things like specialist fabrics, plastics and rubbers. It's frustrating. The moulding companies here say, 'We can't do that,' then you talk to someone in China, and they say, 'Yeah, we can do that tomorrow.'

How easy is it to get businesses involved?

Mainly design-led businesses are amenable. This gets put in the too-hard basket by a lot of other businesses; they're either too busy or they don't get it – they don't see the value. We're reorganising and tightening the processes for generating these ideas so the products are closer to what companies know. For instance now, instead of getting together a group of companies that specialise in fabrics, electronics and petrochemicals, it's a group of companies that do lights, floor coverings and furniture, so we know we're going to get something like a domestic artefact.

And if you put the first three specialists together, what could you get?

Chemically enhanced next-generated dog outerwear. A dog jacket that monitors its heart-rate. Who knows?

**Vision and Values in
Design Management**

Design
directions

Design
transformations

Design
advocacy

Design
alliances

Where next?

This section will discuss key developments
in both society and the changing business
environment, focusing on how new markets
and industries are emerging, and how
technological advances are forcing designers
to adapt and respond to uncertainty within
the creation process. As a consequence of
turbulent market forces and new modes of
working, the role and definition of design has
considerably changed, placing it within the
very DNA of the organisation, in the way it
acts and behaves and the many strategic
benefits that it has to offer.

Figure 1
Greater Manchester Police fully exploits the
use of design throughout all aspects of its
activities.

Emergent issues
in design

CSR and design

Innovation in
services

Where next?

174|175

Future challenges and opportunities

Accelerating social and technological change is rapidly altering our contemporary world and the way in which we perceive it. New ideas, shifting paradigms, traditional models of working practice are becoming obsolete, being replaced by virtual networks and organisations, all contributing to seismic shifts in our everyday lives. The emergence of new world economies are quickly eroding common orthodoxies and long-held beliefs, forcing us to re-evaluate the way in which we consume and value goods and services. It is reasonable to suggest that change and social transformation is happening on a gradual but continual basis, gently nudging us into uncharted territory in one direction or another. Social transformation and technological advancements are two of the biggest drivers promoting change. Their effects are permeating throughout every aspect of our lives; some significant, others more discreet and often invisible. Like it or not, change is the only constant factor in our lives. So how does this affect us and, in particular, the services and products that we in the design industry are tasked to conceive and create?

First, over the last decade in the UK we are witnessing a significant move towards the use of design within the public sector. Local government, the Driving and Vehicle Licensing Agency (DVLA), public transport and the police are amongst the many agencies providing key services. All are embracing design in the way they produce designed material and communication systems to forge closer relationships with their primary stakeholders. Healthcare is another burgeoning growth area where patients and end-users are placed central to the delivery and experience of healthcare provision. This often entails the application of design to increase and enhance the provision of healthcare through ease of communication; well designed, comfortable environments and user-centred products that remove the fear of medical examination and treatment.

Taking the issue of 'experiencing' design further, in particular the rise of the 'experience' economy, the business guru James Gilmore articulates that the next competitive battlefield will lie in staging 'sensuous' experiences with which to wow and seduce the consumer. Companies of all kinds must adopt the mindset of a theatre director, using the goods and services that they want to sell as props for a memorable event. Disney theme parks were held up as the way forward; in Disneyland, employees are called 'actors'; visitors are 'guests' and the entire theme park is a stage where dreams become reality.

What good is an intangible experience you may well ask? According to established theory, experiences are valued because memories last longer than material goods, which are prone to wear and tear. To create a memorable experience that appeals to a specific market segment through the delivery of a product or service, or both, involves a deep understanding of the end-user in terms of their values and aspirations. This issue leads us to the fracturing of market segments into micro-niches where customers are constantly demanding a higher degree of personalisation in what they purchase and consume. Design can offer and provide new ways of identifying and capturing untapped emergent market needs, leading to the creation of new-to-the-world products and services. By embracing and utilising complex methodologies early within the design process, unanticipated needs and purchasing decisions can be identified and incorporated within the final designed outcome.

'In an increasingly global world, our ability to invent, design and manufacture the goods and services that people want is more vital to our future prosperity than ever.'
Tony Blair

**Vision and Values in
Design Management**

Design
directions

Design
transformations

Design
advocacy

Design
alliances

A new landscape of change?

Purchasing decisions are moving beyond the benefits for the consumer to benefits for society as a whole, leading to the rise of the 'compassionate' consumer. Why? With increasing concerns over global catastrophe, famine, poverty and child labour, ethical consumers are looking towards major organisations and examining their motives and business practices through an ethical, compassionate lens of questioning. Sustainability, environmental despoliation and ethical policies are all under scrutiny, leading to a dramatic shift in consumers' purchasing decisions. Consumers are now demanding a more responsible code of practice by the major organisations in our lives. As we look towards organisations for 'responsible' change, they themselves are undergoing radical change in terms of both their organisational structure and everyday working practices.

With the advent of new ICT technologies, new forms of joint ventures and collaborative partnerships are being initiated on a daily basis, with the emergence of virtual organisations. The European Airbus A380 (a joint venture between EU member states and leading manufacturing organisations), is testament to virtual design and cross-border production networks, all collaborating in harmony to produce a radical, eco-efficient aircraft that is set to change industry expectations and the experience of contemporary air travel. Through these dynamic changes in society and industrial practice, design is central to leading change in the way ideas are conceived, developed and commercialised. As a consequence of this pivotal role within the creation process, the very nature of design and managing the process of design has considerably changed. Designers are having to acquire new skills, develop new vocabularies, adopt and apply experimental methodologies to cope with the demands of transformative business and non-commercial professional arenas.

So the role of design management has significantly changed within the last ten years and undoubtedly it will considerably change again over the next ten years. Design is increasingly becoming more of a visionary asset in the way organisations operate, perceive and (re)think future horizons for continual development and sustainable growth. Is design best served through inspirational leadership at boardroom level, or is its value more acute when applied intelligently throughout every sphere of organisational operation? These key issues will continually be debated, but one thing that cannot be overstated is that design is a powerful weapon in the strategic armoury of the organisation, and more so today than ever before.

Figure 1
The Airbus A380 is the largest passenger airliner in the world, making its maiden flight in 2005 from Toulouse, France.

'Innovation, and therefore creativity and design, is viewed by the UK Treasury as one of the five drivers of productivity and as such is seen to be critical to the economic development of national and regional economies.'
Andrés Rodigruez-Pose

Emergent issues
in design
CSR and design
Innovation in
services
Where next?

176|177

TURN IN YOUR KNIFE
BEFORE SOMEONE
TURNS IT ON YOU.

Wrap your knife in cardboard
and hand it in anonymously at
any police station.

NATIONAL KNIFE AMNESTY
May 24 - June 30

Home Office

Figure 2
In 2006 the UK's Home Office Crime
Reduction unit launched a National Knife
Amnesty campaign. A series of creative
posters and an amnesty brand were
designed to help local police forces include
their own activities within the nationwide
campaign.

**Vision and Values in
Design Management**

Design
directions

Design
transformations

Design
advocacy

Design
alliances

Interview
Professor James Woudhuysen

James Woudhuysen is Professor of
Forecasting and Innovation at De Montfort
University, Leicester. Amongst other
achievements, Woudhuysen helped instal and
test Britain's first computer-controlled car
park; led an international multi-client study
of consumer e-commerce; and reorganised
worldwide market intelligence at Philips
Consumer Electronics. He is also the author of
several books and he has consulted or given
keynote speeches for 20 of the Fortune
Global 500 corporations.

Emergent issues
in design

CSR and design

Innovation in
services

Where next?

178|179

For the benefit of our readers who are unfamiliar with your area of activity, can you provide a brief overview of forecasting and innovation and why it's so important to organisations?
No overview can be given of either forecasting or innovation within the space of a page. But the ability to predict the future, and actively shape it through innovation, is something that most organisations are very poor at. Gaining that ability isn't easy, but can help direct expenditure and effort in a useful manner.

The role and application of design is going through radical change, in part through globalisation and continual technological developments; what do you consider to be the biggest challenge that the designer needs to both understand and overcome?
The biggest challenge is to master, uphold and yet take a critical attitude toward technological innovation.

With the erosion of geographic and cultural boundaries, and avenues for international joint ventures, greater opportunities for the organisation are increasingly becoming available; however, to realise these opportunities, organisations need to anticipate future changes within both industry and society – what are the first key steps that they could take to develop a 'future-thinking' consciousness?
They need to challenge their prejudices and do scholarly research on industrial and social history and on what forecasters say about their sector. They need to have this research regularly and formally discussed.

At the moment [2008] the UK government is promoting numerous initiatives and the benefits of innovative activity within the organisation to remain competitive on an international stage; what else would you suggest to ensure the success of this strategy?
The government's expenditure and direction on innovation reveal its ignorance of science, engineering and IT. Numerous initiatives are part of the problem; they won't ensure success.

In a way this question follows on from the last one, how can the UK economy remain competitive in the face of growing economies such as China, India and Brazil?
I am not concerned with UK competitiveness against other rivals. However, the UK needs to recover the importance of science, technology, research and development and manufacturing and pay less attention to financial services and the professions of social control.

In the face of global warming, ozone depletion, climate change and demands on industry to radically restructure and rethink current practice – where does design and the designer take responsibility and the initiative to lead change?
The designer needs to lead change by refusing to hector people about their need to alter their behaviour through greater 'awareness'. He or she can play a part in improving the human side of innovation in energy supply – not in trying to get 'users' to conserve energy, buy ethically and all that. Designers should stay away from the pulpit.

In terms of design, let's say maturing and having to adopt more responsible practice, do you have any thoughts on how design can contribute to the issue of crime reduction (I am thinking more of global crime, i.e. terrorism, fraud and counterfeiting)?
It is ridiculous to think that design can reduce crime. This is an attempt – one of many – to turn designers into a new priesthood of social engineers. Crime has a number of causes, and design is not one of them. To make, say, a council estate less prone to vandals is to deal with symptoms, not causes. In the case of fraud, designers can be responsible in the sense that, outside the 9 to 5, they can ask more questions about the deal between British Aerospace and Saudi Arabia – something that the Serious Fraud Office is not prepared to do.

Let's say if we fast-forward 10–15 years, what do you think would be the greatest challenges that we in the design community need to counter?
Right now and then, it's the refusal to read books and go beyond fads. The obsession with brands and with ethics is a major barrier to advance.

James, to conclude, is there anything else that you would like to add or raise or stress that you consider of great importance to the design profession in terms of future critical engagement?
Critical engagement is the right thing. Precisely what the design community lacks.

'It is ridiculous to think that design can reduce crime. Crime has a number of causes, and design is not one of them.'
Professor James Woudhuysen

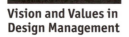
Chapter summary

The world is an ever-changing and turbulent place with common orthodoxies and long-established structures being fragmented and reconfigured on a continual basis. Consequently, design is having to keep readjusting its focus and core remit to accommodate and embrace these constant demands. Technology is getting faster, smaller, less expensive and more available. Organisations are forced to adapt and adopt change, taking on new responsibilities and broader societal commitments. The issues of crime, sustainability and globalisation require new skillsets, again placing further demands on the designer. However, all these emergent issues present fertile and rich sources of inspiration and opportunities for proactive, ambitious firms that wish to succeed and flourish within today's business environment.

Revision questions

Based on what has been discussed, you should now be able to answer the following five questions.

1 With the rise of radical new technologies, shifting demographic segments and emergent markets in the Far East, what other opportunities can you foresee for companies wishing to develop new products and services?

2 Why do you think CSR commitment and practice is a prerequisite for business success? Or do businesses need to bother with CSR at all?

3 Can you think of any celebrated examples of an organisation adopting CSR practice? Why are they considered successful, do you think?

4 Service innovation offers many benefits and rewards to the company; could you identify a company that could innovate through service development?

5 What do you consider to be the future challenges for organisations in the next ten years? How could designers face these challenges and use them to their own advantage?

Emergent issues
in design

CSR and design

Innovation in
services

Where next?

180|181

Further recommended reading

Author	Title	Publisher	Date	Comments
Blowfield, M. and Murray, A.	*Corporate Responsibility: A Critical Introduction*	Oxford University Press	2002	This much-needed textbook examines the multiple dimensions to corporate responsibility. It creates a framework that presents a historical and interdisciplinary overview of the field; a summary of different management approaches; and a review of worldwide trends.
Gladwell, M.	*The Tipping Point: How Little Things Can Make a Big Difference*	Abacus	2002	*The Tipping Point* provides a way of interpreting what factors have contributed to a certain epidemic or trend. A page-turner of ideas and highly readable and stimulating.
Hohmann, L.	*Innovation Games: Creating Breakthrough Products and Services*	Addison Wesley	2006	*Innovation Games* is organised in two parts. The first describes each of the 12 games. The second provides sample processes and templates to help the reader organise their team, plan and run a game, and incorporate the results into their product development plans. A great introduction to the discipline.
Levitt, S.D. and Dubner, S.J.	*Freakonomics: A Rogue Economist Explores the Hidden Side of Everything*	Addison Wesley	2007	This book does two important things – it challenges the reader to really think about the causes of things, and it makes modern economic thinking interesting and accessible to the mass audience. It's also a good-fun read; for all these reasons it should be applauded.
Wootton, A.B. and Davey, C.	*The Crime Lifecycle: Guidance for generating Design against Crime ideas*	DAC Solution Centre, Salford	2004	Two well-respected authorities on the subject share their views and unique insights into embedding crime resistant 'thinking' within the design process. Challenging but accessible; if you are interested in 'designing against crime' then look no further than this book.

Conclusion

Design management has changed considerably over the last 30 years, from its inception of managing and organising the product development process at an 'operational' level through to its role as key constituent of business activity. One thing does remain: design is still notoriously difficult to quantify in terms of its impact and many benefits.

Design has many roles to play within the organisation. On reflection, it has varying levels of application; these range from minimal impact, it mostly being used as a tool to cosmetically improve the appearance of a product, right up to being at the core 'DNA' of business operation.

Through its many faceted roles, design management has the ability to shape business decision making and operation by influencing key individuals within the organisation. With end-consumers and customers demanding greater transparency and honesty in business activity, extra demands have been placed on the organisation to fulfil these obligations.

Orchestrating future vision

This book has offered a strong and persuasive case for design investment. Investment not just in the form of financial spreadsheets or 'bricks and mortar', but more of a strategic and meaningful investment in establishing a culture that fosters a greater awareness and appreciation of what design can truly deliver. Section one discussed the value of design and its value in monetary terms; it looked at investing financial resources to add value to both existing and anticipated products and services with the eventual aim of sustainable differentiation and long-term competitiveness. Investment can be fruitful in nurturing and fostering a climate for design 'thinking', whereby risk-tasking and exploring possibilities through design can reap significant rewards. At this point it may be pertinent to ask, 'What is design?' By having a broader understanding and appreciation of design, its value and impact could be more widespread and central to business activity. It could be suggested that design goes far beyond 'doing' and the final embodiment of that process. It is more akin to an all-encompassing philosophy that permeates throughout every aspect of organisational activity. As Raymond Turner and Alan Topalian frequently and passionately argue, 'Design manifests strategic intent.' And to achieve this, the organisation has to be fully equipped and passionately driven by a holistic design vision.

Unknown opportunities

So how does an organisation start to develop a design consciousness? Where does design thinking begin and end? Who is responsible for this vision and how does it start? These may be simple questions, but the answers are complex. How does an organisation take an evolutionary leap into the unknown and uncharted waters of design leadership? Perhaps, it could be argued, this process and ambition begins within the comfortable confines of education and learning. Every one of the contributors to this book was once a student; most were involved in the study of design in a practical sense, be it typography, product design, textiles and so forth. When they were students, design management was a fledgling subject almost unheard of within the design profession. However, through their practice, understanding and experience, they have come to fully appreciate the value of design and the benefits that it has to offer. If we take this forward and argue that the readership of this book is truly international, with each individual having their own viewpoint and understanding of design management rooted in their own particular cultural and professional context, then design management becomes something much more. Through this 360 degree interpretation of the discipline, design management could potentially take an evolutionary leap in its ongoing development. This book has offered an honest and very broad account of design in both practice and vision; however, amongst its many shortcomings it does not provide a gateway or prescriptive plan for future development. In a way, it offers an examination of emergent topics and ways of understanding that require further exploration beyond the parameters of this book. Who is best equipped to answer this challenge? I will leave it to you.

New beginnings

We are living and working in a century of rapid development. Change is relentless; it affects cultural, political, social, technological and environmental factors that fundamentally inform and shape our lives. Through these strong, dynamic and constantly changing factors beyond our control, history and understanding need to be recontextualised within contemporary practice. Design management is no different; it requires a fresh perspective built upon the edifice of past exploration and debate. One aspect of the future that can certainly be agreed upon is that it is uncertain and unpredictable. To many managers, this thought is horrifying and deeply challenging, requiring an inner confidence previously not required nor expected; however, to designers, this challenge is embraced with relish. As design management takes its next stage in evolutionary development, we ask, 'Who is leading this change?' and 'Who are the beneficiaries of this change?' The answers may not lie within the pages of this book but hopefully within the aspirations of its readership.

Vision and Values in Design Management

Design
directions

Design
transformations

Design
advocacy

Design
alliances

Contacts

Andy Cripps
www.andycripps.co.uk

Aynsley China Ltd
Sutherland Road
Longton
Stoke-on-Trent
Staffordshire
United Kingdom
T +44 (0) 1782 339401
www.aynsley.co.uk

Buxton Wall Product Development Ltd
3 Parsonage Road
Heaton Moor
Stockport
Cheshire
SK4 4JZ
United Kingdom
T +44 (0) 161 4322351
www.buxtonwall.co.uk

CBI
Tubs Hill House
London Road
Sevenoaks
Kent
TN13 1BL
United Kingdom
T +44 (0)1732 468610
www.cbi.org.uk

CIPA
The Chartered Institute of Patent Attorneys
95 Chancery Lane
London
WC2A 1DT
United Kingdom
T +44 (0)20 74059450
www.cipa.org.uk

Design Council
34 Bow Street
London
WC2E 7DL
United Kingdom
T +44(0)20 74205200
www.designcouncil.org.uk

Evoke Creative Ltd
Suite F9 Oaklands Office Park
Hooton
Cheshire
CH66 7NZ
United Kingdom
T +44 (0)151 3281617
www.evoke-creative.co.uk

Haley Sharpe Associates Ltd
11-15 Guildhall Lane
Leicester
LE1 5FQ
United Kingdom
T +44 (0)116 2518555
www.haleysharpe.com

Henley Centre
6 More London Place
Tooley Street
London
SE1 2QY
United Kingdom
T +44 (0)20 79551800
www.hchlv.com

IDEO
IDEO Palo Alto
100 Forest Avenue
Palo Alto
CA 94301
USA
T +1 650 2893400
www.ideo.com

Imagination@Lancaster
The Roundhouse
Lancaster University
Bailrigg
Lancaster
LA1 4YW
United Kingdom
T +44 (0)1524 592982
www.imagination.lancaster.ac.uk

KTP
KTP Programme Office
Momenta
Didcot
Oxfordshire
OX11 0QJ
United Kingdom
T +44 (0)870 1902829
www.ktponline.org.uk

Livework
Studio 401 Lana House
118 Commercial St
London
E1 6NF
United Kingdom
T +44 (0)20 73779620
www.livework.co.uk

London Development Agency
Palestra
197 Blackfriars Road
London
SE1 8AA
United Kingdom
www.lda.gov.uk

PACEC
504 Linen Hall
162-168 Regent Street
London
W1B 5TF
United Kingdom
T +44 (0)20 70383571
www.pacec.co.uk

PDD Group Ltd
85-87 Richford Street
London
W6 7HJ
United Kingdom
www.pdd.co.uk

PDR
UWIC Western Avenue
Cardiff
CF5 2YB
United Kingdom
T +44 (0)29 20416725

Staffordshire University
Faculty of Arts, Media and Design
College Road
Stoke-on-Trent
ST4 2XW
T +44 (0)1782 294415
www.staffs.ac.uk

Trevi
The Bathroom Works
National Avenue
Kingston Upon Hull
HU5 4HS
United Kingdom
T +44 (0)1482 470788

University of East London
Docklands Campus
Royal Albert Docks
University Way
London
E16 2RD
United Kingdom
www.uel.ac.uk

Picture credits

All diagrams redrawn by Rupert Bassett.

Page 17
Figure 1 provided courtesy of Apple. Figure 3 provided courtesy of Kodak. Figure 4 © CHANEL / Photo Daniel Jouanneau. Figure 6: photograph by Richard Davies, provided courtesy of Universal Design Studio. Figure 7: photograph by Chris Gascoigne, provided courtesy of Virgile and Stone.

Page 19
Figure 5 provided courtesy of The Co-operative.

Page 31
Figure 3 provided courtesy of IDEO. Figure 5 provided courtesy of Apple.

Page 40
Figure 1 provided courtesy of Peter Saville Studio.

Pages 43–45
All images provided courtesy of Trevi.

Page 54
Figure 1 © Braun GmbH. Figure 2 provided courtesy of Honda. Figure 3: Oakley Hijinx sunglasses © 2008 Oakley, Inc.

Pages 56–61
All images provided courtesy of Aynsley China.

Page 71
Figure 1 provided courtesy of Fritz Hansen: the Egg chair, designed by Arne Jacobsen in 1958. Manufacturer: Fritz Hansen www.fritzhansen.com. Photographer: Piotr & Co.

Page 77
All images provided courtesy of Mario Ortiz.

Pages 78–79
All images provided courtesy of Alan Pavel Mendez.

Page 81
All images provided courtesy of Jian Ye Deng.

Pages 85–89
All images provided courtesy of Haley Sharpe Design.

Page 96
All images provided courtesy of Katsuhisa Kida/FOTOTECA.

Page 98
Figure 1 provided courtesy of Neff.

Page 101
Figure 1 provided courtesy of Festo: Festo's driving simulator Airmotion_ride. Photographer: Walter Fogel.

Page 111
Figure 2 copyright © Boeing.

Pages 112–117
All images provided courtesy of Buxton Wall.

Pages 127–131
All images provided courtesy of PDD/Exertris.

Pages 138–139
All images provided courtesy of Dr Christiaan de Groot.

Page 146
Figure 1 provided courtesy of Eurofighter GmbH/Geoffrey Lee.

Page 156
Figure 1 © John Cobb/Greenpeace. Image provided courtesy of Greenpeace.

Pages 159–163
All images © Cityspace Limited, 2006–2009.

Page 166
Figure 1 reproduced by kind permission of Xerox (UK) Ltd.

Page 167
Figure 2: Siemens Press Picture.

Page 174
Figure 1 © Bill Morris/GMP.

Page 176
Figure 1 © Airbus.

Glossary

Brainstorming
Creative problem solving through group activity, often used in the initial design concept development stages. It involves a variety of differing techniques to creatively generate a list of ideas related to a achieving a specific goal.

Brand
A symbol, term, design, name or any other feature that clearly identifies a product or service distinct from those of other rivals. The legal term for a brand is 'trademark'.

Brand repositioning
An attempt to change consumer perceptions of a particular brand. For example, VW successfully repositioned the Skoda brand.

Business to business
This term is most commonly referred to as 'B2B'; transactions between non-consumer purchasers such as manufacturers, wholesalers, distributors and so on.

Cannibalisation
The percentage of demand for either a new product or service that comes from the erosion of demand (i.e. sales) for the organisation's current product or service range.

Collaborative new product development
This occurs when two or more organisations work together to develop and commercialise a product or service. Collaborative development is different from simple outsourcing in its level of depth within the partnership.

Competitor analysis
Process of understanding and analysing a competitor's strengths and weaknesses, with the aim that an organisation will find competitive positioning differences within the marketplace.

Concept
A visual description of an idea that includes its core features and consumer benefits, coupled with a broad understanding of technology requirements.

Concept generation
The process by which new product ideas are developed. This term is interchangeable with idea generation or ideation.

Concept screening
The evaluation of possible concepts during the initial stages of product development. Potential concepts are evaluated for their fit with business strategy and development costs and potential financial rewards.

Consumer
The most broadly ranging and all-encompassing term for a firm's target audience. It does not differentiate between whether the person is a buyer or a user of the product or service.

Consumer needs
What a consumer would like a product to do for them. Also, what particular problem the consumer would like to have solved.

Continuous innovation
The continual altering of a product to improve performance and benefits to the consumer. Technology-led products demand continuous improvement in order to remain competitive within the marketplace.

Core competence
The capability at which an organisation does considerably better than their rivals, offering distinctive competitive advantage in order to retain customers.

Cross-functional teams
A multidisciplinary team with members drawn from various departments within the organisation – usually from marketing, manufacturing, finance and purchasing.

Decline stage
The last stage of a product's life cycle.

Demographic segmentation
The statistical description of a human population. Characteristics usually include gender, age, education and marital status.

Design champion
A key individual who takes a passionate interest in seeing that a process or particular design concept is taken forward to commercialisation.

Direct marketing
The process of sending promotion material to a named person within an organisation.

Early adopters
Customers who buy into new products very early within its life cycle stages.

Empathic design
A detailed method for uncovering latent customer needs. Observational studies of the product(s) in use are the core essence of empathic design.

Ethnography
A qualitative and descriptive research methodology for studying the customer and end-user in relation to their environment.

Firefighting
An unanticipated problem requiring the diversion of resources within the design development process.

Focus groups
A strongly qualitative market research technique, where participants are gathered in a room under the supervision of a moderator. Discussion focuses on a consumer problem, product or potential solution to a problem.

Fuzzy front end
The initial stages of the design development process, preceding the more formal stages of idea development. During this stage activities are often unplanned, chaotic and unstructured.

Geographic segmentation
Dividing the market into certain geographic regions e.g. towns, cities and neighbourhoods.

Growth stage
The second stage of the product life cycle. This stage is characterised by a surge in sales and market acceptance.

Initial screening
The first decision to allocate resources (financial and human) on a project.

Introduction stage
The first stage of the product life cycle. Products move very quickly from this stage to the next: growth.

Learning organisation
An organisation that continuously tests and updates the experience of those within the organisation and transforms it into improved processes and knowledge.

Manufacturing design
The process of determining the manufacturing process that will be used to produce a new product.

Market development
Taking existing products or services to a new set of consumers or end users.

Market research
Analysing and collecting data on the environment, customers and competitors for purposes of business decision making.

Marketing mix
The strategy of the organisation consisting of product, price, place and promotion (also known as the '4Ps').

Marketing planning
A written document that plans the marketing activities of an organisation for a given period. It usually covers environmental analysis and marketing mix strategies.

Mass marketing
The promotion of a product or service to all consumers.

Maturity stage
The third stage of a product's life cycle. This stage is characterised by slowing sales due to market saturation.

New-to-the-world product
A product or service that has never before been available to consumers or producers.

Niche marketing
The process of concentrating resources and efforts on one particular market segment.

Open-ended questions
Questions that encourage the respondent to provide their own answers; for example, 'Why did you buy those particular shoes?'

Outsourcing
The process of procuring goods or services from another firm.

Perceptual mapping
A quantitative market research technique used to gain a deeper understanding of how consumers think about current and future products.

Porter's 5 forces
Analysis framework devised by Michael Porter by which an organisation can evaluate its capabilities versus its competitors.

Product development strategy
An overarching strategy that informs and guides the product innovation programme.

Product lifecycle
The four key stages that a product moves through on entering the marketplace: Introduction, Growth, Maturity and Decline.

Quality by design
The process used to design quality into the product, service or process from initial idea to commercialisation.

Relationship marketing
Creating a long-term relationship with existing customers. The aim is to build strong customer loyalty.

Return on investment (ROI)
A standard measure of project profitability, this is the discounted profits over the life of the project expressed as a percentage of initial investment.

Segmentation
The process of dividing a large market into more discrete sections, with each section holding similar views about the product or service.

SWOT analysis
A model used to conduct a self appraisal of an organisation. It looks at internal strengths and weaknesses and external environmental opportunities and threats.

Target market
A group of consumers or potential customers selected for marketing.

Value added
The process by which tangible product features or intangible service attributes are combined with other features and attributes.

**Vision and Values in
Design Management**

Design
directions

Design
transformations

Design
advocacy

Design
alliances

Index

Page numbers in *italics* denote illustrations.

ACTIVboard *112–13*, 114–16, *117*
added value 15–16, 59, 187
Adshel 159–64
advocacy 40, 95–143
alchemy 99
alliances 38, 55, 144–81
    see also collaboration
'antennae', designer's 30, 40
Apple *17*, *31*, 33, 82
Associate design graduates 58, 60
Australia 73
awareness of design 53, 58
Aynsley China 56–62

B2B (business to business) 22, 186
BCS (British Crime Survey) 150
Beijing Industrial Design Centre 72
benefits of design 14–15, 24–35, 64
    see also value of design
blue-sky thinking 30, 123
boardroom decisions 41, 45, 53, 121–3
brainstorming 69, 186
brands 15, 186
the brief 43, 115, 141, 158, 160–1
British Crime Survey (BCS) 150
brokerage operational model 136
'bundling' services 166–7
business to business (B2B) 22, 186
Buxton Wall consultancy 102–3, 113–18

cannibalisation 186
Cawood, Gavin 74–5
CBI (China Bridge International) 83
CBI (Confederation of British Industry) 107
championing design
    see design champions
change 15, 146–53, 174–9, 183
    championing 37–8, 40–1
    culture 32
    need for 57, 85
    see also transformative design
Chartered Institute of Patent Attorneys
(CIPA) 105
chemistry 99
China 55, 72, *73*, 80–3
China Bridge International (CBI) 83
CIPA (Chartered Institute of Patent
Attorneys) 105
Cityspace 140–1, 158–64
clients, case studies 102–3, 116
coalition development 40
cohesion operational model 136
COINs (collaborative innovation networks)
    135
collaboration 38, 55, 76–91, 126–43, 186
    see also alliances
combinatorial thought 135

commercialisation of products 20–1, 82
commitment 33, 157
communication 19, 68–9, 121, 125
    collaboration and 137–8
    of vision 36–45, 123
company opportunities 107
'compassionate' consumption 145, 149, 176
competitiveness 14, 16–17, 35, 57, 156, 179
competitor analysis 186
complexity, service innovation 170
concept, definition 186
concept development 115, 123, 128–9
    see also product development
concept generation 102, 186
concept screening 136, 186
Confederation of British Industry (CBI) 107
consciousness of design 53, 58
consultancies 28–9, 60, 79
consumers
    definition 186
    needs 35, 55, 186
    see also customers
continual monitoring services 168
continuous innovation 186
Cooper, Rachel 11, 64–5
Co-operative Bank *19*, 33
core competences 186
core values 19
Corfield Report 97
corporate social responsibility (CSR)
    11, 67, 149, 152–7
cost factors 59, 65, 124
Cottam, Hilary 35
Cox Review 22–3
creativity 32, 66, 69, 100, 103
    see also value creation
crime reduction
    11, 140–1, 150–3, 158–64, *177*, 179
Cripps, Andy 68–9
cross-functional teams 106–7, 186
Cruz Megchun, Beatriz Itzel 76
CSR
    see corporate social responsibility
culture 32, 66, 100
customers
    engagement 99
    expectations 7, 16–17, 108–10, 149
    see also consumers
customisation 109, 148, 170

Danish Design Council (DDC) 71
Davey, Caroline 152–3
DDC (Danish Design Council) 71
de Groot, Cristiaan 134–5, 172–3
decline stage of product 21, 186
demand-driven innovation 108
demographic change 147
demographic segmentation
    28, 124, 148, 175, 186–7
departmental boundary-crossing 26–7
design
    definition 26, 183

stages of 53, *54*
design alliances
    see alliances
Design Atlas 124–5
design champions
    7, 11, 36–8, 40–1, 95, 142, 186
    see also advocacy; leadership
Design Council, UK 71
The Design Experience (Press and Cooper)
    64–5
Design Forum Finland (DFF) 72
Design Institute of Australia (DIA) 73
design leadership
    see leadership
design-led innovation triggers 105, 107
design management
    definitions 52–63
    vs design leadership 97, 99, 101
design for manufacturability (DFM) 21
Design Wales service 74–5
designers as strategists 123, 131
Designing Demand programme 22–3
DesignSingapore Council 73
detailing stage of design 116
DFF (Design Forum Finland) 72
DFM (design for manufacturability) 21
DIA (Design Institute of Australia) 73
direct marketing 186
'distributed' design teams 87
drivers
    innovation 104–18
    product development 25, 43
    see also triggers

early adopters 186
economic context
    11, 70–1, 74–5, 80, 128, 152–3
educational courses 11, 78–9, 80, 83
embedded systems 86
empathic approach 125, 186
empirical approach 125
engagement 99
ethnography 186
Evoke Creative 43–5
Exertris 126–32
'experience' economy 147, 168, 175
exploration in leadership 98
external consultancies 28–9, 60

failure, fear of 100
feedback, product design 103
financial services 168
Finland 70, 72
'firefighting' 186
flexible approach 125
focus groups 186
forecasting 179
free-thinking approach 125
future development 98, 175, 179, 183
    see also growth
'future proofing' designs 162
fuzzy front end 186

geographic segmentation 186
globalisation 38, 75, 155
    see also international collaboration
Gorb, Peter 121
growth of business 60, 84–90, 98
    see also future development
growth stage of product 21, 186

Haley Sharpe Design 84–90
Harun, Richelle 22–3
healthcare design 11, 18, 19, 175
Henley Centre 147
holistic approach 64–9, 120
Hothouse 134–9, 172–3

idea filtering 136, 186
Ideal Standard 42–5
IDEO consultancy 31, 32
IJV (international joint ventures) 55
image 18
implementation stage 97, 116, 123
in-house design 28–9, 56–7, 60
inclusivity 156
incremental modifications 26–7
India 72
individuals in design 37
    see also design champions
industrial design 78–9, 80, 82
industry consolidation 38
'influence', design champions 37
information technology (IT) 84–90
initial screening 186
innovation 38, 44, 53, 54
    collaboration 126–35
    definition 105
    drivers 104–18
    forecasting 179
    holistic approach 69
    levels of 123
    service sector 11, 166–71
inspirational leadership 98
intangible benefits 6, 41, 64, 135, 149
    see also benefits of design
integration of design 53
'intent', design champions 37, 40
international collaboration 55, 76–91
international joint ventures (IJV) 55
internet 135, 158–9, 161
introduction stage of product 21, 186
investment in design 35, 155, 183, 187
IT, design for 84–90

Japan Design Foundation (JDF) 73
Jevnaker, Birgit 26–7
joint ventures 55

Knowledge Transfer Partnerships (KTP)
    25, 58, 60
Korean Institute of Design Promotion 71
KTP
    see Knowledge Transfer Partnerships

LDA (London Development Agency) 22–3
leadership 7, 11, 95–103, 122, 142
    case studies 44
    creativity 32, 69, 100
    stages of design 53
    see also design champions
learning environments 19
learning organisations 186
leasing services 168
Lenovo China 82
London Development Agency (LDA) 22–3

'Magnificent Seven' attributes 125
maintenance services 168
managerial creativity 100
    see also design management
manufacturing design 20–1, 68–9, 186
market development 186
market fragmentation 148, 175
market pull 105–6
market research 75, 123, 187
market segments 28, 124, 148, 175, 186–7
market value 65
marketing 27–8, 75, 121, 186–7
mass customisation 109, 148
mass marketing 187
maturity stage of product 21, 187
Mexico 76–9
modularisation 160, 162
motivation 156
multidisciplinary teams 44, 126–32

national design policies 70–5
need for innovation 105
new product development (NPD)
    20–1, 25–7, 59, 186
    see also product development
new technology opportunities 106
new-to-the-world products 105, 134, 187
niche marketing 187
Nokia 31, 99, 149
non-renewable energy sources 148–9
NPD
    see new product development

Olins, Wally 18
open-ended questions 187
open innovation 135
operation/support services 168
operational models 136
opportunity sources 104–7, 175, 183
organisational activities 25–33, 58, 100
organisational value 66
Ortmans, Laurent 169
outsourcing 170, 187

PACEC consultancy 15
partnerships 25, 58, 60
    see also alliances
PDD consultancy 127–32
PDMA 105
perception of design 53, 56–62, 120

perceptual mapping 187
perfectionism 125
performance, championing 38
performance value 66
PLC
    see product life cycle
policy creation 70–5
political approach 125
Porter's 5 forces 187
Prendiville, Alison 34–5
Press, Mike 64–5
process 20–1, 26–7, 34, 66, 136
product creativity 100
product design 16, 17, 82, 103, 168
product development
    case studies 115, 128–9, 160–2
    costs 59
    drivers 25, 43
    new products 20–1, 25–7, 59, 186
    process 20–1, 26–7
    strategy 187
    see also innovation
Product Development and Management
Association (PDMA) 105
product life cycle (PLC) 21, 186–7
production improvements 20
project manager role 131
projects 102, 131, 138
Promethean Limited 113–18
prototype testing 129, 130
purchase finance services 168

quality by design 187
quantifiable benefits 24–35, 64
    see also benefits of design
Quinlan, Peter 140–1, 159–62, 161

R&D (research and development) 82
recognition reward 40
relationship management 99, 103, 187
repair services 168
research and development (R&D) 82
'restyling' design stage 53
return on investment (ROI) 35, 187
rewards 40, 107, 169
risks of innovation 107, 169
Robson, Stephanie 169
ROI (return on investment) 35, 187

Saga Group 147
Sanderson, David 56, 58
segmentation 148, 175, 186–7
service sector 11, 17, 18, 166–71
servicisation 170
'silent' design 121
Singapore 73
small businesses 22–3, 75, 103, 135
Smart Point units 141, 158–64, 159, 163
SMEs 22–3, 75, 103, 135
social responsibility 11, 67, 149, 152–7
social value 67
societal change 147, 175

**Vision and Values in
Design Management**

Design
directions

Design
transformations

Design
advocacy

Design
alliances

'soft' benefits 25, 33
stakeholders 30
strategic design 14–19, 24, 30–1, 35, 101,
120–32
   case studies 58
   China 82
   collaboration 137
   emerging issues 176
   levels of 16
   process 27
   stages of 53
style adding value 59
suppliers 108, 116
Supply Chain Council 108
supply-driven innovation 108–9, 112–18
sustainable lifestyles 149
Svengren Holm, Lisbeth 26–7
SWOT analysis 23, 187

tangible benefits
   see quantifiable benefits
target market 75, 187
Teaching Company Schemes
   see Knowledge Transfer Partnerships
technology
   convergence 11, 150
   creativity and 103
   emerging issues 147, 175, 179
   pushing innovation 105–6
   see also information technology
'third way' design 29
time economy 147
Topalian, Alan 97, 101, 183
trademarks 15
training courses 83
   see also educational courses
transformative design 32, 50–93
   see also change
Trevi showers 43–5
triggers
   innovation 104–5
   product development 26, 43
   see also drivers
triple bottom line 153
Turner, Raymond *96*, 97, 101, 183

UK design policies 70–1, 74–5
universities
   see educational courses
user research 115

value creation 64–7
value of design 14–24, 33–5, 59, 64–7, 187
   see also benefits of design
values of companies 121, 157
virtual organisations *146*, 148, 176
vision communication 36–45, 123
Voice Over Internet Protocol (VOIP) 158–9,
161

Wales 74–5
Wall, Alan 102–3

Wootton, Andrew 152–3
world market 70
Woudhuysen, James 178–9

Xerox *166*, 167

Ye Deng, Jian 80
York, Peter 148

Quotation sources

Page 20
Tony Blair, The UK Innovation Report, 2003

Page 25
Cooper and Press, 1995

Page 27
Sir George Cox, 2005

Page 33
Cooper and Press, 2003

Page 37
Design Council National Survey of Firms, 2005

Page 41
CBI 'Understanding Modern Manufacturing', 2007

Page 42
Design in Britain, Design Council, 2005

Page 46
Design in Britain, Design Council, 2005

Page 54
Whyte, Salter, Gann and Davies, *Investing in Design to improve export potential*, 2002

Page 55
Design Council National Survey of Firms, 2005

Page 57
Design Council Briefing: the impact of design on business, 2008

Page 58
NESTA, Hidden Innovation in the Creative Industries, 2008

Page 59
HM Treasury, The Cox Review of Creativity in Business: building on the UK's strengths, 2005

Page 60
NESTA, Hidden Innovation: how innovation happens in six 'low innovation' sectors, 2007

Page 65
Design Council, 2008

Page 67
Design in Britain, Design Council, 2005

Page 82
The Boston Consulting Group, 2009

Page 83
Chinese Design Industry Association, 2007

Page 97
Elbert Hubbard, 1859–1915

Page 99
Design in Britain, Design Council, 2005

Page 100
Design in Britain, Design Council, 2005

Page 105
Stephen Byers, Ritec International

Page 109
Bill Moggridge, IDEO

Page 111
Jonathan Ive, Apple

Page 122
Design in Britain, Design Council, 2005

Page 139
James Harkin, *Big Ideas*, 2008

Page 148
James Harkin, *Big Ideas*, 2008

Page 151
Dr Caroline Davey and Andrew Wootton
Design Against Crime Solution Centre

Page 154
Design in Britain, Design Council, 2005

Pages 156–7
Corporate Social Responsibility: a Government update, 2008

Page 166
Design in Britain, Design Council, 2005

Page 170
Charles Leadbeater, *Innovate from Within*, 2002

Page 175
Tony Blair, The UK Innovation Report, 2003

Page 176
Rodriguez-Pose, *Is R&D Investment in Lagging Areas of Europe Worthwhile?* 2001

Vision and Values in Design Management

Design
directions

Design
transformations

Design
advocacy

Design
alliances

Acknowledgements

This book is dedicated to
Alice and Theo Gittins

Special thanks to

Leafy, Caroline and Rachel at AVA Publishing
for their endless patience and support
throughout this project. Rachel Cooper at
Imagination@Lancaster for being Rachel.
Andrew Wootton, Caroline Davey and Nigel
Howe at Salford University to whom I owe so
much. Kathryn Best for her insightful
wisdom regarding all things Design
Management! Graeme and Alice Russell for
their constant and enduring understanding
which will never be forgotten but always
immensely appreciated. Peter Quinlan at
Cityspace for his valuable contribution and
endless energy regarding the development
of the Smart Point case study. Lastly, to
Jennifer (Liverpool) Brown and Saeeda
(Manchester) Seddon who wonderfully
'bugged' me between 2003 and 2006.

Thanks to

The list is endless, but thanks must go to
Alan Wall, David Sanderson, Richelle Harun,
Alison Prendiville, David Raffo, Andy Cripps,
Gavin Cawood, Alistair Haley, Alan Topalian,
David Humphries, Margaret Bruce, Lucy
Daly, Michael Thomas, Bill Hollins, Bob
Jerrard, Jonathan Vickery, Amy Smith,
James Woudhuysen, Roy Chilvers, Serena
Selva, Anna Vowles and Karen Yair.